AF477936

Patterns of
Consciousness

Richard Haven

Patterns of Consciousness

An Essay on Coleridge

THE UNIVERSITY OF MASSACHUSETTS PRESS · 1969

FOR JOSEPHINE

'animae dimidium meae'

Preface

In HIS PREFACE TO *A Grammar of Motives*, Kenneth Burke speaks of a photograph of "two launches, proceeding side by side on a tranquil sea. Their wakes crossed and recrossed each other in almost an infinity of lines. Yet despite the intricateness of this tracery, the picture gave an impression of great simplicity, because one could quickly perceive the generating principle of its design." Many interpretations of human activity, which includes art, literature, and philosophy, might be described as attempts to put the launches, the "generating principle," in the picture and thereby to transform perplexing intricacy into intelligible pattern.

We need not argue over the infinity of lines. Scholarship delineates the tracery. But we do argue over the generative principle since, in most cases, more than one seems to 'work.' And since more than one 'works,' no one is 'right.' I see nothing amiss with this so long as the interpreter does not insist that what he uses for 'launches,' for a generative principle, is the only principle, is the ontological X, and that the infinity of lines is only and no more than his intelligible pattern. Those charts of colored dots used to test color blindness contain many figures, though each eye sees only one. As a man is, so he sees. This essay is an attempt to trace a figure which I see in Coleridge. I do not need, I trust, to continue to say that it is not the only figure, or the 'right' one, but only a figure, an intelligible pattern, which I see.

The pattern which I see in Coleridge's work is one which appears in his prose as well as in his poetry, and a substantial part of this book is devoted to a consideration of the development and character of some of his speculative ideas. I have not, however, included any comprehensive discussion of Coleridge's published prose works per se, and the reader will find that, while I have drawn on the published prose in various ways, I have relied much more heavily on notebooks, marginalia, and letters. This may seem to some readers a serious deficiency, and I should perhaps therefore explain that, since the 'generative principles' with which I am concerned have their origin in Coleridge's consciousness, in his own experience of 'being,' the notebooks, the marginalia, and the letters are, so to speak, closer to the point of origin than the works which he prepared for publication, and in which he was to some degree concerned to adapt his statements to what he conceived to be the demands of public comprehension. Coleridge liked to suggest that Plato and even Kant kept secret or revealed only to initiates their most profound and esoteric doctrines. Whatever shortcomings this suggestion may or may not have as applied to Plato or Kant, it reveals, I think, something about Coleridge.

Some parts of this essay derive from a dissertation written some years ago and I am indebted to Carlos Baker and the late R. P. Blackmur for their criticisms of that work. Other parts derive from my editing of Coleridge's voluminous marginalia on Jacob Boehme for the forthcoming *Collected Coleridge* and I owe a great deal both to Kathleen Coburn, the general editor of that monumental work, and to the editor of the "Collected Marginalia," George Whalley, for their generosity in sharing with me something of their great knowledge of Coleridge. This essay owes much to the careful and repeated reading of Robert F. Gleckner, some of whose suggestions I have adopted and some of whose criticisms I fear I have failed to meet. I am also indebted to the criticism of Peter Heller, Robert Tucker, and Leone Stein, who have all read the manuscript at one stage or another of its development. And I owe more than I can say to discussions over the years with G. Armour Craig, Robin Skelton, and Charles McDonald.

I wish to thank the Clarendon Press, Oxford, for permission to use material from E. L. Griggs's edition of *The Collected Letters of Samuel Taylor Coleridge*, and the Bollingen Foundation for permission to use material from *The Notebooks of Samuel Taylor*

Coleridge, edited by Kathleen Coburn. I am further indebted to Miss Coburn for allowing me to read the proofs of the still unpublished third volume of her edition of the notebooks, and to Mr. Alwyne Coleridge and the Bollingen Foundation for permission to include extracts from this and from other still unpublished manuscript materials which will appear in forthcoming volumes of the *Collected Coleridge*. I also wish to thank the *Journal of the History of Ideas* for permission to incorporate in Chapter 3 parts of my article "Coleridge, Hartley, and the Mystics" which originally appeared in that journal. I am grateful to the Research Council of the University of Massachusetts for several grants-in-aid.

My obligations to the work of other scholars and critics of Coleridge is very great, and no doubt greater than I realize. But in view of the availability of bibliographies of modern scholarship and criticism, it seems both impractical and unnecessary to attempt to include here one more survey of existing views of the works and issues discussed in this essay. In a period in which critical and scholarly publication is so voluminous, it seems to me that the once traditional practice of trying to incorporate in each new discussion a compendium of what has preceded it becomes self-defeating, a case of the rolling stone gathering *too much* moss. I have therefore included in the text and in the notes only references to those works on which I have specifically drawn or with which I specifically wished to take issue. This by no means exhausts my obligations. But between this and the whole of my reading over many years, I could draw no meaningful line. If my practice here seems insufficient or ungracious, I hope that the complete bibliography of Coleridge criticism and scholarship on which, with several others, I am presently engaged, may make some sort of amends.

While this essay was in proof, I belatedly discovered an important article by R. A. Durr ("'This Lime-Tree Bower My Prison' and a Recurrent Action in Coleridge") which, though in somewhat different terms, anticipates a central element in my discussion. And I apologize for omitting it, except for an addition to note 5 of the Introduction, from consideration in the pages which follow.

Amherst, Massachusetts, 1969

Contents

                                        'Tis not merely

The Human being's Pride that peoples space
With life and mystical predominance;
Since likewise for the stricken heart of Love
This visible nature, and this common world,
Is all too narrow; yea, a deeper import
Lurks in the legend told my infant years
That lies upon that truth, we live to learn.
For fable is Love's world, his home, his birth-place;
Delightedly dwells he 'mong fays and talismans,
Divinities, being himself divine.
The intelligible forms of ancient poets,
The fair humanities of old religion,
The Power, the Beauty, and the Majesty,
That had their haunts in dale or piny mountain,
Or forest by slow stream, or pebbly spring,
Or chasms and wat'ry depths; all these have vanished.
They live no longer in the faith of reason!
But still the heart doth need a language, still
Doth the old instinct bring back the old names,
And to yon starry world they now are gone,
Spirits or Gods, that used to share this earth
With man as with their friend; and to the lover
Yonder they move, from yonder visible sky
Shoot influence down; and even at this day
'Tis Jupiter who brings whate'er is great,
And Venus who brings everything that's fair!
          SCHILLER, *Piccolomini*, II.iv
          (translated and adapted by Coleridge)

Pay particular attention, I beseech you, to these things; in
that way you may understand me, a person who may per-
haps seem mad—or at least see why I am mad.
          GIORDANO BRUNO (as translated in *The Friend*)

As a man is, so he sees.
          WILLIAM BLAKE

As we experience the world, so we act.

R. D. LAING

Truth has more than one mode; scientific knowledge is only one of its modes. There is another mode, which is knowledge of self. Scientific knowledge is a stricter mode than this, in a definable sense, but it is not truer; it is not certain.

J. BRONOWSKI

One excellence of the Doctrine of Plato, or of the Plotino-platonic Philosophy, is that it never suffers, much less causes or even occasions, its Disciples to forget them-selves, lost and scattered in sensible Objects disjoined or as disjoined from themselves. It is impossible to under-stand the Elements of this Philosophy without an appeal, at every step & round of the Ladder, to the fact within, to the mind's Consciousness—and in addition to this, in-stead of lulling the Soul into an indolence of mere atten-tion . . . [it] rouses it to acts and energies of creative Thought & Recognition—of conscious re-production of states of Being.

COLERIDGE, *Notebooks*, III, #3935

Introduction

E. K. CHAMBERS CONCLUDED HIS BIOGRAPHY of Coleridge with the words: "So Coleridge passed, leaving a handful of golden poems, an emptiness in the heart of a few friends, and a will-o'-the-wisp light for bemused thinkers." This remark has often been quoted as evidence that its author failed to appreciate or to do critical justice to the talents and accomplishments of his subject. But the sense of disappointment with a performance which seems only rarely to justify the promise is one which even the most devout Coleridgeans must sometimes share, and share not only with Chambers, whose sympathy and insight may well be called in question in this instance, but with Coleridge's friends and, indeed, with Coleridge himself. That Coleridge in his later years worked much harder than has sometimes been thought, that he wrote much more than was finished or published, is now common knowledge. But while we should now add to the traditional selections, to Chambers' "handful," a few more poems, we can find few neglected masterpieces, though many unwritten ones. The neglected poetry remains for the most part far inferior, marked not infrequently by a memorable passage, but marred and sometimes overwhelmed by lapses into sentimentality and mere rhetoric. Remove the "handful," and Coleridge ceases to be a great poet. Remove a score or so more, and he ceases to be even a very superior one and sinks to a level somewhat below Southey and Crabbe.

Nor do efforts to enhance Coleridge's stature as, in any strict sense, a philosopher fare very much better. This is not only because he was so often derivative, because his most sustained and systematic philosophical arguments are those which follow most closely the thought of someone else, usually Kant, Schelling, or Steffens. More important is the fact that, as philosophy, Coleridge's work—including the 'Magnum Opus' so far as we have it and so far as we are able to guess at what it might have become—is now of little more than academic or historical interest, remembered and sometimes read not for itself but because its author also wrote "The Rime of the Ancient Mariner" and *Biographia Literaria,* or because as the Sage of Highgate he so profoundly influenced the first generation of Victorians.

The universe which Coleridge envisioned seemed to him coherent; a universe in which all "extremes meet" and in which everything is an analogue of everything else. He wrote in an appendix to *The Statesman's Manual:*

> I seem to myself to behold in the quiet objects, on which I am gazing, more than an arbitrary illustration, more than a mere *simile,* the work of my own fancy. I feel an awe, as if there were before my eyes the same power as that of the reason—the same power in a lower dignity, and therefore a symbol established in the truth of things. I feel it alike whether I contemplate a single tree or flower, or meditate on vegetation throughout the world, as one of the great organs of the life of nature.[1]

Such a vision is noble but by no means unique. It has inspired many amateur and some professional philosophers. The shelves of second-hand bookshops contain innumerable forgotten works by forgotten writers whose vision of wholeness, whose purposes and even methods approximate Coleridge's own, and who were as successful or unsuccessful as he in transforming that vision into an intellectually acceptable body of systematic thought. He was anxious to avoid 'mysticism' and 'enthusiasm,' to prove that his vision of unity was consistent with and corroborated by the discoveries of a rational and experimental science and psychology. But he depended too much on theories that have proved untenable. The new light which he thought he saw in German *Naturphilosophie* proved a false dawn, and the grand abstractions of Schelling and Steffens were ultimately more of a hindrance than a help. Late in life, Coleridge remarked that he felt that he might have been more useful as a thinker had he never read the Germans. It is a sentiment we may well echo.

Neither the materials which have only recently become generally available with the publication of letters and notebooks, nor those which are still to come greatly alter this situation. If anything, they serve to increase our disappointment with much of the hitherto published work. Passages of fresh insight and brilliant suggestion make us better able to understand the admiration and even awe which Coleridge aroused in many of his friends and contemporaries, but make us, like them, the more acutely aware of what it seems he might have done and did not do.

All this, familiar though it is, needs, I think, to be repeated. Impressed by the undeniable subtlety and brilliance of Coleridge's mind but confronted with little more than a mass of fragments, we may be too easily led to extrapolate, to try to create some part, at least, of what Coleridge left undone. An attempt to complete "Christabel" is a harmless if trivial pastime. Attempts to complete or systematize Coleridge's speculative writings may be equally trivial but much less harmless. They are apt to be trivial because they possess neither historical validity nor contemporary value. They may not be harmless because, in giving us what is in fact not Coleridge, they may obscure the interest and value of what *is* Coleridge. Confronted with a difficult poem, many readers resort to paraphrase, to the substitution for the difficult poem of a simpler and more easily managed alternative. Similarly, confronted with so fragmented and diverse a body of work as this, the reader may feel the need of something in terms of which he can relate the various parts to each other and reduce the whole to manageable and intelligible form. But as the paraphrase is not the poem, so such an extrapolation is not Coleridge's philosophy.

And Coleridge's actual work is important not merely as the fragmentary beginnings of something else, but as it is, in itself. To agree with many other critics that Coleridge was a failure as a philosopher, even to admit all that his most formidable critic in this respect, René Wellek, can say, is not at all to dismiss the bulk of his prose as of no value. The kind of negative judgment which I have outlined is the result of certain kinds of expectations and demands. They are expectations and demands which Coleridge often invited, but they do not provide the most fruitful or even the most valid basis for a consideration of his work. Let us accept Coleridge's failures. Then, as those hunting the whale sometimes found in a rotten and worthless carcass, ambergris, so we may find in Coleridge's fragments something more interesting and finally more significant than the systematic philosophy which he could not produce.

His least sympathetic critic will agree that even when he is most closely following the work of another, Coleridge continually astonishes and delights us with flashes of original observation, insight, and suggestion, with those "fine isolated verisimilitude[s] caught from the Penetralium of mystery" which Keats felt he too often let "go by." These are not, as the figure might suggest, merely nuggets embedded in an otherwise uninteresting matrix, or, in Coleridge's words, "poetic partridges" driven away by a "laborious metaphysical bustard." They might often more accurately be described as the foci of Coleridge's thinking. He was an acute and indefatigable observer of his own mind, his own experience. He was at his best when drawing most heavily on that observation. He longed, he once said, to find "some principle that was derived from experience, but of which all other knowledge should be but so many repetitions under various limitations, even as squares, triangles, etc., etc., are but so many positions of space." [2] His "philosophical opinions" were "blended with, or deduced from, . . . [his] feelings." [3] As he wrote of Plato, he "thought deeply within himself of the goings-on of his own mind . . . and then looked abroad to ask if this were a dream or whether it were indeed a revelation from within, and a waking reality." [4] There have been many studies of what happened when Coleridge "looked abroad." There have not been many which tried to consider what he found when he "thought deeply within himself of the goings-on of his own mind," and the extent to which this determined what he thought and wrote.

Nothing has a merely verbal history. The work of any writer, whether of poetry or philosophy, derives in part from the nature of his own experience, however traditional he may be and however indebted to the formulations of others. This is particularly important in the case of Coleridge whose reliance on his own intuition is often obscured by the range of his reading and the extent of his 'borrowings.' An understanding of Coleridge, and especially of the relation between his poetic and his speculative work, requires, I believe, an examination of the genesis from experience, from the 'goings-on of mind,' to formulation, as well as the study, so often undertaken in the past, of the relation of his formulations to those of others whom he had read, by whom he was influenced, or from whom he had borrowed. While many studies of Coleridge's poetry, and of that of other Romantics as well, have shown such a concern, there has not to my knowledge been an attempt to make it the basis for a consideration of the whole of his work.[5] What follows, then, may be seen as the beginning, though by no means the fulfillment, of such an attempt.

As an aid to establishing more clearly a point of departure, I should like to introduce two statements. The first is from Erich Neumann's *The Origins and History of Consciousness*. "Every figure in a work of art," Neumann says, ". . . requires a dual interpretation, that is to say, a 'structural' interpretation based on the nature of the figure itself, and what we might call for short a 'genetic' interpretation which regards the figure as the expression and exponent of the psyche from which it springs. . . . The fact that the poet's conscious mind uses extraneous material for the creative process . . . does not disprove the inner associations presupposed by the genetic interpretation, for the selection and modification of this material are decisive and typical of the psychic situation." [6] I should like to add to this a remark by Herbert Read in *The Forms of Things Unknown*. The object which the artist creates, says Read,

> is the objective correlative of an emotion, a mood, an idea, or an intuition; in brief, the realization of a state of consciousness. . . . Consciousness . . . does not exist apart from the object we are conscious of; but we can induce consciousness by seeking a correlative for feeling. . . . The object the artist creates, therefore, corresponds to his state of consciousness; it is his consciousness of that object; it was not first present *in* consciousness, and then expelled like an egg: it grew into consciousness as it germinated . . . .[7]

Read is speaking of a concrete object, "a plastic configuration, sounds, colours, shapes, masses accessible to sensation," and both he and Neumann are concerned with the genesis of works of art. But what they say is often true as well of abstract or theoretical formulations. The function of an 'object,' verbal or otherwise, as a correlative for consciousness depends not only on a qualitative correspondence but also on structure, on, to use Read's term, "configuration." And the same configurations may be embodied in a poem or in a scientific or philosophic theory, though the latter when so regarded is being treated as art rather than as science or philosophy.

A genetic interpretation of a work may thus not only add to our understanding of the work itself. If we find analogous structures in various areas of a man's work, if, in our particular case, we find them in Coleridge's poetry, in his scientific speculations, and in his metaphysics, and if they derive at least in part from the "goings-on of his own mind," then a genetic interpretation may enable us to see relationships between these various areas which are not apparent when we examine them as historians of ideas.

Some years ago, Kenneth Burke promised a study of Coleridge in which he would use recurrent "associational clusters" as "objective bridges for getting from one area [of his work] to another." [8] Burke has not yet produced his "symbolic analysis of Coleridge's writings," but from the examples which he gives in this preliminary discussion, it is evident that he connects recurrent "clusters" with specific situations in Coleridge's personal experience; with his marital problems, for instance, or his drug addiction. Such patterns may no doubt be found, though I question many of Burke's particular interpretations, but they are not what are suggested by Coleridge's aforementioned comment on Plato. It was partly to distinguish what was unique in his own experience from what was actually or potentially common to the experience of all men that, Coleridge thought, Plato "looked abroad to ask if this were a dream, or whether it were indeed a revelation from within, and a waking reality." Plato, he continued,

> employed his observation as the interpreter of his meditation,
> equally free from the fanatic who abandons himself to the wild

workings of the magic cauldron of his own brain mistaking every form of delirium for reality, and from the cold sensualist who looks at death as the alone real, or life of the world, by not considering that the very object was seen to him only by the seeing powers . . . .[9]

Coleridge was concerned with mental goings-on, with psychic configurations which he took to be of general rather than individual occurrence. The writers who attracted him when he looked abroad were those in whom he thought that he found evidence confirming the validity of experiential discoveries that he himself had made.

Neumann is, of course, a disciple of Jung. But the acceptability of genetic interpretation does not depend upon any doctrinaire psychological position. For neither Neumann nor for Jung himself does an archetypal image exist as such in the unconscious, to be, in Read's words, "expelled like an egg." The image is rather the correlative of the unconscious, the form in which the unconscious becomes conscious. This does not require that the image be always the same or that it be latent in the unconscious like an undeveloped photograph, but only that it have those qualities or configurations which enable it to serve as a correlative. Moreover, such a correlative may be an abstract formulation as well as a poetic vision. The recurrence of the same configuration or even the same image may be genetically explained on the assumption that certain structural characteristics are recurrent in human consciousness. This assumption is not confined to Jungean psychology and certainly does not necessarily involve Jung's theories concerning the basis for such recurrence. I do not, therefore, propose another essay in what often passes for 'Jungean' criticism, but only an examination of those configurations which, in his introspective contemplations, Coleridge first discovered in himself, which he tried to express in his poetry, and which became the essential basis of his speculative thought. "As we experience the world, so we act." [10] As a man discovers himself-in-the-world to be, so he writes.

Neumann distinguishes a "genetic" from what he calls a "structural" interpretation, "based on the nature of the figure itself." As will already be apparent from my remarks, I should prefer to say that genetic interpretation involves structural analysis insofar as structure is genetically determined. I shall therefore rather draw a line between genetic and historical interpretation, both of which may involve structural analysis. The two are not mutually exclusive. The configurations which serve one writer as a correlative of a state of consciousness may also have served other writers as well and may have, therefore, a history which one can trace. Yet still it is the state of consciousness which demands this configuration rather than another. The genetic interpretation is concerned with structural *analogies* where the historical interpretation is concerned with structural, or other, *antecedents.*

However illuminating it may sometimes be, historical interpretation, and most especially the study of 'sources,' involves an implicit acceptance of those very 'Newtonian' principles which all the major Romantics in varying ways and to varying degrees rejected. As historians, we see a work, whether of art or otherwise, as an event in time, and we see the individual character of that event as the result of prior events. In much the same way, Newton and his successors considered objects and individuals as the results of prior causes, as items, as *discrete* items, in a temporal sequence. But for the Romantic, even for Wordsworth who most of all seems to see the individual consciousness as shaped by 'Nature' in time, the essential relationship is, so to speak, not horizontal but vertical. The individual is *subject*, not just *subject to;* the cause, not just the result, of its environment. What the eye sees depends upon the eye. "May God us keep / From Single vision and Newton's sleep!"

In recent years, Coleridge has, along with other Romantics, frequently been called a 'visionary.' [11] The term is one which is now commonly used to describe experiences and poems which earlier critics have called 'mystical.' The reasons for the change in terminology have been cogently argued by, among others, Mark Schorer in *The Politics of Vision* and Northrop Frye in *Fearful Symmetry.* Properly speaking, 'mysticism,' both agree, is a "technique" whose object is "a form of spiritual communion with God which is by its very nature incommunicable to anyone else," [12] and true mystics are rarely if ever poets. Although "one type blends into the other" [13] and visionary poets and philosophers may be "mystical in spots," [14] "most of the poets generally called mystics might better be called visionaries, which is not quite the same thing." [15]

René Wellek has remarked that "nobody has ever argued that Coleridge was a genuine 'mystic,' " [16] and not all critics would agree that he should even be called a 'visionary.' Coleridge was much concerned, especially in his published writing, to distinguish himself from the 'mystic,' the 'enthusiast,' the 'fanatic,' to show that his views were in accord with logic and reason. This is an important matter and one which I shall discuss later. Nevertheless, he shared with Wordsworth and Blake a reliance on the cognitive value of experience which involves something more or other than a knowledge of an objective physical universe. Whatever his or our explanation may be of such experience and of its expression, I shall without further apology refer to it as 'visionary.'

Moreover, I shall insist that there is a relationship, which should not be disregarded, between 'genuine' mysticism and the kind of 'vision' which we find in Coleridge, and between both and some other types of 'abnormal' experience. Certainly there are distinctions which can and should be made.[17] But we might do well to remember Coleridge's insistence on the importance of 'distinction' without 'difference': distinction, that is, which does not deny an underlying unity. While Coleridge objected to being called 'mystical,' he still, as we shall see later,[18] presents the mystic and the 'true philosopher' as having shared the same experience, the same way of being, and they are saved by this from "the heartless sobrieties of a Locke, a Paley, or a Dugald Stewart!" [19] Insofar as we may take him to exemplify his own notion of a 'true philosopher,' I shall argue that up to a point, at least, he was right, and that this becomes important in the consideration both of the evolution of his own ideas and of his use of other writers, whether mystical or nonmystical. The shared experience may be as important a determinant of poetic or theoretic expression as is the influence of one work on another which is traced by the historian of ideas.

The nature of 'mystical' experience has been the subject of much discussion and some controversy. The possibility of what William James defined as a different "kind of consciousness," [20] of a loss of the sense of self and of an awareness of or feeling of union with what seems to be the life or spirit or essence of the universe, with 'God,' is too well documented to be denied.[21] Whether all such experiences, those of the saint, the 'nature mystic,' the madman, the taker of drugs, and a considerable number of more ordinary people, are 'the same' is, and will continue to be, a matter of profound disagreement. For the purposes of this discussion, however, it is not necessary to insist that such experiences are identical but only that they are analogous. Disregarding the context of belief in which a 'mystical' experience occurs or is reported, we find repeatedly a patterned relationship between 'union' and disunion, between 'vision' and ordinary perception, between ecstasy and alienation. Since this recurrent pattern is not confined to one religion, one culture, or one age, it would seem to be experiential in origin rather than merely doctrinal or ideological, "datur," as Coleridge puts it, "non intelligitur." And since it occurs alike in the reports of 'saints,' of 'nature mystics,' and of 'madmen,' we are justified in saying that in this respect, at least, their experiences are the same, that they exhibit a common structure.

Coleridge saw such a pattern in his own experience, and he recognized or thought that he recognized it, sometimes clearly and sometimes obscurely evident, in much that he read. It was this which led him to see the whole history of philosophy as a series of approximations to a truth which he hoped, though vainly, to expound. Earlier thinkers, he liked to say, were wrong only because they were imperfectly in the right. In many of them, he thought that he found an echo of his own introspection but combined with assumptions, beliefs, dogmas, and superstitions which he could not accept. His object and his problem was to reconcile what he found to be true in them with the science and psychology which had played so large a part in discrediting them, to show that the pattern was not inseparable from false ideologies and to find new and acceptable terms in which to express it.

Speaking of Thomas Hobbes in *The Seventeenth Century Background*, Basil Willey writes:

What will seem 'true' or 'explanatory' to any age or individual is what satisfies current demands and interests. What has this writer most urgently demanded from life? is the question we must consistently ask ourselves. The original impulse towards, say, 'materialism,' or 'idealism,' is usually something sublogical; not, that is, a 'conviction' resulting from an intellectual process, but a quite simple set of the whole being towards a particular way of life. The direction once given, the subconscious affirmation once made, the character of the metaphysical superstructure is determined accordingly.[22]

Any student of Coleridge would agree that there was in him such a "sublogical something" which led him to turn to "idealism" rather than "materialism." And he repeatedly affirmed his reliance on intuitive convictions. "Believe me, Southey," he wrote, "a metaphysical solution that does not instantly *tell* for something in the Heart is grievously to be suspected as apocryphal." [23] And in a notebook, he complained of "the Philosopher of London & Paris" that he did not "go into his own Nature, look at it stedfastly, & observe whether or no . . . it or the part of it in question, corresponds with the Statement [.]—O no! this would be a sort of Ventriloquism in his Opinion/ his poor Asthmatic Soul feels by a moment's Self-introiting as if he had been already 3 days & 3 nights in the Jonas-Prison of an Odd-fish's Belly." [24]

In the first chapter of *Coleridge on Imagination*, I. A. Richards writes:

Coleridge was not, I suppose, a good philosopher; he made too many mistakes *of the wrong kind*. He mixed with his philosophy too many things which did not belong to it, he let accidental and inessential prejudices too much interfere. In spite of them he took the psychology of the theory of poetry to a new level. For causes whose force will be experienced by anyone who follows Coleridge with any closeness he could not help adding into and developing again out of this relevant psychology a huge ill-assorted fabric of philosophic and theological beliefs which is not, I think, a relevant part of it. But it is, as I see it, an elaborated transformed *symbol* of some parts of the psychology.[25]

I cannot wholly agree with Richards' later exposition of the "relevant psychology," nor can I agree with the implication that the psychology of which the philosophy is a 'symbol' is itself a set of theoretical formulations. I do believe, however, that Coleridge's philosophy should be seen not as an unsuccessful attempt at a logical analytical system but, like his poetry, as a projection, an "elaborated transformed symbol," of his own psychological experience. It is because of this that we so often find in Coleridge what appear to be startling anticipations of later writers whose primary concern has been the study and analysis of human consciousness. Coleridge, one is almost tempted to say, was a born psychologist trying to write as a metaphysician.

This view is supported both by such explicit comments on the nature of philosophy as I have already mentioned and by certain characteristics of Coleridge's manner of writing. One of the most striking things about the many speculative remarks scattered through the notebooks and letters is the extent to which they seem to grow out of his own observation or introspection, the frequency with which he seems to arrive at some idea not as the result of consideration of an abstract problem but from dwelling on some particular experience of his own. It is thinking of the illness of his child that leads him to assert: *"Life, Power, Being!*—organization may & probably *is* [sic], their effect; their *cause* it *cannot* be!" [26] After describing how "the further I ascend from animated Nature . . . the greater becomes in me the Intensity of the feeling of Life . . . ," he goes on to suggest "that Death exists only because Ideas exist/ that Life is limitless Sensation; that Death is a child of the organic senses, chiefly of the Sight; that Feelings die by flowing into the mould of the Intellect, & becoming Ideas; & that Ideas passing forth into action reinstate themselves again in the world of Life. And I do believe, that Truth lies inveloped [sic] in these loose generalizations." [27] Such judgments, and these instances may easily be multiplied, may be susceptible of logical formulation, but as they are here expressed they look for support not to logic but to experience, or, as Coleridge would say, to the 'heart.'

A similar dependence appears at times in terms which Coleridge uses, as in the opposition here of 'life' and 'death' or the familiar remark in *Biographia Literaria* that "the products of the mere reflective faculty partook of Death." This is a common and crucial distinction in Coleridge, but the words 'life' and 'death' in such contexts do not represent logical categories; they denote qualities of experience, the same qualities which we find in "The Ancient Mariner" and in "Dejection."

These statements rest upon intuitively apprehended qualitative distinctions, and in this they are consistent with Coleridge's assertions as to the nature of philosophy. Philosophy for him was not so much a means of arriving at the 'truth' as it was a means of exposition of a truth already 'felt.' "Deep thinking," he wrote to Poole, "is attainable only by a man of deep Feeling, and . . . all Truth is a species of Revelation." [28] In a notebook, he wrote of

> the dignity of passiveness to worthy Activity when men shall be as proud within themselves of having remained an hour in a state of deep tranquil Emotion, whether in reading or in hearing or in looking, as they now are in having figured away one hour/ O how few can transmute activity of mind into emotion/ yet there are who active as the stirring Tempest & playful as a May blossom in a Breeze of May, can yet for hours together remain with hearts broad awake, & the Understanding asleep in all but its retentiveness and receptivity/ yea, & the Latter evinces as great Genius as the Former/ [29]

"Language & all *symbols* give *outness* to Thoughts/ & this the philosophical essence & purpose of Language/" [30] A valid metaphysical formulation will "tell for something in the Heart" because it provides such "outness" for what was first discovered in introspection. Thus in a letter to Thomas Clarkson, Coleridge introduced some remarks on the nature of God and the Soul by saying:

> What the Spirit of God *is*, and what the Soul *is*, I dare not suppose myself capable of conceiving: according to my religious

and philosophical creed they are *known* by those, to whom they are revealed. . . . *Datur*, non intelligitur. . . . The only reasonable form of question appears to me to be, under what connection of ideas we may so conceive and express ourselves concerning them, as that there shall be no inconsistency to be detected in our definitions, and no falsehood felt during their enunciation, which might war with our internal sense of their actuality. . . .[31]

And in a marginal note on the works of Jacob Boehme, he wrote that "in all knowledge" we must distinguish between "the mode of acquiring, and the mode of communicating it." The first of these, he continued, is "Intuition, or immediate Beholding." The second is "the *art* of reasoning, by acts of abstraction, which separate from the first are indeed mere shadows, but, like shadows, of incalculable service in determining the rememberable outlines of the Substance." [32]

The term 'Reason' which Coleridge came to attach to 'immediate beholding' may well have been derived from Kant, but it meant to him something outside the limits of Kant's epistemology. While Coleridge on many occasions made use of the Kantean concept of *Vernunft*, Reason in what was to him the "highest as well as the most comprehensive sense," [33] referred to a kind of experience which Kant, whom he once criticized as "a wretched Psychologist," [34] did not admit.[35] Reason, he said in an unpublished note, is not a faculty of the individual mind "but a Presence, an Identification of Being and Having." [36]

We speak of ourselves as possessing reason; and this we cannot otherwise define than as the capability . . . of beholding, or being conscious of, the divine light. But this very capability is itself that light, not as the divine light, but as the life or indwelling of the living Word, which is our light; that is, a life whereby we are capable of the light, and by which the light is present to us, as a being which we may call ours, but which I cannot call mine; for it is the life that we individualize, while the light, as its correlative opposite, remains universal.[37]

Reason, for Coleridge, is the apprehension of 'reality' by, so to speak, being real, and is distinguished from discursive consciousness as a different level of existence. The note on Boehme which I have just cited continues: "Qui vere discit, intuendo discit: ast intueri, sensu spirituali, vult idem ac *esse existentialiter.* Quantum sumus, intuemur. [He who learns truly learns by contemplating: but to contemplate, in the spiritual sense, means the same as to be in an existential sense. To the degree to which we are, we contemplate]." [38] And he wrote in *The Friend:*

> The groundwork, therefore, of all pure speculation is the full apprehension of the difference between the contemplation of reason, namely, that intuition of things which arises when we possess ourselves, as one with the whole, which is substantial knowledge, and that which presents itself when, transferring reality to the negations of reality, to the ever-varying framework of the uniform life, we think of ourselves as separated beings, and place nature in antithesis to mind, as object to subject, thing to thought, death to life. This is abstract knowledge, or the science of the mere understanding. By the former, we know that existence is its own predicate, self-affirmation, the one attribute in which all others are contained, not as parts, but as manifestations. It is an eternal and infinite self-rejoicing, self-loving, with a joy unfathomable, with a love all-comprehensive. It is absolute; the absolute is neither singly that which affirms, nor that which is affirmed; but the identity and living *copula* of both.[39]

In contrast to such "contemplation of reason," to the "immediate beholding of 'truth,'" speculative thought, the "*art* of reasoning, by acts of abstraction," is, or should be, the communication of truth, to oneself and to other people. Philosophical concepts thus become, for Coleridge, "propaideutic," and, at least in the case of the ultimate truth, God, "mythical." In his own very free translation of a passage from an unidentified "Greek philosopher," he wrote, "those notions of God which we attain by the process of the discursive Understanding the Soul will contemplate as *mythical* when it exists (for its own consciousness) in union (or co-presence) with the Father, and is feasting, as a guest in his House, on the Truth of the absolute Being and in a *pure* Splendor." [40] Philosophy is what the conceptualizing intellect can make of the experience of the "contemplation of reason," or, in the words of Evelyn Underhill, "the comment of the intellect on the proceedings of spiritual intuition— . . . classifying its data, criticizing it, explaining it, and translating its vision of the supersensible into symbols which are amenable to dialectic." [41]

If such was Coleridge's position, two important conclusions follow. In the first place, his use of the work of other writers need not be seen simply or primarily in terms of influence. While he may well make use of the symbols and arguments of other men, one who regards reasoning as a means of exposition of the truth will differ from one who regards reasoning as a means *to* the truth in his attitude towards what other men have written. He may admire, but he will not be convinced by, the force of logic alone, since for him the validity of the conclusion does not depend upon the validity of the logical argument which supports it. He is more concerned to find adequate symbols than irrefutable arguments. Conversely, he may find value in a work which seems logically indefensible. This is characteristic of Coleridge. The fact that "the originality, the depth, and the compression of the thoughts; the novelty and subtlety, yet solidity and importance of the distinctions; the adamantine chain of the logic [of Kant's philosophy] . . . took possession of me as with a giant's hand" [42] did not in the least prevent him from the first from differing radically and fundamentally from Kant where the limits of knowledge were concerned, or from thinking him "but suspicious Authority" [43] on the powers of the human mind. Nor did his awareness of the "gross ignorance" of the Neoplatonists in physics and psychology,[44] of the bizarre obscurities of Boehme, of the superstitions of Paracelsus, prevent him from finding in them if not a more lucid exposition, at least a more significant grasp of reality than he found in the most *logical* empiricists. What he looked for, and what he often borrowed, was not a new 'world view,' but a language, a system of "symbols . . . amenable to dialectic" in which the "contemplation of reason" could be expressed.

In the second place, Coleridge's philosophical work appears, as I have already suggested, as primarily symbolic and descriptive rather than logical and systematic. Simply to assert that he conceived of Reason "in the highest . . . sense" as essentially a faculty of 'mystical' insight would be only to repeat what has been said, and sometimes denied, in the past. But if what is involved in such insight is not merely a vague will to believe but a recognizable kind of experience, then it is possible to examine the philosophy not as a more or less incoherent and derivative system, but as a symbolic projection of such experience. And this in turn would suggest that when philosophy replaced poetry as Coleridge's primary activity, the language and symbols of philosophy came to serve some of the same functions that had earlier been served by the language and symbols of poetry.

In the first two chapters, then, I shall examine some aspects of the pattern which I think emerges in Coleridge's poetry. And in the remainder of this study, I shall consider in relation to that pattern what seem to me some central elements in his philosophical and critical speculations.

Chapter I

"THE RIME OF THE ANCIENT MARINER" remains the central document in Coleridge. Not only is it generally acknowledged to be his most accomplished poem, the one to which over many years he devoted the most care and attention, it is also, as Miss Coburn's edition of the Notebooks makes beautifully clear, the work in which he best knew himself and in which he most fully embodied those patterns of experience which dominate his work both before and after. Passages foreshadowing the poem are scattered through earlier poems and notebooks, and later entries clearly show, in Miss Coburn's words, "the unconscious subjectivity of the poem . . . emerging into something like consciousness." [1]

Many years ago, Leslie Stephen said that with a little ingenuity one could find in "The Ancient Mariner" all of Coleridge's philosophy,[2] and any number of ingenious critics have found reflected in the poem theoretical ideas which Coleridge held at one time or another. Insofar as the statement is true, however, it is true not because of philosophical concepts which preceded the poem and were symbolically embodied in it, but because the poem is the final and successful culmination of a series of efforts to create in a poetic object an 'objective correlative' for 'inner' phenomena which the philosophy tries to account for in abstract theoretical terms. As Humphry House has written, "the whole poem is part of the exploration [of the mysteries and uncertainties of mental life]. It is part of the experience which led Coleridge into his later theoretic statements (as of the theory of the Imagination) rather than a symbolic adumbration of the theoretic statements themselves." [3]

Even Robert Penn Warren admits that the themes which he finds in the poem need not have pre-existed in its author's mind.[4] And Irene Chayes, who sees the Mariner as "an embodiment of the potentialities of error by the human mind" in the light of passages from *Biographia Literaria* and *Aids to Reflection,* concludes that "this poem may have suggested or opened the way for more complex and more subtle meanings than Coleridge at the time of original composition would have been able to formulate discursively."[5] My point, however, is that the poem is not merely a stage on the way to theoretical formulation any more than it is the product of such formulation. Poem and theory are analogues with a common basis in experience, and we need to consider not only the relation of poem and theory, but of both to that common basis.

The poem does not appeal to the rationalizing intellect. It presents experience for contemplation, not speculation. It makes us powerfully aware of possible modes of consciousness, but it explains nothing, either explicitly or implicitly. Explanation and theory do not constitute the meaning of the poem, but are another possible way of dealing with the same areas of experience, another kind of language.

Writing in *Biographia Literaria* of Wordsworth's Intimations Ode, Coleridge said,

> the ode was intended for such readers only as had been accustomed to watch the flux and reflux of their inmost nature, to venture at times into twilight realms of consciousness, and to feel a deep interest in modes of inmost being, to which they know that the attributes of time and space are inapplicable and alien, but which can yet not be conveyed save in symbols of time and space.[6]

To some degree this applies to "The Ancient Mariner" as well. The poem is a narrative, a record of events apparently consecutive in time and contiguous in space. It is a narrative of a voyage to the other side of the world and also, as nearly any critic would agree whatever his interpretation of the poem, of a mental or spiritual voyage. The Mariner not only leaves the familiar world of village, church, and lighthouse to travel to strange and desolate seas; he also leaves the world of ordinary experience to discover extremes of agony and ecstasy. This mental voyage does not take place in time and space but rather moves out of it. The poem begins and ends in time (though we do not know exactly when) and space (though we do not know exactly where). But at the center of the poem, time and space cease to be essential coordinates. The ship is static in a boundless sea unmoved by wave or wind. The days of the Mariner's ordeal are numbered, but by that oldest of 'mystic' numbers, *seven*, which is qualitatively suggestive rather than temporally definitive.

The world of time and space is the world of ordinary consciousness, at least for modern Western man. It is our way of locating things and selves in relation to each other, and it underlies our definition of those things and selves. The Mariner does not go from this place to that place, from this time to that time. What changes is not his location but his relation to the world around him, the structure, so to speak, of his experience. The watersnakes whose beauty he blesses are the same creatures whose loathsomeness repelled him. The world of lovely lights and sweet sounds is the same 'place' as that in which his anguished soul was an alien. The consciousness that shrank in upon itself in an agony of isolation is the same as that which opens out in a gush of love. The realist looks to experience, but in experience, the Mariner discovers, there is another dimension than time and space, a dimension in which the boundaries between subject and object, between *I* and *it* are not fixed but fluid.

I shall discuss in a later chapter Coleridge's efforts to reconcile in theory what he knew from experience with what he accepted from the empirical tradition of his day. The poem wisely attempts no such theorizing, through symbolism or otherwise. It rather dramatizes the confrontation. By his physical presence, the Mariner stands as a bridge between the familiar and the unfamiliar, between the commonplace reality of the outer, public world and the extraordinary reality of the inner world of consciousness. The Wedding Guest is confronted by the Mariner, by skinny hand, grey beard, and glittering eye. The Mariner is a fact. And by his "strange powers of speech" he persuades the Wedding Guest that his tale is also a fact. But the Mariner cannot explain; he can only describe. Faced with that description, the commonplace mind is at a loss: the hermit prays, the pilot "falls down in a fit," the pilot's boy goes mad, the Wedding Guest departs "like one who has been stunned." The Mariner knows what happened to him, but he does not understand what happened. His was an experience of overwhelming significance, but he can state that significance only in conventional and traditional terms: "He prayeth best, who loveth best / All things both great and small." These are the only words in which he can sum up for himself what he has to teach, the only formulation, it may be, which the Wedding Guest, the pilot and his boy, or the hermit could understand. But this is only the rationalized residue; this is not what stuns or maddens the matter-of-fact mind. The Mariner is compelling not as commentator but as a witness, as he who simply tells what it is that he has seen. His final response may seem a simpleminded platitude. But in the still center of the poem, he has known the limits of human consciousness.

Not only do the Mariner and those who see and hear him not explain; Coleridge in various ways artfully suppresses the reader's natural tendency to rationalize, forces us to 'suspend disbelief,' drives us beyond what we believed. The vividness and brilliance of the imagery give the events of the Mariner's narration an extraordinary intensity and immediacy, confront us with them as physical things as the Wedding Guest is confronted with the Mariner's "glittering eye." But our need to rationalize is, so to speak, diffused and drawn off. We are there as in a dream, but, as in a dream, we do not consider where we are. The Mariner tells his tale to the Wedding Guest, and the whole is told us by the completely impersonal matter-of-fact narrator of the opening and closing stanzas. Intensely present, the events are vaguely remote from our normal frame of reference. Because we do not know where we are, we do not know what labels we should apply. We are therefore forced, again like the Wedding Guest, simply to watch and listen.

The gloss which Coleridge later added is a further step in this artful isolation of the experience from rationalization and explanation. As E. E. Stoll remarked in the course of making quite another point,[7] the gloss belongs to a world as remote from us, as incredible to our rational minds, as the world of spectre-barks and spirits from the land of mist and snow. It is one more voice, one more frame, a circle at one more remove from the immediate 'facts' which are presented to us. The gloss seems like a commentary, but it provides a psychological rather than a rational satisfaction. Our questions are answered with learned allusions to Michael Psellus or the Jew Josephus, and we accept, our disbelief transmuted for the moment into faith.

Jung tells a story of a difficult patient with whom he could make little progress because, as he puts it, "my patient's animus was steeped in Cartesian philosophy and clung so rigidly to its own idea of reality that the efforts of three doctors—I was the third—had not been able to weaken it." One day, as the patient was recounting a dream involving a golden scarab,

> suddenly I heard a noise behind me, like a gentle tapping. I turned around and saw a flying insect knocking against the window pane from outside. I opened the window and caught the creature in the air as it flew in. It was the nearest analogy to a golden scarab that one finds in our latitudes, a scaraboid beetle . . . which contrary to its usual habits had evidently felt an urge to get into a dark room at this particular moment.[8]

The incident seemed to the patient, and also to Jung himself, to be more than chance. She seemed to be confronted with an impossible matter of fact, with the result that "her natural being could burst through the armour of her animus possession." She rose, like the Wedding Guest, a wiser if not necessarily a sadder woman.

Something like this happens in the poem. It happens to the Wedding Guest who discovers that there are more things in heaven and earth than had been dreamt of in his philosophy. It happens to the reader, for the poem has the Mariner's power of speech. We are made to share the Mariner's experience to such a degree that we are forced to acknowledge its reality, to realize that in form and quality if not in circumstance, what happened to him may happen to us. And one great achievement of the poem is that it permits us, compels us, to contemplate these possibilities of experience which our rational intelligence normally will not let us admit.

The Mariner's experience is impossible; his tale is incredible. His experience is impossible because we 'know' that spectre-barks, figures of Death and Life-in-Death, and spirits from the land of mist and snow do not 'exist.' We know this both because we have never seen such things and because our rational understanding of the universe convinces us that such things cannot be. This, however, we can explain in various ways. Insofar as we read the poem as narrative, we can explain them as the Mariner's hallucinations—perhaps to some degree we should, since they also become ours. Insofar as we assume that the poet intended a further meaning, we may translate them; we may, that is, substitute for them a set of ideas, as critics have frequently and ingeniously done.

But the Mariner's experience is impossible, at least to the Cartesian mind, in another and more important way. He not only sees impossible *things*. He experiences extremes of agony and ecstasy, of alienation and communion which have no place in a Cartesian view of reality. Yet it is precisely to this experience of alienation and communion that we respond, and which in our depths we recognize. And our recognition makes us realize that the Mariner's experience is not impossible or even unique. It is rather something which we have trouble accounting for, and which we normally therefore disregard or, more usually, suppress.

The quality of the Mariner's experience as distinct from the "symbols of time and space" by which it is conveyed becomes clearer when we see it in relation to other accounts couched in different terms. We may, as I have already suggested, find such accounts among the writings of various mystics who also describe both the agony of the isolated self and the ecstasy of communion, both what Boehme calls the "Dark World" of "bitterness" and "hardness" and the "Light World" of "sweetness," "fluidity" and "Divine Play." [9] We may find them too in other poets, most obviously in other Romantics, who were similarly concerned to explore modes of consciousness. The fall of Blake's Urizen into isolated selfhood is a striking example, and no better illustration could be found of the Mariner's condition when he feels himself alone in the universe than Blake's plate of Urizen crouched in a state of almost catatonic withdrawal. But there are analogies as well, if fainter ones, in Wordsworth, in Shelley, and in Keats. And we seem to find them, as we now well know, in descriptions of some forms of psychosis and of the influence of certain drugs.

I do not wish to suggest that Coleridge was a madman or that "The Ancient Mariner" should after all be taken as an opium dream any more than I wish to suggest that he was an unrecognized saint or bodhisattva, but I do wish to turn for a moment to an account from the literature of psychosis, from John Custance's *Wisdom, Madness, and Folly,* written while the author was suffering from recurrent attacks of acute mania and depression. The value of such an account lies in the fact that while it describes experiences in some respects, at least, analogous to those of the Mariner, it does so in very different language, and it avoids problems of influence or ideological intent. It therefore enables us to distinguish more clearly between what may belong only to the correlative image and what may be characteristics of possible states of consciousness and may therefore be 'given' in experience itself.

Mania and depression, as the terms imply, seem to be two different but equally 'abnormal' states, sometimes separated by periods of 'normal' consciousness. For Custance, one of these was a state of extreme exultation, the other of unimaginable horror. In the state of exultation, which he calls a "universe of bliss," the world seemed suddenly transformed:

> The whole aspect of the world about me began to change . . . .
> The whole of infinity seemed to open up before me, and during the weeks and months which followed I passed through experiences which are virtually indescribable. The complete transformation of 'reality' transported me as it were into the Kingdom of Heaven. The ordinary beauties of nature, particularly, I remember the skies at sunrise and sunset, took on a transcendental loveliness beyond belief.[10]

Custance experienced what he calls a "breach in the barriers of individuality," an ecstatic sense of harmony or oneness with the universe, of communion with all things and all people. He felt an overwhelming 'love' for all things: nothing, not even the most loathsome, repelled him. And he experienced "strange flashes of insight" in which it seemed "as though all truth, all the secrets of the Universe were being revealed, as though I had some clue, some Open Sesame to creation." The corresponding "universe of horror," on the other hand, exhibited features which were "precisely the reverse of those of the manic [state]." There was "a sort of strengthening of the barriers of individuality, a hardening of the shell of the ego. I seem shut into myself, withdrawn from real contact with the outer world, as also from contact with God." He was now repelled by all things and paralyzed by guilt and fear.

The Mariner's ordeal is also at first one of isolation, and like Custance's it is isolation in a universe of horror, a horror directly associated with his own sense of guilt. He is first isolated from human society, cut off from his fellow men by their condemnation, their "evil looks," and by the fact that thirst makes speech impossible. Then with the death of his fellows, as the anguish deepens, he finds himself alone in a strangely alien world of burning sun and burning sky, alone in a universe without pity. Custance remarks how he seemed surrounded by what was loathsome and disgusting. So too the Mariner finds himself surrounded by "a thousand thousand slimy things":

> I looked upon the rotting sea
> And drew my eyes away;
> I looked upon the rotting deck,
> And there the dead men lay.

Custance found himself overwhelmed by guilt, convinced of his own damnation, utterly cut off from 'God.' The Mariner, turning his eyes from the rotting sea and the rotting ship, similarly finds no relief from Heaven:

> I looked to heaven and tried to pray;
> But or ever a prayer had gusht,
> A wicked whisper came, and made
> My heart as dry as dust.

At the nadir of his depression, Custance says, "I lay in my bed in the ward of the hospital dominated above all by an overpowering

sense of fear . . . . I lay as motionless as I could, covering my head
as a rule with the bedclothes, partly to shut out the sights and sounds,
partly as a sort of instinctive reaction." [11] The Mariner too, and also
without success, tries to withdraw:

> I closed my lids and kept them close,
> And the balls like pulses beat;
> For the sky and the sea, and the sea and the sky
> Lay like a load on my weary eye,
> And the dead were at my feet.

Naked on a rotting ship, with nowhere to hide and with the symbol
of his guilt hung round his neck, he is exposed to the glaring immensity of a merciless universe. In all that wide world of sea and
sky, there is nothing to nourish or sustain him, nothing which does
not stand in opposition to his anguished self.

As for Custance the 'manic' phase of his illness seemed the exact
opposite of his depression, so the Mariner's salvation is the reversal
of his torment. Love replaces anguish; what was loathsome becomes
indescribably beautiful; what repelled, attracts:

> Beyond the shadow of the ship,
> I watched the water-snakes:
> They moved in tracks of shining white,
> And when they reared, the elfish light
> Fell off in hoary flakes.

> Within the shadow of the ship
> I watched their rich attire:
> Blue, glossy green, and velvet black,
> They coiled and swam; and every track
> Was a flash of golden fire.

No longer cut off from God, he can pray once more. The universe
bursts into life and is filled with music.

Custance was insane. He had no control over such states of mind
and was overwhelmed and incapacitated by them. But they may
occur, if perhaps with less intensity, in more 'normal' people. They

are not something utterly different from a 'sane' consciousness, but are rather, so to speak, something underlying or surrounding it. "Normal life and consciousness of 'reality,'" Custance writes, "appear to me rather like motion along a narrow strip of table-land at the top of a Great Divide separating two distinct universes from each other." [12] Put in another way, these two states seem to 'lead out' of ordinary consciousness in opposite directions which may be characterized by Custance's figure of the "barriers of individuality," the distinctions between the self and the not-self. In the direction of 'depression,' there is a constant intensification of these 'barriers,' a sort of progression through distinction, division, antipathy, alienation. "If I were asked," Custance says, "to characterize in the briefest possible way, the whole experience of the depressive phase, I would describe it as a total reaction of repulsion between those fundamental poles of all being as we perceive it, which can be roughly designated as the individual and the environment, the 'I' and 'Not I,' the ego and 'the other,' the perceiver and the perceived (including inner perceptions), or even as the soul and God. The basis of that repulsion seems to be fear or 'anxiety,' to use the word generally employed to translate the Freudian concept of 'Angst.'" [13] In the other direction, that of mania, there is a feeling of attraction, a lessening of 'barriers,' a loss of the sense of self as something apart.

Thus described, the states of mania, depression, and 'normal' consciousness seem not so much three separate psychic areas as different points in a single pattern, a continuum whose extremes are utter alienation and complete communion, and one of whose essential variables is the intensity of the sense of self. The Mariner's voyage, we might almost say, is the record of the evolution of a self, the history of an ego. The world of the Wedding Guest, who is only a guest at the wedding, an observer of the ritual but not a participant, is a world in which selves are public objects defined by their social relationships as bride or groom or next of kin. The Mariner's preference for the church rather than the marriage feast, his desire

> To walk together to the kirk,
> And all together pray,
> While each to his great Father bends,

> Old men, and babes, and loving friends
> And youths and maidens gay!

is the result of his discovery that the depths of the self are known not in social relations but in relation to the universe and to 'God.' To leave the social world as he has done, to find oneself alone in the immensity of the universe, is to experience a terror and a beauty which no mortal mind can long sustain. He has returned to be in, though he can never again be entirely of, the social world. But having had such experience, he can only see the limits of that world as false, its definitions as shams, the pageantry of the marriage feast as insubstantial. The homely image of men kneeling and praying together reflects his awareness of and his need to connect his two worlds, the two modes of being he has known and cannot now escape.

The Mariner is not mad, though to the Wedding Guest he at first seems mad. But his position has again something in it akin to that of the mad as described by R. D. Laing:

> Psychotic experience goes beyond the horizons of our common, that is, our communal sense.
>
> What regions of experience does this lead to? It entails a loss of the usual foundations of the 'sense' of the world that we share with one another. Old purposes no longer seem viable; old meanings are senseless; the distinctions between imagination, dream, external perceptions often seem no longer to apply in the old way. External events may seem magically conjured up. Dreams may seem to be objective reality. But most radical of all, the very ontological foundations are shaken. The being of phenomena shifts and the phenomenon of being may no longer present itself to us as before. There are no supports, nothing to cling to, except perhaps some fragments from the wreck, a few memories, names, sounds, one or two objects, that retain a link with a world long lost. This void may not be empty. It may be peopled by visions and voices, ghosts, strange shapes and apparitions. No one who has not

experienced how insubstantial the pageant of external reality can be, how it may fade, can fully realize the sublime and grotesque presences that can replace it, or that can exist alongside it.

When a person goes mad, a profound transposition of his place in relation to all domains of being occurs. His center of experience moves from ego to self. Mundane time becomes merely anecdotal, only the eternal matters. . . . An exile from the scene of being as we know it, he is an alien, a stranger signalling to us from the void in which he is foundering, a void which may be peopled by presences that we do not even dream of. They used to be called demons and spirits, and they used to be known and named. He has lost his sense of self, his feelings, his place in the world as we know it. He tells us he is dead. But we are distracted from our cosy security by this mad ghost who haunts us with his visions and voices, which seem so senseless and of which we feel impelled to rid him, cleanse him, cure him.[14]

The Mariner, that greybeard loon, also disturbs our "cosy security," but since he is only a character in a poem, we do not try to cure him; we explain him away.

The Mariner begins his voyage merely as one of a group: it is not until the last line of Part I that he uses the word 'I': "I killed the albatross." Until then, he has used only the plural pronoun, the collective 'we.' It is with his unmotivated, inexplicable act of violence that he becomes a self-conscious individual rather than a social unit. In the succeeding stanzas, it is, with few exceptions 'I' and 'they.' It is thus that we become individual to ourselves, thus, in Blake's terms, that we enter the world of 'experience.' 'I' discover myself by discovering the difference between 'I' and 'it,' by opposing, resisting, killing, 'it.' The Mariner who has hitherto been indistinguishable from his fellows, who has done nothing, now becomes the one individual, the dominant actor: "I beheld . . . I bit . . . I sucked . . . I cried." But the Mariner's very existence as an individual leads directly to his agony, as he finds himself not only apart but alone, an alien ego in a universe of 'it,' tortured by the isolation of his own selfhood, a selfhood so rigid that "I could not die."

The Mariner is a point, pinned at the still center of the universe. He cannot move because there is no context against which he can move: he is a part of nothing. The only relationship he is conscious of is that of 'not-I.' His emergence from this state of complete alienation begins, appropriately, with movement:

> The moving Moon went up the sky,
> And nowhere did abide:
> Softly she was going up,
> And a star or two beside—

He becomes aware of movement as, in his intolerable self-isolation, he begins to discover himself in the universe around him. We may be reminded of Coleridge's comment that,

> in looking at objects of Nature while I am thinking, as at yonder moon dim-glimmering thro' the dewy window-pane, I seem rather to be seeking, as it were *asking*, a symbolical language for something within me that already and forever exists, than observing any thing new. Even when that latter is the case, yet still I have always an obscure feeling as if that new phaenomenon were the dim Awaking of a forgotten or hidden Truth of my inner Nature/ It is still interesting as a Word, a Symbol! It is Λόγος, the Creator! and the Evolver! [15]

The Mariner sees the moving moon not simply as an alien event but as one intelligible in terms of feelings of which he simultaneously becomes aware. She moves "softly" and "nowhere did abide." And this awareness is immediately followed by the realization that the "slimy things" which repelled him are beautiful, are not after all alien but are joined to him by the love which "gushed from my heart" and led him to bless them "unaware."

In a fragment from *Osorio* entitled "The Dungeon," written about a year before "The Ancient Mariner" but published with it in *Lyrical Ballads,* Coleridge described a somewhat similar transformation. The criminal, "Each pore and natural outlet shrivell'd up / By ignorance and parching Poverty" until "His energies roll back upon his heart, / And stagnate and corrupt," is imprisoned, surrounded by

> . . . friendless solitude, groaning and tears,
> And savage faces, at the clanking hour,
> Seen through the steams and vapours of his dungeon,
> By the lamp's dismal twilight! So he lies
> Circled with evil, till his very soul
> Unmoulds its essence, hopelessly deform'd
> By sights of ever more deformity!

Nature, in contrast,

> Healest thy wandering and distemper'd child:
> Thou pourest on him thy soft influences,
> Thy sunny hues, fair forms, and breathing sweets,
> Thy melodies of woods, and winds, and waters,
> Till he relent, and can no more endure
> To be a jarring and a dissonant thing,
> Amid this general dance and minstrelsy [.]

In "The Dungeon," however, the emphasis falls on the difference between two distinct physical environments, that which confirms 'deformity' and that which heals, so that the state of mind seems the product of external circumstances. The Dungeon is 'there' and Nature is 'there' and a man may be in one place or the other. The Mariner's prison is his own selfhood: he stays in the same 'place'; the elements in his experience remain the same. It is the configuration that changes.

The blessing of the watersnakes marks the end of the Mariner's isolation. He discovers that he can pray once more, and the burden of the Albatross, the *thing* which he killed and thereby made a thing, drops from his neck and sinks "like lead into the sea." The events which immediately follow also involve release and relief. The anguished 'I' finds unconsciousness in sleep. Thirst is relieved by rain. Thirst of course is traditionally associated with spiritual dryness and rain with the reawakening of life. But even without such traditional association, the rain would be meaningful here. Kenneth Burke's equation of the rain with the physical relief of urination[16] may be an exaggerated suggestion, but he is quite right in sensing that the rain, like the sinking of the Albatross, conveys a feeling of release, of letting go. The alienated ego is knotted up like a constricted muscle. Alienation disappears, we might say, with the relaxation of the ego.

The Mariner does not lose consciousness permanently, nor does he return to his original state of what might be called preindividuality. He awakes, but to a new state of awareness. He no longer feels his own body:

> I moved, and could not feel my limbs:
> I was so light—almost
> I thought that I had died in sleep,
> And was a blessed ghost.

An 'I' is present, but with two minor exceptions ("the body and I pulled at one rope"; "I took the oars") it does not act except to see, to hear, to pray. It is an 'I' which is a consciousness but not an actor. The last four verbs which the Mariner utters are *see, know, teach, tell*.

As the Mariner's sense of self has changed, so has his awareness of the universe around him. His release began with his awareness of motion, and the universe is now full of movement.

> The upper air burst into life!
> And a hundred fire-flags sheen,
> To and fro, they are hurried about!
> And to and fro, and in and out,
> The wan stars danced between.
>
> .   .   .   .
>
> Around, around, flew each sweet sound,
> Then darted to the Sun;
> Slowly the sounds came back again,
> Now mixed, now one by one.

Instead of a universe of things, he is aware of a harmony of sensation, of sound and color. At the beginning of his voyage, before his meeting with the Albatross and before he had become an 'I,' the Mariner was also surrounded by light and sound, but the light was "a dismal sheen" and the sounds were those of ice which "cracked and growled, and roared and howled, / Like noises in a swound!" Lowes has remarked that anyone who has been knocked senseless knows what it is to "come up through those bizarre and sinister noises" as consciousness returns.[17] It is not too much to suggest that they precede self-consciousness for the Mariner, whereas the sweet sounds and lovely lights, the exquisite harmony, come afterwards, and the consciousness of *things* lies in between.

The Mariner's new situation is precarious. He has not simply entered into Paradise. The "curse" can, and does, return. He is "in fear and dread. . . . Because he knows, a frightful fiend / Doth close behind him tread." Moreover, his new world is as strange, as inexplicable, as far from the one he left so long ago, as was that of his anguished isolation. Coleridge once wrote that "the dim Intellect *sees* an absolute oneness, the perfectly clear Intellect *knowingly perceives* it. Distinction and plurality lie in the Betwixt." [18] The Mariner never quite emerges into that clear light. He remains an ordinary, in his own terms a rational, man who has had extraordinary experiences, who has known unearthly terror and unearthly beauty, who like Plato's philosopher and like Dante, returns to the cave, but unlike them returns only as a witness who does not understand and cannot interpret his own tale. He is perhaps closer to Keats who, at the conclusion of a not wholly dissimilar experience, says "Fled is that music:—Do I wake or sleep?"

This lack of comprehension, of which I have spoken earlier, is important in connection with the often debated moral significance of the poem. While the Mariner suffers after killing the Albatross, and while this suffering is seen as penance, the moral status of the act is by no means clear. It was not until the addition of the gloss many years after the original composition of the poem that it was specifically labelled a "crime," and even then its criminal nature is unexplained. The sense of selfhood as contraction, disjunction, alienation, producing a world of destructive antagonism rather than harmonious interaction runs throughout Coleridge's writing, and in his later work is explicitly associated with the explanation of evil. But at the time of the poem, his theoretical position was less certain. In "Religious Musings," he had presented a contrast between one who thinks "his self, his own low self the whole" and one who "by sacred sympathy might make / The whole one self, self that no alien knows." But in "The Eolian Harp," the sense of the universe as melody leads only to reproof by the orthodox and more serious eye of Sara, and in "Reflections on Having Left a Place of Retirement," the contemplation of "Omnipresence" is said to involve "feelings all too delicate for use" and is dismissed in favor of social action.

"The Ancient Mariner" does not embody a moral conclusion but presents a fact of experience which has profound moral implications. It is a measure of Coleridge's artistry that he does not here, as he does elsewhere, pursue those implications. Wordsworth's 'answer' to "The Ancient Mariner," "Peter Bell," ostensibly so much more 'realistic,' is in fact a far more theoretical poem. We are told exactly why Peter does as he does and the whole poem is informed with the author's conception of moral regeneration. The Mariner's act produces dire consequences, but it has no antecedents. It is willful yet inexplicable: it simply happens.[19] It is significant that six years after he had written the poem, Coleridge could still speculate about a similar episode in which sailors tried to shoot a hawk that had attempted to land on the ship carrying him to Malta: "Poor Hawk! O strange lust of Murder in Man!—It is not cruelty/ it is mere non-feeling from non-thinking."[20]

It may well have been the presence in the poem of the notion of penance and later the addition of the term "crime" that led Coleridge to remark that the poem had too much moral, that it should have been like the story in which a genie must kill a man because the man threw away a date pit which put out the eye of the genie's son. The words *crime* and *penance* imply moral judgment, but moral judgment, if it is to be meaningful, implies conscious action or intention. The Mariner does not intend. He does not begin to think or feel until he has acted. He and his fellows judge his act only as they become aware of its consequences. The act of violence that tears apart the self from the not-self is like the casting of the date pit:

only the results prove its significance. And even they do not prove it surely and entirely evil: as in Blake, it is only by knowing the world of experience that the Mariner can become, like the Wedding Guest, a sadder but a wiser man. Whether the wisdom was worth the sadness is a question the poem does not answer.

For the most part, what I have said concerns not the whole poem but the Mariner's tale which is contained within the poem. As I have read it, the Mariner's tale is a 'myth' whose 'meaning' is not a set of ideas and attitudes but a psychic process in itself preconceptual but whose form and qualities are externalized, made available to contemplation in the concrete object of the poem. The myth is significant both for the psychic process which it embodies and for the manner of the embodiment, the symbolic rather than literal use of language, the production of concrete images which, because they are structurally and qualitatively identical with the psychic process, provide an objective correlative for what can otherwise be known but not conceived.

But the whole poem, which includes the myth, is a 'fable' in which both of these aspects of myth are related to the communal world of ordinary thinking and ordinary language. This is the thought and language of the impersonal narrator and of the writer of the gloss, who describe a series of things and events and, in the case of the gloss, comment upon them. It is the language of the Wedding Guest, the Hermit, the Pilot and his Boy. The language of the Mariner does not work in the same way nor embody the same kind of thinking. That is why he is disruptive, compelling but inexplicable. The Wedding Guest cannot simply assimilate the facts of the Mariner's experience to the patterns of facts which he already knows; he must add new dimensions to his thinking.

The fable therefore 'means' in a different way from the myth. As characters in the fable, the Mariner and the Wedding Guest have an ideological as distinct from a psychic significance. The Poet confronts his audience; the Prophet or Seer confronts the world of "single vision and Newton's sleep"; the *mental* traveller confronts the resident of the physical world of time and space. Elements in the Mariner's tale may also function as elements in the fable, and many critics have interpreted the entire poem in this way. But as elements in the myth, they do not function in the same way, and their 'meaning' cannot be reduced to a concept or a set of concepts.

The relation between literal narrative, fable, and myth which I am suggesting may perhaps be seen as in some degree analogous to the much more formal distinctions which Dante describes in his famous letter to the Can Grande della Scala. The fable, we might say, contains both allegory and trope, and its meaning can be abstracted and restated. The meaning of the myth, however, is the anagoge, and because it is nonconceptual, it can be expressed only by a symbolic pattern.

The position of "The Ancient Mariner" in relation to other parts of Coleridge's work involves both the myth and the fable. At the beginning of this chapter, I referred to Leslie Stephen's remark that with ingenuity one could find all of Coleridge's later philosophy in "The Ancient Mariner," and I suggested that insofar as this was true, it was because the poem was "an objective correlative for 'inner' phenomena which the philosophy tries to account for in theoretical terms." The sense of experience as a continuum between extremes of alienation and communion, between the contraction of self and the expansion or dissolution of self, is not only found in many of Coleridge's other poems but is an underlying pattern in his speculative thought as well. Coleridge believed, as have many others, that the fundamental structure of consciousness was the same as the fundamental structure of the external universe, that, in his own terms, an 'Idea' in the mind (defined not as a concept but as a genetic pattern) corresponded with a 'law' in the world of physical phenomena. And the fundamental structure which he found given in consciousness and which he thereafter tried to show was also implicit in physical phenomena, was the structure which he embodied in the myth of the Mariner.

It is not only as myth, however, that the poem is related to other areas of Coleridge's writing; it is also relevant as fable. Coleridge was not only a Mariner, a witness to the possibilities of experience. He was also enough a child of the eighteenth century to believe that reality could be understood as well as known, and understood ultimately in terms acceptable to an 'enlightened' rational mind. In the development of Coleridge's thought, the problem posed by the confrontation of Mariner and Wedding Guest is as important as the Mariner's experience itself.

In an appendix to *Aids to Reflection*, Coleridge presents "a sort of allegory or parable" to illustrate the difference between mysticism and philosophy. The story concerns three men, each of whom visits and describes "an *oasis* or natural garden" situated in "a wilderness or desert." The first, "a poor pilgrim . . . pursuing his way in the starless dark with a lantern in his hand," is led to the oasis by "chance or his happy genius." He sees the beauties of the oasis by the light of his lantern, but then, "scared by the roar and howl from the desert," he flees, and in his haste and fear, "shadows and imperfect beholdings and vivid fragments of things distinctly seen blend with the past and present shapings of his brain. Fancy modifies sight. His dreams transfer their forms to real objects; and these lend a substance and an outness to his dreams." When at last he meets with other men and tells of his experience, "his narration is received as a madman's tale." Such a man, Coleridge adds, is the "enthusiastic mystic" Jacob Boehme. The second man, also a traveller, visits the oasis by moonlight, and "the moonshine, the imaginative poesy of Nature, spreads its soft shadowy charm over all, conceals distances, and magnifies heights, and modifies relations; and fills up vacuities with its own whiteness, counterfeiting substance; and where the dense shadows lie, makes solidity imitate hollowness; and gives to all objects a tender visionary hue and softening." This is "a Mystic . . . of a nobler breed—a Fenelon." The third man, the philosopher, is "the residentiary, or the frequent visitor of the favored spot, who has scanned its beauties by steady daylight, and mastered its true proportions and lineaments." [21]

The striking applicability of this parable to "The Rime of the Ancient Mariner" has been noted by a recent critic, Irene Chayes.[22] But Miss Chayes uses it only to support her thesis that the Mariner like the mystic is in error. I have already discussed the fact that the Mariner does not understand, cannot explain what has happened to him. But he has had, nevertheless, a "vision shadowy of truth." In Coleridge's parable, the oasis of life in the desert of normal consciousness is real, not an error. And the true philosopher "will discover that both pilgrims have indeed been there. He will know, that the delightful dream, which the latter tells, is a dream of truth; and that even in the bewildered tale of the former there is truth mingled with the dream." [23] The philosopher can recognize the truth in the dream because he has "thought deeply within himself of the goings-on of his own mind" and has found the same oasis in his own experience. His role is to convey the true lineaments of that oasis to fellow travellers who have never consciously been there, to bridge the gap between Mariner and Wedding Guest. And this was the consistent aim of Coleridge's speculative thinking.

The relationship between the seer and the rational man was a problem for Coleridge the poet as well as for Coleridge the thinker and not only in "The Ancient Mariner." And it was a problem which as a poet he rarely solved both to his own complete satisfaction and to ours. Any number of poems are more or less seriously marred by the intrusion of what he once called "metaphysical bustards," [24] of a discursive voice which is often shrill and labored, and which attempts to explain rather than express. He seems then to write not as he felt, but as he felt he must, and we can only guess to what extent this was the result of his own need to make his contemplative vision intelligible and relevant to the public world of thought and action and to what extent it reflected what he took to be the demands of his audience. Like Wordsworth, he believed the poet to be a "man speaking to men" and in some sense in their language. In "The Ancient Mariner," as we have seen, he protected his divergence from the ordinary language of men, from ordinary ways of thought, by dramatizing the problem of communication within the poem. But it is significant that even so, after the initial adverse reaction, he republished the poem with the apologetic and explanatory title "A Poet's Reverie," if not a madman's dream. And the unwritten essay on the supernatural in poetry which was promised as a prefix to the poem and whose contents we can in part deduce from Coleridge's many fragmentary remarks on the subject would have served as further justification and explanation. Even more revealing is the fact that he delayed for years the publication of one of his own masterpieces, and finally published it as a "psychological curiosity" with a lengthy explanation not of what it 'means' but of how it came to be written, an explanation, we might say, intended to forestall the objections of those who might be expected like the Squire in Wordsworth's "Peter Bell" to cry,

> Hold . . . against the rules
> Of common sense you're surely sinning;
> This lead is for us all too bold;
> Who Peter was, let that be told,
> And start from the beginning.

It was, certainly, a cry that he heard from contemporary reviewers.[25] For us, "Kubla Khan" needs no such explanation, is not a fragment. For Coleridge, or at least for his anticipated audience, it, like so many of his 'unfinished' poems, required something more, something to make it rationally as well as mythically complete. To the discursive mind, "The Ancient Mariner" is at least coherent if incredible as narrative. "Kubla Khan" is not.

A similar point could be made about a number of other poems. "Christabel" remained a fragment because, I think, Coleridge could never work out, as he did for "The Ancient Mariner," a narrative structure that would 'contain' his myth. A number of verses which Coleridge never published and which E. H. Coleridge included as "Fragments" are fragments only in that they lack an intelligible discursive or narrative framework. Consider, for example, Fragment 55:

> His native accents to her stranger's ear,
> Skill'd in the tongues of France and Italy—
> Or while she warbles with bright eyes upraised,
> Her fingers shoot like streams of silver light
> Amid the golden haze of thrilling strings.

This is made a fragment by the first two lines. Without them, it could almost be the work of a modern imagist. The first two lines are the beginning of an attempt to give the image a narrative setting, an intelligible *raison d'être*.

Fragments 2 and 49 are free from such vestigial encumbrances:

2

Sea-ward white gleaming thro' the busy scud
With arching Wings, the sea-mew o'er my head
Posts on, as bent on speed, now passaging
Edges the stiffer Breeze, now, yielding, drifts,
Now floats upon the air, and sends from far
A wildly-wailing Note.

49

Water and windmills, greenness, Islets green;—
Willows whose Trunks beside the shadows stood
Of their own higher half, and willowy swamp:—
Farmhouses that at anchor seem'd—in the inland sky
The fog-transfixing Spires—
Water, wide water, greenness and green banks,
And water seen—

Perhaps these do not quite stand alone, have not quite "come right
with a click." But if so it is not because they lack a narrative which
would provide an occasion for them or a didactic statement which
they could illustrate. And if there may be doubt about these, there
can be none about "Phantom," which Coleridge wrote before 1805
and which was finally included nearly thirty years later in the last
edition of his poems.

All look and likeness caught from earth
All accident of kin and birth,
Had pass'd away. There was no trace
Of aught on that illumined face,
Uprais'd beneath the rifted stone
But of one spirit all her own;—
She, she herself, and only she,
Shone through her body visibly.

A generation raised on "In the Metro" and "The Red Wheelbarrow"
requires no more, if as much.

Some years ago, Jacques Maritain argued that the distinction between 'classical' and 'modern' poetry lay in the fact that in the classical poem, "creative intuition" originating in the "preconscious life of the Intellect" must in search of expression pass "mainly through full-grown and definitely formed images . . . and through concepts existing under the regime of the logos. . . . The work of words, bound to this logical organization, had, thus, a *double signification* . . . the first of which . . . belongs to the realm of rationalized and socialized communicability." But in the modern poem, "creative intuition in search of expression is not bound to pass through reason-dominated concepts and full-grown images which have been logically organized. The creative process is free to start developing in the nest of dynamic unity of image and thought where the music of intuitive pulsations takes place, and where emotion and nascent images are pregnant with virtual intelligibility." The "internal organization" of the poem depends "only on the transreality to be signified." [26] Whether we think in Maritain's terms of "transreality" or in terms of psychic pattern, we might say that Coleridge was moving towards a 'modern' poem but that this movement was inhibited by his own acceptance of 'classical' demands which were finally incompatible with his own artistic impulse.[27]

At the outset of this chapter, I said that "The Ancient Mariner" remains the central document in Coleridge. It was, to a much greater degree, obviously, than he was aware at the time of its original composition, the astonishingly adequate symbol not only of much that he had experienced in the past but of much that was still latent within him. We might well apply to it a passage which he wrote in his notebook on the way to Malta at a time when the poem was much in his mind:

Poetry a rationalized dream dealing [?about] to manifold Forms our own Feelings, that never perhaps were attached by us consciously to our own personal Selves.—What is the Lear, the Othello, but a divine Dream/ all Shakespeare, & nothing Shakespeare.—O there are Truths below the Surface, in the subject of Sympathy, & how we *become* that which we understandly [sic] behold & hear, having, how much God perhaps only knows, created part even of the Form.—[? and so] good night—[28]

Because the poem stands in this relation to Coleridge, it seems both the culmination of what went before and the foreshadowing of much that was still to come. I should like to turn now first to a consideration of some of what went before and then to some of what came later, especially in metaphysics and critical theory, keeping in mind "The Ancient Mariner" as our best image of the Coleridge from whom the whole body of work derived.

Chapter 2

IT WAS ONCE COMMON TO REGARD "The Ancient Mariner," "Chrisabel," and "Kubla Khan" as the products of an almost miraculous development in Coleridge's poetical powers, of which his earlier work offered little if any anticipation. Few critics would now maintain such a position. Since G. M. Harper's seminal essay on the so-called "conversation poems,"[1] some at least of the earlier poems have received substantial critical attention and have been recognized as achievements worthy in themselves and important in the development of English Romanticism. And since Lowes' profoundly influential study, there has been general recognition of the fact that the poems of the *'annus mirabilis'* did not come into being *ex vacuo*, that a part at least of their history may be traced in images that appear in earlier poems and notebooks. In his recent study of "Kubla Khan," for instance, Marshall Suther approaches the problem of the 'meaning' of the poem through an exhaustive examination of all the related images which he can discover.[2]

In view of such developments, it is all the more surprising that there should be so little attention paid to the *pattern* of development which the early work reveals or to the degree to which it foreshadows "The Ancient Mariner." At least a partial exception must be made for Max Schulz's *The Poetic Voices of Coleridge,* for Schulz has argued that "Coleridge's poems are the work of an artist seeking definite ends" and that his various poetic "voices" represent his attempts to evolve "a style natural to him and his time."[3] But he sees "The Ancient Mariner" as a "magnificent" experiment in a style which led nowhere and which was discarded in favor of others which came closer "to realizing [his] ideal of poetry."[4] While there is much that is valuable in Schulz's study, his argument leaves him in the unfortunate position of having to present some of Coleridge's greatest poems as in some ways inferior to a quantity of relatively minor verse which, in terms of his schema, represents a stylistic advance. And his treatment of "The Ancient Mariner" as an instance of a soon to be discarded style, obscures its position in the mainstream of Coleridge's development.

If, like Schulz and some other critics, we consider "The Ancient Mariner" as essentially a literary ballad, then we may see it only as Coleridge's most successful effort in a genre that includes "Christabel," "The Three Graves," "The Ballad of the Dark Ladié," "Love," "Alice du Clos," and "Baron Guelf of Adelstan."[5] But if we read it as in the previous chapter, then we may find it more closely akin to earlier poems in other genres than to other ballads; we may see it as the culmination of Coleridge's efforts to "put together some form to fit [the feeling]"[6] and of his concern with the myth of the mental wanderer. Coleridge's work prior to 1798 may easily seem a potpourri of 'voices.' Like most poets, he imitated and experimented. But, especially if we exclude the *juvenilia* and the topical and occasional verse, we do find a major line of development. We find a continuing effort to give poetic form to certain states of mind, particularly 'visionary' states. We find the development of that fusion of inner and outer, subjective and objective, private and public that W. K. Wimsatt described in "The Structure of Romantic Nature Imagery"[7] and which M. H. Abrams has brilliantly developed in "The Greater Romantic Lyric."[8] And we find a persistent concern with the problem of relating what has often if misleadingly been called 'noncognitive experience' and symbolic expression with 'public' experience and communal language. We find, that is, some of the problems of "The Ancient Mariner."

I shall examine several poems briefly and three in considerable detail in which these concerns appear and in which we can trace something of the evolution of three central patterns which we found in "The Ancient Mariner." The first of these is the figure of some sort of a journey both physical and mental, the figure of the traveller and the oasis. The second is what I may call the pattern of

Mariner and Wedding Guest, embodying the confrontation, and sometimes the attempted reconciliation, of different modes of being, of thought, of language. The third is what I shall call, borrowing a term from Albert Gérard,[9] the systolic pattern, the pattern of expansion and contraction which is so marked a feature of many poems. These three are, as Coleridge might say, distinguishable rather than different. The Mariner confronts the Wedding Guest in the role of returned traveller. The journey out and back may be a form of the systolic pattern. But the distinction can be made and it helps to simplify thinking and discussion.

In the chapter entitled "The Halted Traveller" which opens his study of Wordsworth, Geoffrey Hartman suggests that "it might be useful to consider the Romantic Lyric as a development of the surmise." The term is derived from Milton's "Lycidas" and, presumably, from the last lines of Keats's "On First Looking into Chapman's Homer." The poetic projections of 'surmise,' Hartman says, "add up to more than their sum: they revive in us the capacity for the virtual, a trembling of the imagined on the brink of the real, a sustained inner freedom in the face of death, disbelief, and fact. . . . The reflective stopping of the poet, which is like the shock of self-consciousness and may express it in a mild and already distanced form, is a general feature of Romantic lyricism." [10] He proceeds to speak of

> the influx of an unusual state of consciousness which is quickly normalized. A Wordsworth poem is then seen to be a reaction to this consciousness as well as its *expression*. . . . The supervening consciousness, which Wordsworth names Imagination in *Prelude* VI, and which also halts the mental traveller in the Highlands, is *consciousness of self raised to an apocalyptic pitch*. The effects of 'Imagination' are always the same: a moment of arrest, the ordinary vital continuum being interrupted; a separation of the traveller-poet from familiar nature; a thought of death or judgment or of the reversal of what is taken to be the order of nature; a feeling of solitude or loss or separation.[11]

As Hartman's remarks suggest, the patterns which I have enumerated are by no means exclusively Coleridgean. The sense in which

Hartman uses the term 'surmise' does not exactly fit my purpose, but Coleridge is not exactly Wordsworth, however alike they may sometimes seem to be. Coleridge's traveller is not 'halted' in quite the same way; there is not the same sense of 'usurpation' that is so important to Wordsworth, nor is the "unusual state of consciousness" so quickly, or so easily, "normalized." Coleridge is more likely than any other major Romantic except Shelley (or Blake if he be included in the pantheon) to try to push beyond "the trembling of the imagined on the brink of the real" to the assertion of vision. But there is recurrently in Coleridge both the figure of the traveller and the interruption of the 'normal' linear sequence of events by a discovery or an awareness which stops or cuts across that linear sequence.

Coleridge's traveller does not usually embark on a voyage so obviously extraordinary as is that of the Mariner; more commonly his journey is no more than a country stroll. But from the juvenile sonnet "Life" to "The Ancient Mariner" itself, Coleridge's most characteristic stance is that of one moving in terms of time and space from the ordinary to the extraordinary and, in most instances, returning again to his starting point. One does not, I think, stretch the point too far in saying that this is the pattern of all the 'conversation poems.' As the Mariner between his departure and return discovers the visionary beauty of the watersnakes, so does the poet leave his "pretty cot" and climb a hill to contemplate what "seem'd like omnipresence"; so does he, at least in imagination, escape his "Lime-Tree Bower" and wander to a spot where he beholds "such hues as veil the almighty spirit." Even "The Eolian Harp," "Frost at Midnight," and "The Nightingale" exhibit, if less obviously, a similar essential structure.

All of these except "The Ancient Mariner" might be called meditative poems, and a country walk, actual or imagined, had long been a conventional setting for meditation. The degree to which Coleridge's figure of the traveller diverges from the convention and becomes an element in a poetic structure which embodies the peculiar shape and movement of the poet's mind becomes apparent, however, when we look at a series of poems in which the figure appears, beginning with an early and still conventional one. Among Coleridge's juvenile poems is a sonnet dated September, 1789:

As late I journey'd o'er th'extensive plain,
Where native Otter sports his scanty stream,
Musing in torpid Woe a Sister's pain—
The glorious prospect woke me from the dream.
At every step it widen'd to my sight—
Woods, meadows, verdant hills, and barren steep
Following in quick succession of Delight—
Till all—at once my ravish'd eye did sweep!
May this (I cried) my course thro' life pourtray!
New scenes of Wisdom may each step display,
And knowledge open, as my days advance:
Till, when Death pours at length th'undarkened day,
My eye shall dart thro' infinite expanse,
While Thought suspended lies in Transport's blissful trance! [12]

There is here nothing new or distinctive in the use of landscape or journey, nor in the conception of life to which the contemplation of the landscape gives rise. It was over sixty years earlier that Dyer in "Grongar Hill" had described how "Wide and wider spreads the vale" and had shown how "Thus is nature's vesture wrought, / To instruct our wand'ring thought," and many a wandering bard before and since had found a moral meaning in the scene which spread before him. Coleridge merely draws a commonplace moral analogy from a conventional description. Precisely the same sort of thing appears in Southey's 1794 sonnet "On Lansdown Hill" which Coleridge praised [13] and sent to Mary Evans.[14]

Although Coleridge later in his familiar criticism of Bowles complained of such a use of description as "a trick of moralizing everything" which "proves faintness of Impression," [15] it is of course not infrequent in his own maturer work. "Rudely vers'd in allegoric lore," he could turn a mountain into "The Hill of Knowledge" ("To a Young Friend"), could see in an early blossom "dim analogies" with the death of Chatterton and the oppression of Poland ("On Observing a Blossom"), could trace in a wind-blown myrtle leaf the fate of a fallen woman ("To an Unfortunate Woman"). There are traces of such moralizing even in the first two of the conversation poems: in "The Eolian Harp," jasmin and myrtle are "Meet emblems

. . . of Innocence and Love"; and in "Reflections on Having Left a Place of Retirement," the song of the invisible skylark is equated with "the inobtrusive song of Happiness."

Elisabeth Schneider has argued [16] that this is the only kind of 'symbolism' which Coleridge employed, but while such use of images as 'emblems' persists, we begin very soon to find something else as well. In the pattern established by Dyer and other earlier 'nature poets,' the structure of the poem is determined by the sequence of the objects observed, and the speaker matches these observed objects with appropriate reminiscences or moral reflections. This matching is the kind of process which Coleridge was later to term the mechanical fancy. The succession of objects provides a succession of opportunities for the speaker to find apt analogies or reminiscences, but there is no change or development in the *manner* in which he sees or thinks. Increasingly, however, Coleridge seems concerned to express in his poems changes not in what the speaker sees, but in *how* he sees. And whatever physical movement occurs in the poem serves not to provide a change of objects for consideration but an analogue for a movement of mind.

A hint of a new development may be found in a still largely conventional poem written six years after "Life": "Lines composed while climbing the left ascent of Brockley Coomb, Somersetshire, May 1795":

> With many a pause and oft reverted eye
> I climb the Coomb's ascent: sweet songsters near
> Warble in shade their wild-wood melody:
> Far off the unvarying Cuckoo soothes my ear.
> Up scour the startling stragglers of the flock
> That on green plots o'er precipices browze:
> From the deep fissures of the naked rock
> The Yew-tree bursts! Beneath its dark green boughs
> (Mid which the May-thorn blends its blossoms white)
> Where broad smooth stones jut out in mossy seats,
> I rest:—and now have gain'd the topmost site.
> Ah! what a luxury of landscape meets
> My gaze! Proud towers, and Cots more dear to me,

> Elm-shadowed Fields, and prospect-bounding Sea!
> Deep sighs my lonely heart: I drop the tear:
> Enchanting spot! O were my Sara here!

Whereas in the earlier poem, description of the landscape is confined to one very general line ("Woods, meadows, verdant hills, and barren steep"), it here occupies eleven of the sixteen lines. Instead of merely saying "I journey'd . . . it widen'd . . . Till all—at once my ravish'd eye did sweep," Coleridge here conveys both his journey and the unfolding of the landscape through the description. We are given, however derivative the language, an account of an experience rather than merely the basis for an analogy. And in fact no analogy is drawn. Perception leads not to moral reflection but to sighs, tears, a feeling of enchantment, a longing for Sara. Weak though they be, the last two lines are an attempt to articulate an emotional response which is a part of the experience described rather than an intellectual response *to* it.

The conclusion of the poem is disappointing because the speaker's response is *asserted* and in banal language, and because the "luxury of landscape" is reduced to a neoclassic *"prospect bounded by* the sea." The speaker's experience, we might say, is reduced to and bounded by conventional language; the boundless reverberations of experience are conceived as a "spot," as what we can frame or label and carry away with us or give to someone else. But there is a little more to it than this. Physically, there is only one direction in the poem: upward towards the mountaintop. But the speaker climbs "With many a pause and oft reverted eye," and when at last he sees the world spread before him, it includes the "Cots more dear to me" from which he came and where, presumably, his Sara remains. This backward looking ascent reflects a state of mind. On the one hand, the speaker moves eagerly towards the revelation which awaits him; the *"startling* stragglers" and the yew tree which "bursts" from the fissures of the rock prepare for the "Ah!" with which he greets the sudden vision. But he looks back as well as forward; he cannot lose himself in the sublimity of the view; his response is "bounded" by his longing for Sara; the last line echoes the first:

> With many a pause and oft reverted eye
>
> .   .   .   .
>
> Enchanting spot! O were my Sara here!

All this does not mean that the poem is more than mediocre. But it does mean that Coleridge is using the traveller and the landscape in a different way from what appears in "Life." The description of the climb does not provide the *occasion* or *excuse* for the expression of thoughts, but rather serves to *dramatize* a state of mind, to define the shape of a consciousness.

As I would not imply by the length of my comment that the poem is more than mediocre, neither would I suggest that it involves the kind of 'vision' of which I have spoken earlier, though in some respects it is very closely akin to poems in which such a vision is expressed. There is, nevertheless, some hint at least of what I called the systolic pattern. And if there is no confrontation nor occasion for confrontation of Mariner and Wedding Guest, the "oft reverted eye" perhaps foreshadows something of the condition in which that confrontation arises.

From these early poems, I shall now turn to three in which Coleridge's divergence from convention becomes increasingly clear and increasingly significant: "Reflections on Having Left a Place of Retirement" (1795), "The Eolian Harp" (1795), and "This Lime-Tree Bower My Prison" (1797). On the basis of the dates of the earliest known versions,[17] the second of these is a slightly earlier poem than the first, but the familiar text is one which evolved over a period of time, and "The Eolian Harp" reveals, I think, a stage of development somewhat beyond that of "Reflections."

In "Reflections on Having Left a Place of Retirement," Coleridge again used the figure of a mountain climb but to much greater effect and with more interesting results. The figure appears in the second of the poem's four sections:

> But the time, when first
> From that low Dell, steep up the stony Mount
> I climb'd with perilous toil and reach'd the top,
> Oh! what a goodly scene! *Here* the bleak mount,

The bare bleak mountain speckled thin with sheep;
Grey clouds, that shadowing spot the sunny fields;
And river, now with bushy rocks o'er-brow'd,
Now winding bright and full, with naked banks;
And seats, and lawns, the Abbey and the wood,
And cots, and hamlets, and faint city-spire;
The Channel *there*, the Islands and white sails,
Dim coasts, and cloud-like hills, and shoreless Ocean—
It seem'd like Omnipresence! God, methought,
Had built him there a Temple: the whole World
Seem'd *imag'd* in its vast circumference:
No *wish* profan'd my overwhelméd heart.
Blest hour! It was a luxury—to be!

In his recent study, *Coleridge and the Abyssinian Maid*, Geoffrey Yarlott says of this passage:

> In the second stanza the lens widens, enlarging from the 'dell' until it encompasses the panoramic view from the nearby mountain-top. The 'But' with which this stanza commences marks an antithesis between microcosm and macrocosm, and forms a hinge on which the thought-movement of the poem swings . . . . As Coleridge describes his difficult ascent of the 'stony Mount' which walls in the 'dell,' one is half-prepared for 'Chattertonian' euphoria but, instead, we are given a carefully ordered description of the panorama outspread before him. Though he walks apart from men, his thoughts remain with them, so that instead of seeking the windy heights he pauses to identify places of human interest—the 'seats, and lawns, the Abbey and the wood, / And cots, and hamlets, and faint city-spire.' This renewed concern with human habitations suggests a reawakening of moral and political concerns.[18]

While I agree with much of what Yarlott says about the poem, it seems to me that he somewhat misrepresents the movement of this passage, and that his description applies better to a similar but significantly different passage in "Fears in Solitude":

> On the green sheep-track, up the heathy hill,
> Homeward I wind my way; and lo! recalled
> From bodings that have well-nigh wearied me,
> I find myself upon the brow, and pause
> Startled! And after quiet sojourning
> In such a quiet and surrounded nook,
> This burst of prospect, here the shadowy main,
> Dim-tinted, there the mighty majesty
> Of that huge amphitheatre of rich
> And elmy fields, seems like society—
> Conversing with the mind, and giving it
> A livelier impulse and a dance of thought!
> And now, belovéd Stowey! I behold
> Thy church-tower, and, methinks, the four huge elms
> Clustering, which mark the mansion of my friend;
> And close behind them, hidden from my view,
> Is my own lowly cottage, where my babe
> And my babe's mother dwell in peace!

Here the same situation, the same setting *is* used to convey a return of the mind to friends and family. But in "Reflections" this is not the case. The speaker's vision moves not merely from object to object, but from the most concrete, the most clearly perceived, to the most distant and elusive, a movement emphasized by the italicized words "*here*" and "*there*." In "Fears in Solitude," the movement is from the "shadowy main" *here* to the fields, the village, the house *there*. But in "Reflections," as the speaker's vision moves from the mountain "*here*" at his feet, down through the fields, past abbey, woods, and villages, to the city spire faint in the distance, and then to the dim coasts, cloud-like hills, and shoreless ocean, the concrete precise image becomes more distant, its outlines less distinct, more easily merged into one totality, until

> It seem'd like Omnipresence!

There is an order, a structure, but it leads not to "human interest" but to a moment in which there is, significantly, no concern with past or future, no concern with practical purpose. The experience satisfies all desire:

> No *wish* profan'd my overwhelméd heart.
> Blest hour! It was a luxury—to be!

In this section of the poem, then, the imagery parallels a movement of mind from the specific perception to an all-embracing vision in which specific perceptions become parts of a felt whole, and the increasing shadowiness of the visual images as they merge in the distance conveys this movement, this experience. What is only seen becomes absorbed in what can only be felt ("Omnipresence"). We may be reminded of the notebook passage in which Coleridge wrote:

> Unconsciously I stretched forth my arms as to embrace the Sky, and in a trance I had worshipped God in the Moon/ the Spirit not the Form/ I felt in how innocent a feeling Sabeism might have begun/ O not only the Moon, but the depth of Sky!—the Moon was the *Idea;* but deep Sky is of all visual impressions the nearest akin to a Feeling/ it is more a Feeling than a Sight/ or rather it is the melting away and entire union of Feeling & Sight/ [19]

or of the comment in a letter that "the further I ascend from animated Nature . . . the greater becomes in me the intensity of the feeling of Life. Life seems to me then a universal spirit, that neither has, nor can have, an opposite. God is every where, I have exclaimed, & works every where; & where is there *room* for Death?" [20]

The mountain passage, however, includes only seventeen of the seventy-one lines of the poem, and seems to have little logical relation to what precedes and follows it. The first section (lines 1–26) is a description of Coleridge's cottage at Clevedon and of an occasion when "A wealthy son of Commerce saunter[ed] by" and called it "a Blesséd Place." The third section (lines 43–62), which Harper takes to be the poem's climax, is a didactic statement rejecting "feelings all too delicate for use" in favor of active involvement in the cause of social justice. And the fourth (lines 63–71) looks forward to the soothing effect that memories of the "dear Cot" will have and expresses the wish for a time of equality when "all had such." Without the mountain passage, these three sections would form a conventional descriptive-moralizing poem, and the mountain passage seems on this level an unnecessary intrusion. It is introduced, in the middle of a broken line, with an awkward transition: "But the time, when first . . . I climb'd." It is referred to only once in the remainder of the poem, in the line which immediately follows it:

> Ah! quiet Dell! dear Cot, and Mount sublime!

And here the reference is merely to the mountain, a place to be catalogued along with the Dell and the Cot. Not even the word "sublime" is sufficient to comprehend the experience of omnipresence, the luxury of being.[21]

The passage interrupts the development of the descriptive-moralizing poem because in it the speaker moves not only from one place to another, from the bounded Dell to the mountaintop, but from one level of experience to another, from the perception of a sequence of things to an awareness of "something one and indivisible."[22] And the transition is awkward in part because this involves a movement from one sort of language to another, from the language of 'public' experience to the language of 'inner' experience.

Most of what is described in the first section of the poem is what would be noticed by any conventional observer: the cottage with a rose peeping through the chamber-window; the "little landscape" which "refresh'd the eye"; the commercially minded citizen of Bristol who is led by the scene to "muse / With wiser feelings"; and finally the sound of the "viewless sky-lark's note." Where the speaker's response enters, it is formalized in a 'public' rhetoric, in terms which his "sweet girl" or any reader might use. The sight of "Bristowa's citizen" pausing on his Sunday stroll leads him to reflect "methought, it calm'd / His thirst for idle gold"; and he interprets the skylark's note to his "Belovéd" as "the inobtrusive song of Happiness," using it, as we have seen before, as an emblem.

The second section of "Reflections," the mountain passage, is not so much descriptive and didactic as dramatic. The speaker is not merely an observer and commentator standing apart from what he describes, nor are the images interesting only for themselves or for the ideas which they suggest. The speaker is now involved in an experience which is intrinsically significant: its meaning is its form, not some idea with which it may be linked in a formal simile. The images, as we have seen, reveal the movement of the speaker's mind from one mode of apprehension (the perception of things) to another (the apprehension of wholeness). As a result, the comparison "it seem'd like Omnipresence" is significantly different from the earlier comparison of the skylark's song to the "song of Happiness." In the latter instance, a word denoting an abstract idea (happiness) is associated with a word denoting a conception of a specific thing (a skylark's song). Each term in the comparison is separately intelligible, and the conception of neither is altered by the comparison. The word "Omnipresence," however, derives much of its meaning from the lines which precede it. Without them, it is a vague, possibly a meaningless term; by them it is given, so to speak, an experiential reference.[23]

The poem ends, as many critics have noted,[24] where it begins. It begins and ends in a spot which the reader, like the citizen of Bristol, may easily share, in the familiar world of things and ideas embodied in conventional rhetoric. But in between, the poem rises to a level which we may recognize and talk *about*, but where conventional rhetoric is no longer appropriate or adequate, where experience is a whole not an aggregate, where the distinction between things, between perceiver and perceived, dissolves.

In one significant respect, we may now say, the first section does anticipate and prepare for the second. In spite of the emphasis on conventional images and reflections, there is also a pervasive concern with sensation which is not clearly differentiated or defined. This is revealed by the use of auditory as opposed to visual imagery. The ear is less objective than the eye. We are told of a place which is silent except for "The Sea's faint murmur," a sound at the periphery of consciousness. "Bristowa's citizen" is "Hallowing his Sabbath-day by quietness." The skylark is "Viewless," known by sound, not sight; or if by sight, then "haply for a moment seen / Gleaming" like a sudden apparition. The analogy with the "song of Happiness," also "inobtrusive" and "only heard / When the Soul seeks to hear; when all is hush'd," may reduce this to a 'public' statement, but we have also perhaps been prepared for another kind of understanding of what may be known by the quiet soul, the listening heart.

To some extent this justifies the apparent awkwardness of the "but" which introduces the second section and which does, as Yarlott says, provide a sort of "hinge on which the thought-movement of the poem swings." [25] The first section describes a peaceful and pleasant scene such as anyone might see and in terms which anyone might use. *But,* we might say, there is more to it than 'peace' and 'pleasure,' more than can be conveyed by descriptive catalogue and reflective comment, more than we are at first aware of in the bounded dell of our minds. We may sense something "at silent noon, and eve, and early morn"; we may respond to "the viewless skylark's note." *But* if we would know and express what we feel "when all is hush'd, / And the Heart listens," we must ascend from our dell and climb "with perilous toil" the visionary mount.

With line 42,

Ah! quiet Dell! dear Cot, and Mount sublime!

there is again a change in the speaker's language and in his mode of consciousness. Left behind, dell, cot, and mountain are merely objects seen or thought of from a distance as the speaker turns to active involvement in a public world. In this world, the visionary moment seems unreal or unimportant, not a sense of omnipresence but only a feeling "all too delicate for use." Wordsworth could discover in a spot of time the seed of his moral and ethical development, and could move smoothly, as Herbert Lindenberger has so well demonstrated,[26] from a private to a public language. But for Coleridge here, the remembered moment has no such ethical content to carry over and enrich the public and the practical. The ethical order which he accepts derives from other sources, from other kinds of thought, and he has as yet no single language which can reconcile the two. It is worth observing that the two 'visionary' political poems of about this time, "The Destiny of Nations," and "Ode to the Departing Year," are visionary in a very different sense. The personified human passions and social and historical forces in these poems serve as a way of seeing and talking about the public world and themselves provide an ethical context. In "Religious Musings," which I shall discuss in the next chapter, Coleridge does with some success attempt to relate the vision of omnipresence to a practical ethic, but he does so by calling on a variety of philosophical, theological, and poetic sources for assistance.

The last two sections of "Reflections" are neither successful nor convincing. They seem to me an instance of Coleridge writing, as I mentioned in the previous chapter, what he felt he should. The ostensible subject of the whole poem is the rejection of the dell of contemplation in favor of the arena of public action, of the fight for "Science, Freedom, and the Truth in Christ." In that arena, the returned traveller can only dismiss his ascent to another mode of being as a pleasant but useless memory, an amiable spectre which cannot, like the Mariner, compel the attention of a practical world to its stunning tale. Nevertheless, although the poem finally presents such a point of view, the mental journey is there and it is this and not the affirmation of pious intentions which determines the structure of the poem.

Whatever the shortcomings of "Reflections" as a poem, it does clearly contain the three patterns which I mentioned earlier in this chapter. The same patterns and some of the same problems appear also in "The Eolian Harp," a more successful and more complex poem which was begun, but not completed, a few months earlier.[27] "The Eolian Harp" also starts from and returns to the cottage at Clevedon. The opening description is similar but even more explicitly emblematic ("Meet emblems they of Innocence and Love") and even more strongly marked by the suppression of the perception of things in favor of an awareness of qualities of sensation in a "world *so* hush'd": we are told of the fading light in the clouds, the "scents / Snatched from yon bean-field," and again of the "stilly murmur of the distant Sea" so close to the periphery of consciousness that it "Tells us of silence." And it is again the sound of music—though of a wind-harp rather than a nightingale—that provides a bridge from a world of things to participation in a universal harmony, an expanded consciousness. Finally, the poem ends with a return to a 'public' language—though of religious orthodoxy rather than social ethics. The systolic pattern and the pattern of confrontation are clear, and the figure of the journey is faint but not absent.

"The Eolian Harp" has, for the purposes of this discussion, one great advantage in that it exists in several versions, including an early first draft in manuscript, which enable us to trace the poem's development and to see how its pattern, ultimately so similar to that of "Reflections," came into being. The first draft of the poem, "Effusion xxxv" in the Cottle manuscript,[28] gives little hint of such a pattern.

> My pensive SARA! thy soft Cheek reclin'd
> Thus on my arm, how soothing sweet it is
> Beside our Cot to sit, our Cot o'ergrown
> With white-flowr'd Jasmine and the blossom'd myrtle,
> (Meet emblems they of Innocence and Love!)
> And watch the Clouds, that late were rich with light,
> Slow-sad'ning round, and mark the star of eve
> Serenely brilliant, like thy polish'd Sense,
> Shine opposite! What snatches of perfume
> The noiseless gale from yonder bean-field wafts!
> The stilly murmur of the far-off Sea
> Tells us of Silence! and behold, my love!
> In the half-closed window we will place the Harp,
> Which by the desultory Breeze carress'd,
> Like some coy maid half willing to be woo'd
> Utters such sweet upbraidings as, perforce,
> Tempt to repeat the wrong!

We cannot, of course, be certain that when he wrote this draft, Coleridge considered it a complete poem. But I think it is significant that if so considered it is not only very similar to the first section of "Reflections" but seems akin also to such other poems of about the same date as "To the Nightingale" ("Effusion xxiii") and "Lines written at Shurton Bars" ("Epistle I") in which love for Sara is the dominant concern. The description of his response to the music of the nightingale in the first of these may remind us of both "The Eolian Harp" and "Reflections":

> O! I have listen'd, till my working soul,
> Waked by those strains to thousand phantasies,
> Absorb'd hath ceas'd to listen!

But instead of leading to the expression of a new level of consciousness, the nightingale's song becomes only the minor term in a comparison: "all thy sweet diversities of tone / . . . Are not so sweet as is the voice of her, / My Sara." Similarly, in the first draft of "The Eolian Harp," the music merely provides a metaphor for a lover's feelings.[29]

In the version published in 1796, the function of the harp image is radically changed. The poem now continues:[30]

> And now, its strings
> Boldlier swept, the long sequacious notes
> Over delicious surges sink and rise,
> Such a soft floating witchery of sound
> As twilight Elfins make, when they at eve
> Voyage on gentle gales from Fairy-Land,
> Where *Melodies* round honey-dropping flowers,
> Footless and wild, like birds of Paradise,
> Nor pause, nor perch, hov'ring on untam'd wing!
>
> And thus, my Love! as on a midway slope
> Of yonder hill I stretch my limbs at noon,
> Whilst thro' my half-clos'd eyelids I behold
> The sunbeams dance, like diamonds, on the main,
> And tranquil muse upon tranquillity;
> Full many a thought uncall'd and undetain'd,
> And many idle flitting phantasies,
> Traverse my indolent and passive brain
> As wild and various, as the random gales
> That swell and flutter on this subject Lute!
> And what if all of animated nature
> Be but organic Harps diversly fram'd,
> That tremble into thought, as o'er them sweeps,
> Plastic and vast, one intellectual Breeze,
> At once the Soul of each, and God of all?

> But thy more serious eye a mild reproof
> Darts, O beloved Woman! . . . .

In this version, the function of the harp is somewhat ambivalent. No longer the objective correlative of a sentimental passion, it now serves both as a transition to a sense of synaesthetic harmony and as the basis for a metaphysical analogy. In view of the fact that the birds of paradise passage appears independently as a notebook entry[31] and that Coleridge tried to delete it from the 1797 edition, we may reasonably assume that the second of these functions was then his primary concern. We have thus a situation much like that in "Reflections," where the music serves to prepare for the mental shift which follows and which is marked by a physical change of location:

> And thus, my Love! as on a midway slope
> Of yonder hill I stretch my limbs at noon [.]

Only in this case the emphasis is on a speculative rather than an experiential development. And it is this speculation which, under the "mild reproof" of Sara's "more serious eye" is rejected in the last section of the poem.

As Coleridge's passing desire to delete lines 20–25 indicates, the experiential response had already been developed further than the speculative analogy required. Not only, however, did he finally retain these lines, but it was this section of the poem which he further developed in later versions. In 1803, he replaced the birds of paradise with the lines

> Methinks, it should have been impossible
> Not to love all things in a World like this,
> Where e'en the Breezes of the simple Air
> Possess the power and Spirit of Melody!

In 1817, he retained these lines but restored the birds of paradise and further added in the *Errata* for insertion between the birds of paradise and the lines added in 1803, the familiar quatrain,

> O! the one Life within us and abroad,
> Which meets all motion and becomes its soul,

> A light in sound, a sound-like power in light,
> Rhythm in all thought, and joyance everywhere [.]

Finally, in 1828 and thereafter, the poem was printed as we know it, incorporating the additions and with a few changes in wording, of which the most important is the alteration of the third and fourth of the 1803 lines to read

> Where the breeze warbles, and the mute still air
> Is Music slumbering on her instrument.

The effect of these additions is to shift the climax of the poem from the third to the second section, so that it occurs before rather than after the physical movement to "yonder hill," and thus to put the mental journey out of phase with that physical movement. Even the rejected speculations now seem part of the mental return to the public world, and the shift to "yonder hill" corresponds not to a journey from ordinary to extraordinary but to a movement from extraordinary experience to attempted explanation. The second section of the poem now suggests, however, a further kind of journey. In "Reflections," the natural world provides the images by which the movement of mind is rendered. The mountain and the landscape seen from its top are geographically contiguous to the dell from which the speaker ascends. In "The Eolian Harp," however, we move from that same dell to another world, a remote and magical "Fairy-Land," which provides the images of joyous harmony. As a literal ship carries the Mariner on his real but not literal voyage, and becomes a psychic rather than a literal location, so the literal sound of the harp carries the speaker here to a world in which the sounds become Elfins which are melodies which are brightly colored birds. The psychic reality seems in this instance to demand a more than naturalistic imagery.

There is thus again a shift in location, however delicately suggested, which corresponds to a change in consciousness and requires a changed language. While as in "Reflections," the lines of the first section prepare for the second and suggest a fading of the distinctions between thing and thing, and between perceiver and perceived, they still refer to and embody an objective public order.

But, through the instrument of the harp, we move to images which have no such reference, embody no such order. The psychic pattern is liberated from the demands of our material expectations. Fairyland, in which we do not, and are not asked to, believe, anymore than we are asked to believe in spectre-barks or spirits from the land of mist and snow, enables us to be conscious of qualities and patterns of sensation liberated from the conceptual structure of the objective world.

While Coleridge departs from the Wordsworthian principle that the natural world can provide whatever images are needed to express any human experience, he does not, as Wordsworth implied in "Peter Bell," leave the 'real' world for one of fantasy. The experience described is "such . . . as" we might imagine in Fairyland, and such as can be best described in terms which arouse no practical reservations in the breast of a Wedding Guest, but it is still an experience of a human being in a 'real' world, of a 'real' world. And the lines added in 1803 and again in 1817 serve to make this clear. It is in this real world that all things are loved, because it is this real world that is, when so experienced, "fill'd" with a transcendent music of life. As birds of paradise, being footless and wild, can never alight, become static, become objects, so life, of which we can be conscious, cannot rest in the pigeonholes of our conceptualizations, the "mould of the Intellect"[32] but is a "power" in light, in sound, in motion; is all of them and none, is all things and no thing. Similarly the Mariner, after his self-made alienation has ended, enters a world in which, as in Prospero's island, the air is filled with light and sound and motion.

The final section of "The Eolian Harp" is, to most readers, disappointing. This is partly because the language is banal and unconvincing, and partly, as Humphry House[33] and Geoffrey Yarlott[34] have noted, because it has not been revised to keep pace with the additions to the poem, and what was originally a rejection of speculations about the "intellectual breeze" now seems to apply to the whole of the revised and expanded second section. The final section does, however, present a more effective treatment of the predicament of the returned traveller than what we find in "Reflections," chiefly because of the inclusion within the poem in the person of Sara of the conventional audience, the uncomprehending mentality.

Coleridge's apparent readiness to accept the restrictions of that mentality seems artistically unsatisfactory as does the dismissal of the second section of "Reflections" as "feelings all too delicate for use." We may think it a pity that he could not, like Wordsworth in "Tintern Abbey," have for audience someone such as Dorothy in whose eye and voice he could sense not reproof but "the language of [his] former heart," or that, if he must have Sara, he could not let her cry "Beware! Beware! / His flashing eyes, his floating hair!" instead of feeling compelled, so to speak, to pat her hand and say "There, there, I didn't really mean it." But, as Yarlott says, Sara in the poem represents at least to some extent, as does the Wedding Guest, a facet of Coleridge himself. The conflict, the confrontation, was internal as well as external. And however much we may regret Sara, her presence in the poem does enable him to dramatize that confrontation.

Both "Reflections" and "The Eolian Harp" are very imperfect poems, though the latter has moments of great beauty. In neither does Coleridge manage with complete success, as he does in "The Ancient Mariner," his departure, his voyage, and his return to the conventional world. But both reveal some at least of the patterns of "The Ancient Mariner" and of the oasis fable. Both are attempts of the traveller who has found the oasis of life to present it in its relation to the desert and the language of the desert. In both, he is ambivalent about his own position and his own values. But he is discovering as an artist how he can embody in a verbal structure his exploration of his own consciousness.

In "This Lime-Tree Bower My Prison," begun in June of 1797 and published with substantial changes in 1800, the patterns found in these two poems have been brought to a much higher stage of development. We have again a departure, a journey, and a return, though the dell has become a bower and the journey takes place only in the speaker's mind as he imagines himself accompanying his friends on a walk. The climax of the 'journey' is again a moment of ecstatic vision:

> So my friend
> Struck with deep joy may stand, as I have stood,
> Silent with swimming sense; yea, gazing round

> On the wide landscape, gaze till all doth seem
> Less gross than bodily; and of such hues
> As veil the Almighty Spirit, when yet he makes
> Spirits perceive his presence.

And we have again the situation of the returned traveller, though this time, as we shall see, with a difference.

As was the case with "The Eolian Harp," we have fortunately several early versions of "This Lime-Tree Bower" which enable us to see how the poem evolved and thus to see more clearly how it works. As with the other two poems, an important consideration here is the preparation for the moment of vision, the rendering of the movement from ordinary perception, from one mode of seeing to another. In the earliest extant version of the poem, a letter to Southey in July, 1797, that movement is not yet successfully conveyed. The poem then began:

> Well—they are gone; and here must I remain,
> Lam'd by the scathe of fire, lonely & faint,
> This lime-tree bower my prison. They, meantime,
> My friends, whom I may never meet again,
> On springy heath, along the hill-top edge,
> Wander delighted, and look down, perchance,
> On that same rifted Dell, where many an Ash
> Twists it's wild limbs beside the ferny rock,
> Whose plumy ferns for ever nod and drip
> Sprayed by the waterfall. But chiefly Thou,
> My gentle-hearted CHARLES! thou, who hast pin'd
> And hunger'd after Nature many a year
> In the great City pent, winning thy way,
> With sad yet bowed soul, thro' evil & pain
> And strange calamity.—Ah slowly sink
> Behind the western ridge; thou glorious Sun!
> Shine in the slant beams of the sinking orb,
> Ye purple Heath-flowers! Richlier burn, ye Clouds!
> Live in the yellow Light, ye distant Groves!
> And kindle, thou blue Ocean! So my friend
> Struck with joy's deepest calm, and gazing round

On the wide view, may gaze till all doth seem
Less gross than bodily, a living Thing
That acts upon the mind, and with such hues
As cloathe the Almighty Spirit, when he makes
Spirits perceive His presence! [35]

Although the lines in which the moment of vision is described are almost identical with those in the final version of the poem, they remain here an assertion of an experience which the reader can only partially share. We do not identify ourselves with the speaker; we only *hear* him. We do not see a vision; we listen to S. T. Coleridge who sits "Lam'd by the scathe of fire," the skillet of boiling milk which "dear Sara accidentally emptied . . . on my foot,"[36] exhorting Lamb, absent on a walk, to feel the same response to nature that Coleridge would feel were he there. The description of the setting sun provides an analogy as, in the earlier versions of "Effusion xxxv," the eolian harp provided an analogy. But there is a gap between the response which the speaker asserts and what the reader is made to see or feel, a gap that is tacitly acknowledged in the letter to Southey by a footnote: "You remember, I am a *Berkleian*," which asks us to look outside the poem to a philosophical system for understanding. Instead of appearing to be the form in which an experience is realized, the lines seem rather an attempt to translate prior philosophical concepts into the terms of an experience.

A few months later, in October, Coleridge quoted the climactic lines of the poem in a letter to Thelwall in connection with a generalization about his own experience:

I can *at times* feel strongly the beauties, you describe, in themselves, & for themselves—but more frequently *all things* appear little—all the knowlege [sic], that can be acquired, child's play —the universe itself—what but an immense heap of *little* things? I can contemplate nothing but parts, & parts are all *little*—!—My mind feels as if it ached to behold & know something *great*—something *one* & *indivisible*—and it is only in the faith of this that rocks or waterfalls, mountains or caverns give me the same sense of sublimity or majesty!—But in this faith, *all things* counterfeit infinity!—'Struck with the deepest calm of Joy' I stand

> Silent, with swimming sense; and gazing round
> On the wide Landscape gaze till all doth seem
> Less gross than bodily, a living Thing
> Which acts upon the mind, & with such Hues
> As cloath th'Almighty Spirit, when he makes
> Spirits perceive his presence! [37]

Here again the lines are made meaningful through reference to something outside the poem, in this case the statement which precedes them. We can see them as the description of an experience, but they do not themselves communicate that experience. We *understand* them with reference to the prose statement.

In the final version of the poem, the wording of what I have called the climactic lines is almost unchanged, but the effect of the lines has been fundamentally altered by the alteration of the lines which precede them. The alterations are two: the first three lines have been revised,[38] and the first nine lines have been expanded to twenty-six. And it is these alterations that so change our response to the poem that we no longer look or need to look to footnote or commentary for explanation, that close the gap between what the lines mean to the poet and what they mean to the reader.

The revision of the opening lines changes our relation to the speaker in the poem. The opening lines now are:

> Well, they are gone, and here must I remain,
> This lime-tree bower my prison! I have lost
> Beauties and feelings, such as would have been
> Most sweet to my remembrance . . . .

We are no longer made aware of practical contingencies, of the difficulties of Coleridge with dear Sara and boiling milk. We are not concerned with what has happened, with the identity of 'they' who have gone, nor with the reasons for the 'imprisonment.' The setting is now just specific enough to provide a point of contact. We are immediately involved not in contingent problems nor in action, but in contemplation, in reverie. From this initial point of contact, we are led immediately to the "beauties and feelings, such as would have been / Most sweet to my remembrance . . . ," and thus we immediately escape with the speaker from his 'prison': the lime-tree bower, the fixed physical setting, the restrictions of this time, this place, are dissolved as part and symbol of that imaginative process which achieves realization later in the poem.

The second alteration in the final version of the poem is in the next twenty-one lines which are nearly all new and which are devoted to a description of what the absent friends may be seeing. The description is in itself detailed, vivid, 'realistic': a presentation of sensuous images.

        They, meanwhile,
Friends, whom I never more may meet again,
On springy heath, along the hill-top edge,
Wander in gladness, and wind down, perchance,
To that still roaring dell, of which I told;
The roaring dell, o'erwooded, narrow, deep,
And only speckled by the mid-day sun;
Where its slim trunk the ash from rock to rock
Flings arching like a bridge; that branchless ash,
Unsunn'd and damp, whose few poor yellow leaves
Ne'er tremble in the gale, yet tremble still,
Fann'd by the water-fall! And there my friends
Behold the dark green file of long lank weeds,
That all at once (a most fantastic sight!)
Still nod and drip beneath the dripping edge
Of the blue clay-stone.

       Now my friends emerge
Beneath the wide wide Heaven—and view again
The many steepled tract magnificent
Of hilly fields and meadows, and the sea,
With some fair bark, perhaps, whose sails light up
The slip of smooth clear blue betwixt two Isles
Of purple shadow!

The effect of these twenty-one lines is subtle but important. There is here no attempt to make the images suggest anything beyond themselves, but already an effect other than that of ordinary perception has been achieved. By placing us physically not with the 'friends' on the hilltop edge or in the roaring dell but in the lime-tree bower, and then by leaving our physical selves behind, Coleridge has, so to speak, extricated us from the normal physical situation of perception. We are disembodied: we are there not as walkers and doers, not as potentially sore feet, stung eyelids, and hungry stomachs, but only as perceivers and feelers. We have no way in which the trees might stand, no heads which they might shade. The only being which we have is the perception, the feeling of these images.

This situation is carefully maintained. The friends themselves, unnamed, uncharacterized, undescribed, are too vague to provide a new point of view. And Coleridge avoids any verb which would put the image and the reader in a fixed and physical relationship. Not once does he use the verb *to be* which would remind us that we are *here* and the tree or waterfall is *there*. His words do not define a perceiver and a thing perceived; they define perceptions. Nor does he use verbs which define an actor in relation to something acted upon. As in the latter part of "The Ancient Mariner," there is only movement and awareness: "They . . . wander . . . and wind down"; "that dell . . . of which I told"; "my friends behold"; "my friends emerge . . . and view."

As we have no fixed relation to any fixed object, so we are also kept from such absorption in a single image that it can become an exclusive object. We are disembodied and we float, from hill to dell, from tree to waterfall. "As soon as [the mind] is fixed on one image," Coleridge said in a lecture, "it becomes understanding; but while it is unfixed and wavering between them, attaching itself permanently to none, it is imagination." [39] We have not yet arrived at the moment of vision, but we are made ready for it; we are being stripped of the encumbrance of our usual concerns and expectations. When, at the beginning of the second part of the poem, the friends "emerge" from the dell to "wander on in gladness," they, and we, are no longer anywhere in particular but only "beneath the wide wide Heaven." We emerge, we might say, from a place to *no place* and find, as in "Re-flections," the world spread shimmering before us.

With line 27, there is a pause. One of the vague friends is identi-fied as "my gentle-hearted Charles" and described as one who has

> pined
> And hunger'd after Nature, many a year,
> In the great city pent, winning thy way
> With sad yet patient soul, through evil and pain
> And strange calamity!

In the earlier version, these are lines 10–15, and they are separated from the opening lines by six lines of description which do little more than provide a new physical setting. The result is that Charles is as distinct a physical presence as the lamed poet. Now, however, the introduction of Charles does not alter the basic dramatic situa-tion. In spite of the form of direct address, that address comes so late and the dramatic situation has been so firmly established that the addressee is present only as a thought. We do not see Charles as a physical presence nor are we led to locate ourselves in the poem in relation to him. The function of the lines is to strengthen the climax which follows, and they do it by introducing as contrast the thought of those transitory mundane considerations which normally im-prison us, and which without knowing it we left behind at the be-ginning of the poem. The Charles described is not the Charles to whom the landscape is present, but the Charles of London. He is, we may say, akin to the self or the kind of self we have left and which now appears as a figure of the past, a memory.

It is with this realization of the contrast between our present state and the normal mundane 'imprisonment' which we have left that a transformation begins to take place. Notice what happens in line 32:

> With sad yet patient soul, through evil and pain
> *And strange calamity! Ah! slowly sink*
> Behind the western ridge, thou glorious Sun!

In the middle of the line, there is an abrupt change of address and change of tone. The moment is similar to that in which a speaker sharing with his hearer the common ground of a religious faith might turn from the contemplation of mundane existence with "Ah, Christ!" Coleridge, sharing with his reader only a common empirical world, turns not to a named god, but to that world transformed, transcendent. The next few lines are still descriptive, but no longer merely so. The nature which is described is now addressed, and addressed in the language of invocation:

> Ah slowly sink
> Behind the western ridge, thou glorious Sun!
> Shine in the slant beams of the sinking orb,
> Ye purple heath-flowers! richlier burn, ye clouds!
> Live in the yellow light, ye distant groves!
> And kindle, thou blue Ocean!

In the earlier descriptive lines, there was no suggestion of consciousness or personality in the nature perceived. There was only the presentation of a series of sensuous images. Now something new has appeared, but in spite of the form of address, it is not merely a matter of personification. We are not led to see in nature an analogy to human behavior. We seem rather to have lost the distinction between the consciousness which contemplates and the nature which is contemplated. As the landscape is transformed, unified, and set on fire by the light of sunset, so it ceases to be a separate object or a collection of objects: it seems one, and one with the life of the consciousness which contemplates it. In a comment on Wordsworth's line "We see into the life of things" in "Tintern Abbey," Coleridge wrote,

> By deep feeling we make our *Ideas dim*—& this is what we mean by our Life—ourselves. I think of the Wall—it is before me, a distinct Image—here. I necessarily think of the *Idea* & the Thinking I as two distinct & opposite Things. Now ⟨let me⟩ think of *myself*—of the thinking Being—the Idea becomes dim whatever it be—so dim that I know not what it is—but the Feeling is deep & steady—and this I call *I*— . . . identifying the Percipient & the Perceived—.[40]

Something like this is presented in "This Lime-Tree Bower." We are not made to *see* images as distinct from ourselves. We are rather made aware of a single totality in which images melt into, or become the forms of, feeling.

In the next lines of the poem, there is again a change:

> So my friend
> Struck with deep joy may stand as I have stood,
> Silent with swimming sense; yea, gazing round
> On the wide landscape, gaze till all doth seem
> Less gross than bodily; and of such hues
> As veil the Almighty Spirit, when yet he makes
> Spirits perceive his presence.

With the words "stand as I have stood," we are reintroduced to a fixed position, but one in which we can now 'stand' with new awareness. The statements which follow are those which in earlier versions required an introduction or footnote in explanation because when they are taken by themselves, then insofar as they assert more than 'I saw a landscape,' they seem merely 'poetic' embroidery. Now however they appear not as something which needs to be explained or substantiated, but as a restatement of what has happened in the poem. Like the term "Omnipresence" in "Reflections" and the speculations in "The Eolian Harp," they are meaningful not in the context of a conceptual system such as Berkeley's idealism, but with reference to the experience which the returned mental traveller has had and which the reader has been led to share.

The third section of the poem again represents a return, both physically and verbally. But compared with the earlier poems it is a return with a difference. There is not this time the disjunction or the rejection that marked "Reflections" and "The Eolian Harp." The visionary moment is not just a moment in the past: its effects continue. We return to "this little lime-tree bower" but it is now a bower indeed and not a prison. The bower, like the imagined landscape, is suffused with light, with "a deep radiance," which combines with the murmur of the bee and the inevitable so fragrant bean flower in a continuing harmony of sensation. The things which the speaker sees are not only things but are parts of a pattern of light:

>   Pale beneath the blaze
> Hung the transparent foliage; and I watch'd
> Some broad and sunny leaf, and lov'd to see
> The shadow of the leaf and stem above
> Dappling its sunshine! And that walnut-tree
> Was richly ting'd, and a deep radiance lay
> Full on the ancient ivy, which usurps
> Those fronting elms, and now, with blackest mass
> Makes their dark branches gleam a lighter hue
> Through the late twilight: and though now the bat
> Wheels silent by, and not a swallow twitters,
> Yet still the solitary humble-bee
> Sings in the bean-flower!

Having experienced how objects dissolve into "hues / [that] veil the Almighty Spirit," he, and we, can see, experience, things both as objects and as hues of that one light. The situation which seems in the earlier poems to be one of 'either/or' requiring a choice, becomes in "This Lime-Tree Bower" one in which opposites evolve into synthesis. Not only does the solitude of individuation yield to the sense of universal harmony, but the 'return' is not to solitude but to a balance between the individual and the universal, the parts and the whole, so that a simultaneous awareness of both is possible.

As we return to the bower, so we also return to the self. The poem began with a self imprisoned, cut off. "They" were gone and "I" remained, crippled and alone. "Beauties and feelings" which he might have had were "lost." There was even with the thought of those "whom I never more may meet again" a sense of impending death, of isolation and deprivation not temporary but eternal. Now, as the bower is no longer a prison, neither is the self any longer alone. The imagined experience in which the speaker has vicariously participated has led to an awareness of this bower flooded with the same radiance, this heart flooded with the same "delight," as that known by absent "friends." Wordsworth in "Tintern Abbey" can see in Dorothy's wild eyes "what I was once" and know that she will therefore comprehend his words. In "The Eolian Harp," Coleridge could find in Sara's eyes only a "mild reproof," a lack of real comprehension. But here the shared experience is assumed, explicitly with Charles and implicitly with the reader. And if both see the bird, "now a dim speck, now vanishing in light" as it crosses "the mighty Orb's dilated glory," if for both the bird that, in Blake's words "cuts the airy way" becomes "an immense world of delight," then by virtue of that shared vision, the prison of self is broken and communication is possible.

"This Lime-Tree Bower" is in this respect one of Coleridge's most Wordsworthean poems, and it is no doubt important that it was begun on the occasion of the Wordsworths' first arrival at Nether Stowey and reached its final form during the period of the closest intimacy between the two poets. Whatever his influence on Coleridge's attitude towards nature and on his poetic manner, and the influence was certainly reciprocal, Wordsworth most importantly enabled Coleridge to be confident that his experience was shared and valued, that it was sufficient, that it was dependable. For the moment, though only for the moment (Wordsworth never understood "The Ancient Mariner" and it may be questioned how far he understood Coleridge except insofar as Coleridge seemed to agree with him), Coleridge could feel that he had 'fit audience' however few.

The expectation of a sympathetic response appears elsewhere in this year, most interestingly in "The Nightingale," though artistically this is a much less finished poem. "The Nightingale" does not present us with the whole arc of the journey, but is rather written from a point close to that at the end of "This Lime-Tree Bower," after the synthesis has been achieved and in the confidence that it is shared. The music of the nightingale is not so much the herald of a voyage of discovery as the reminder of a discovery already made by the speaker and by his "friends." Together they can consider the contrast between "we [who] have learnt" and they who have not. We are moved from 'here' when we are told of the speaker's experience, how he has heard

> one low piping sound more sweet than all—
> Stirring the air with such a harmony,
> That should you close your eyes, you might almost

> Forget it was not day! On moonlight bushes,
> Whose dewy leaflets are but half-disclosed,
> You may perchance behold them on the twigs,
> Their bright, bright eyes, their eyes both bright and full,
> Glistening, while many a glow-worm in the shade
> Lights up her love-torch,

in which we may recognize the characteristic qualities of sound and glittering light. And we are told also of the "gentle maid," like a priestess "vowed and dedicate / To something more than Nature in the grove," who

> Hath heard a pause of silence; till the moon
> Emerging, hath awakened earth and sky
> With one sensation, and those wakeful birds
> Have all burst forth in choral minstrelsy,
> As if some sudden gale had swept at once
> A hundred airy harps!

But these are presented as instances, recognizable by 'friends,' rather than as unexpected revelations. And at the end we have not *come* back; we are about to *go* back, but only temporarily, only "till to-morrow night."

"This Lime-Tree Bower" and "The Nightingale" might seem almost to point to a disappearance of the problem of the visionary speaker and his audience, of the Mariner and Wedding Guest. But this is not quite the case. In the earlier poems, the Mariner, so to speak, yields to the Guest. In these two poems, the Guest is absent: the address, one might say, is to fellow Mariners. The existence of such does not obliterate those who have not travelled, but it does enable the Mariner to speak with greater confidence, a confidence which appears both in "Kubla Khan," apparently written at about the same time as "This Lime-Tree Bower," and in "The Ancient Mariner" itself. Like the Mariner, the poet-prophet in "Kubla Khan" is an alien figure, separated from the generality of men by what he has experienced. They can protect their narrow selves and world from the impact of his vision only if they

> Weave a circle round him thrice,
> And close [their] eyes with holy dread [.]

But both he and the Mariner speak with authority. They cannot by a look of "mild reproof" be led to dismiss or forget what they have seen.

There is also in these two poems a compression, a symbolic complexity and intensity which the more genial and seemingly casual conversation poems do not strive to achieve. While we can find in them a contrast between the prison of selfhood, the narrow egotism of what Coleridge later described as the "ever anxious Crowd," and the unbounded consciousness of universal harmony, we do not find the tension, the danger as well as the beauty of vision that is revealed in "The Ancient Mariner" and "Kubla Khan." Perhaps with the abandonment of the everyday setting, of the attempt to maintain a naturalistic coherence side by side with the symbolic vision, such a change became possible and points, as I suggested at the end of the previous chapter, towards the further step which Coleridge could only falteringly take towards the purely symbolic poem. Perhaps "The Ancient Mariner" and "Kubla Khan" involved discoveries which made the conversation poem no longer an adequate language for what Coleridge now found to say.

In any case, so far as poetry is concerned, the development of the patterns of which I have been speaking comes virtually to a halt in 1798. The poems written in Germany and immediately thereafter are for the most part topical or occasional verses, translations and adaptations, or, as in the case of the 'Asra' poems, expressions of Coleridge's immediate circumstances and problems. In "Lines written in the album at Elbingerode," the one German poem that might seem reminiscent of the earlier poems, we find an expression of an inability to respond to "the lovely shapes and sounds intelligible" instead of the ascent, the boundless expansion or loss of self, the vision of forms suffused with life and light. The "surging scene" from the top of Brocken, "only limited / By the blue distance," produces no sense of Omnipresence but only a "low and languid mood" of nostalgia and loneliness. Instead of ascent, we have descent:

> Heavily my way
> Downward I dragged through fir groves evermore,
> Where bright green moss heaves in sepulchral forms
> Speckled with sunshine; and, but seldom heard,
> The sweet bird's song became a hollow sound [.]

External forms express a state of mind, but the state of mind is that of the anxious ego which sees and separates.

"Hymn before Sunrise" (1802), Coleridge's adaptation of Frederika Brun's "Ode to Chamouny," does describe a moment in which

> the dilating Soul, enrapt, transfused,
> Into the mighty vision passing—there
> As in her natural form, swelled vast to Heaven!

But the rhetoric of the poem is forced, as if Coleridge were trying to make something happen rather than expressing what had happened, and this impression receives some support from what we know of the circumstances of composition, of the need he felt to pretend that the poem was "involuntarily poured forth" on Scafell and transferred to Chamouny as providing a more appropriate setting than the "humble mountains" of Westmorland.[41]

"Dejection: an Ode," whose original version belongs to the same year as the "Hymn," is a poem of genuine self-exploration and one concerned with the difference between

> that inanimate cold World allow'd
> To that poor loveless ever anxious Crowd,

and a world enveloped in "A Light, a Glory, and a luminous Cloud." It is filled with echoes and images from earlier poems: the eolian harp, the sunset, even the notion that

> thou, my Love!
> Art gazing now, like me,
> And see'st the Heaven, I see [.]

The poem is *about* vision, but it expresses not vision but the failure of vision. A number of later poems and fragments are connected in various, sometimes in very significant, ways with the earlier poems. But they do not present us with further versions of the figure of the mental traveller which we have been considering.

I said something at the end of the Introduction about the problem of Coleridge's failure to continue to develop as a poet in the ways that we might expect, and I shall have something further to say about other aspects of this in Chapter 4. At this point, however, I am concerned with the fact rather than with explanation. The development which does not take place in poetry does take place in metaphysics, and we may trace in Coleridge's philosophy the further evolution, or at least the further ramifications, of the concerns, the patterns, and the problems which we have so far been considering only in terms of poetry. In the next chapter, I shall turn, therefore, to some discussion of Coleridge's philosophical position and its relation to his poetry during the earlier years when poetry was still his primary language. And in the chapters which follow, I shall try to show how, as it seems to me, the patterns of the poetry reappear in, and to a large extent determine the direction of, the speculations which occupied his middle and later years.

Chapter 3

THE OASIS WHICH COLERIDGE'S TRAVELLER FINDS is not an idea or a theory but a way of being. The experience of the oasis may lead to speculation ("And what if all of animated nature / Be but organic harps . . ."; "Henceforth I shall know / That Nature ne'er deserts the wise and pure . . ."), but the speculation follows from the experience; it does not produce it.

The matters which I have discussed in the previous two chapters obviously do, however, have speculative implications. If the Mariner tells of things in heaven and earth undreamt of in the philosophy of the Wedding Guest, then the Wedding Guest has no choice but either to dismiss the tale as the ravings of a grey-beard loon or to modify his philosophy.

Towards the end of *Coleridge the Visionary*, J. B. Beer writes:

> It is characteristic of his range of sympathies that . . . [Coleridge] was also held by the Wordsworthian challenge. Side by side with his visionary world of speculation, there is in his mind a positivist world of rationalist investigation, which he no doubt hoped would eventually be harmonized with it, but which none the less seems at times to contradict it flatly.[1]

The "Wordsworthian challenge" is well described in a famous passage from "The Recluse":

> Paradise, and groves
> Elysian, Fortunate Fields—like those of old
> Sought in the Atlantic Main—why should they be

> A history only of departed things,
> Or a mere fiction of what never was?
> For the discerning intellect of Man,
> When wedded to this goodly universe
> In love and holy passion, shall find these
> A simple produce of the common day.[2]

The poetic challenge in this is one which, as we have seen, Coleridge only intermittently accepted. The philosophical challenge, however, was an essential element in his intellectual make-up and antedated Wordsworth's influence. It was not quite, as Beer puts it, something existing "side by side" with "visionary speculation" and incompatible with it. This implies two divergent paths either of which might be chosen. For Coleridge, there was no such choice. The challenge was the reflection of his need to substantiate not visionary *speculation* but visionary experience. As the Wedding Guest "cannot choose but hear" the Mariner, neither can he, unless he is to remain forever stunned, abandon all other knowledge and become part of the Mariner's dream. He must, like the philosopher of the oasis fable, examine it by the light of common day. The contradiction was there, but it was precisely this which constituted a challenge. It was, he said later, the mind which could overcome the contradiction, which could "find *no* contradiction in the union of old and new" which could feel and might help to unravel the riddle of the universe.[3]

There have been many philosophies which could account for the Mariner's experience, philosophies in terms of which there is nothing incredible in a universe which can be apprehended either as one life manifesting itself in fluid harmonies of sound and color or as a vast and alien immensity, nothing incredible in an individual conscious-ness which can experience itself either as a discrete isolated ego or as melting into that universal music. With many such philosophies —Neoplatonic, alchemical, mystical—Coleridge was familiar and fascinated. He wrote to Thelwall in 1796 that "Metaphysics, & Poetry, & 'Facts of mind'—(i.e. Accounts of all the strange phan-tasms that ever possessed your philosophy-dreamers from Tauth [Thoth], the Egyptian to Taylor the English Pagan), are my darling Studies." [4] As this remark suggests, however, he was drawn by them not as speculative theories but as embodiments of 'facts of mind' which are not 'dreamt of in your philosophy, Horatio.' And it is not essentially a matter of theory that determines their compatibility with the Mariner's universe. The Mariner's universe is a universe of mind; that is, it is a universe whose structure derives from and corresponds to the structure of human consciousness. The same is true of the cosmologies which Coleridge found in various earlier writers, in whom the underlying paradigm, whether consciously recognized or not, is man's experience of his own consciousness. Inevitably, therefore, Coleridge could find in them echoes of his own explorations, recognizable 'facts of mind.'

But in England at the end of the eighteenth century, such philosophies were generally in disrepute, at least among the intellectual establishment. The developments of some two centuries in science, epistemology, and psychology had produced a very different image of reality, a universe of discrete minds and discrete objects which offered little support for the visions of grey-beard loons. The universe bequeathed by Newton and Locke might also be said to reflect the structure of human consciousness, but in a much more limited sense. Instead of taking all modes of apprehension as ways of knowing reality, it is limited to one—discursive thought. Blake said: "The tree which moves some to tears of joy is in the eyes of others only a Green thing which stands in the way."[5] For him, the first possibility was more revealing than the second. But the philosophy of the enlightenment took into account only the things which stand in the way.

There have been numerous accounts of Coleridge's discomfort in such an intellectual environment and of his interest in those earlier writers who, it would seem, could provide a more congenial alternative for one moved by transcendental yearnings for "something one and indivisible."[6] We need to remember, however, that the developments which I have mentioned were not ones which Coleridge could simply reject. Intensive analysis of the nature of the physical world and of the nature and limits of human knowledge from a 'scientific' rather than a teleological point of view had resulted not only in the formulation of specific philosophical and scientific systems, but also, less consciously, in the establishment of new principles of verification, principles which we roughly call empirical, and which came to seem not merely possible premises but common sense and obvious truth. Coleridge was faced, therefore, not so much with a variety of systems with which he could agree or disagree, as with a general way of thinking, an accepted language. He shared the respect of his age for science and scientific theories, the confidence that human experience could be explained as physical nature could be explained, that there were laws of human nature as well as laws of motion. While he was drawn to various earlier visionaries, he was also well aware of what seemed to be their inadequacy, their inability, that is, to meet the challenge of 'enlightened' analysis and criticism. What he required was a means of reconciling the experience of the oasis with acceptable conceptions of physical and psychological reality, of proving to the Wedding Guest that the Mariner and his tale were not fantasies of a disordered imagination.

I have outlined not a philosophy but an attitude towards philosophy, and during these early years, Coleridge did not have a philosophy in any formal sense. In spite of his wide reading and some grandiose plans for further metaphysical study, he saw himself as primarily a poet, and as such he could be fragmentary and eclectic in philosophy without being essentially incoherent or inconsistent. Coleridge said, it is true, that a poet must first of all be a profound metaphysician, but he must be so, he added, implicitly not explicitly, in the heart rather than in "logical coherence" of the head.[7] Philosopical *formulation* is external to the poem. Such formulations may provide confirmation and support; they may provide footnotes. But it is the poem that must possess unity and coherence, and in poetic rather than philosophical terms.

The study of Coleridge is complicated throughout by the extraordinary range and diversity of his reading. And during the early years, it is complicated by the fact that as "with a little ingenuity" we can find his later philosophy in "The Ancient Mariner," so with a little of the same ingenuity we can find in his early reading analogues for many of the leading ideas of that philosophy. It therefore can indeed appear that "side by side" with a temporary allegiance to some current doctrines, there was emerging from the study of Plotinus or Cudworth or Boehme the outlines of a transcendental metaphysic which evolved, with the help of the Germans, into his mature philosophy,[8] and that his intellectual development derived its direction and much of its substance from his reading. I believe, however, that an examination of the available evidence shows that while Coleridge's later work is in important respects a logical development from his early attitudes, it is misleading to consider his early studies primarily as sources of his later ideas, and that to do so distorts his relation both to earlier and to contemporary writers and obscures the nature of what happened during the ten years or so following his return from Germany.

Scholars have found, of course, substantial evidence to support the study of sources. According to Lamb, Coleridge was as a schoolboy at Christ's Hospital already unfolding "in thy deep and sweet intonations, the mysteries of Jamblichus, or Plotinus (for even in those years thou waxedst not pale at such philosophic draughts) . . . ."[9] In 1796, he spoke, as we have seen, of "philosophy-dreamers" from Thoth to Thomas Taylor as his "darling studies."[10] And there are many scattered references, quotations, hints, and allusions which point, or seem to point, to these and similar works. Moreover, in after years, Coleridge himself implied on various occasions that such reading laid at least a major part of the foundation for his later metaphysical position. In 1812, Crabb Robinson reported

> a metaphysical tirade in which Coleridge declared that when many years ago he began to think on philosophy he set out from a passage in Proclus at the point where Schelling appears to be. And here with modifications he, Coleridge, has remained. From Fichte and Schelling he has not gained any one great idea. To Kant his obligations are infinite, not so much from what Kant has taught him in the form of doctrine as from the discipline Kant has taught him to go through.[11]

A few days later Coleridge told Crabb Robinson that "from Schelling he has gained no new ideas, all Schelling has said he having either thought before or found in Jacob Boehmen."[12] In *Biographia Literaria,* he wrote that "the early study of Plato and Plotinus, with the commentaries and the THEOLOGIA PLATONICA of the illustrious Florentine [Ficino]; of Proclus and Gemistius Pletho; and at a later period of the 'De Immenso et Innumerabili' and the *'De la causa, principio ed uno,'* of the Philosopher of Nola [Bruno] . . . had all contributed to prepare my mind for the reception and welcoming of the 'Cogito quia sum, et sum quia Cogito' . . . ." [13] A few pages later appears an expression of indebtedness to Boehme, and of appreciation, at least, for Fox, Law, and "De Thoyras." [14] "The writings of these mystics," he continues, "acted in no slight degree to prevent my mind from being imprisoned within the outline of any single dogmatic system. . . . If they were too often a moving cloud of smoke to me by day, yet they were always a pillar of fire throughout the night, during my wanderings through the wilderness of doubt, and enabled me to skirt, without crossing, the sandy deserts of utter unbelief." [15]

Statements such as these, however, still leave considerable uncertainty as to the nature of the influence exercised by these writers and the period at which it is supposed to have taken place. I suggest that we need to distinguish both two *periods* of influence and two *kinds* of influence.

Of Coleridge's reading of the writers mentioned in *Biographia Literaria* during the period before 1798, there is little external evidence beyond what I have already mentioned. There are, unfortunately, no annotated volumes from these years which would show us clearly not only what he read but what he thought of what he read. Nor are the letters and notebooks of much assistance here. Compared with the later years, there is relatively little in either concerning philosophical speculation, and even less that involves the authors in question. Apart from the remark to Thelwall, the letters before 1798 reveal not a single mention of the reading of any of them except Plato. He did, in 1796, ask a friend to purchase for him a small volume containing selections from Iamblichus, Porphyrius, Proclus, and Plotinus, but if he received and read it, he said nothing about it.[16] He borrowed Cudworth's *True Intellectual System* from the Bristol Library twice, for three weeks in May of 1795 and for a month in November of 1796,[17] and there are in the notebooks a few quotations from Cudworth along with quotations from Proclus and Plotinus which appear to be derived not from the originals but from Cudworth and Jeremy Taylor.[18] A note from 1796 contains phrases which one scholar, J. B. Beer, believes point to Sparrow's translation of Boehme's *Aurora*,[19] and the name "Jacob Behmen" appears without comment in a list of projected works.[20] But this is all.

We have a very different situation for the decade or so following Coleridge's return from Germany when we do begin to have annotated volumes and when we find much more comment in letters and notebooks. During these years, when he buried himself in philosophy, he included in his studies all of the authors mentioned in *Biographia Literaria* with the possible exception of Pletho. After his reference to "a later period," it is not surprising to find him reading Bruno apparently for the first time in April of 1801.[21] But we also find, in the British Museum, an annotated copy of Ficino's *Theologia Platonica*, the work to which Coleridge refers, with his name and "Messina 9 Oct 1805" on the flyleaf. Notebook entries of 1803 indicate a study of Proclus' *Elements of Theology*,[22] and there is, again in the British Museum, Taylor's translation of *The Philosophical and Mathematical Commentaries of Proclus* with several notes clearly indicating a reading between 1802 and 1812. One of these includes the remark that "I have unfortunately never met with the original." In the same library is the four volume 'Law' edition of Boehme's works presented to Coleridge by De Quincey in 1807 or 1808[23] and containing voluminous marginalia showing several periods of careful study after that date. There are no known annotated copies of Plato or Plotinus, but a notebook entry of November, 1803, seems to indicate that Coleridge was reading Plotinus at that time,[24] and in a letter to Sotheby in September, 1802, he wrote, "last winter I read the Parmenides and Timeus with great care." [25]

This alone is enough to suggest that the influence referred to in *Biographia Literaria* and elsewhere may belong at least partly to the years following the return from Germany. But more important, the comments and annotations seem to indicate that it was during these years that *for the first time*, Coleridge began to see in some of these writers the rudiments of an intellectually viable metaphysical *system*.

This involves a point which is too easily overlooked. As a result partly of developments in philosophy since Kant, a modern reader is apt to see in some ancient, medieval, and renaissance writers, possibilities and implications which are by no means self-evident, and we are apt to assume that Coleridge read them in the same way and did so from the beginning. I do not think that this was the case. Speaking of Boehme and others in *Biographia Literaria*, he said: "It has indeed been plausibly observed, that in order to derive any advantage, or to collect any intelligible meaning, from the writings of these ignorant mystics, the reader must bring with him a spirit and judgment superior to that of the writers themselves." [26] The sentiment presumably reflects his own experience. In another passage which I have already repeated, he spoke of those who were a "pillar of fire" by night but a "cloud of smoke" by day. That, I suggest, accurately describes the situation in which he found himself during the earlier period, when he could not yet explain 'by day' what he could nevertheless recognize 'by night,' when he could, like the Wedding Guest, recognize a Mariner's tale as a dream of truth, but could not wholly reconcile it to his intellect.

I have no wish to argue with the notion that, as Beer puts it, "where an image or a sentiment in Boehme [or in others] found an echo in the shapings of his own imagination, it was eagerly taken up into the pattern, and valued for the hint of external confirmation which it offered." [27] But arguments for 'sources' and 'influences' usually suggest more than this. Any support, encouragement, confirmation, is of course an influence on a writer whether it comes from what he reads or from a sympathetic friend. But when we discuss sources and influences, we usually mean that a writer is to some degree dependent upon them, that he would not have thought and written as he did without them, that he finds in them ideas which he would not otherwise have had. In this sense, influence or source is one thing, and confirmation or support another.

I have already said that the patterns which I have discussed in the poetry have a psychological basis, that they derive not from theories but from the nature of human consciousness. Certainly Coleridge read and was fascinated by visionary and mystical philosophers. But he did not need to read them in order to acquire the 'idea' of a visionary apprehension of the universe: such apprehension is a matter of experience, not of theory. Certainly, too, there was in some of them an attempt to explain the physical world in a manner consistent with visionary or mystical experience, and this again fascinated and probably encouraged him. But it was precisely this attempt that he found for some time particularly difficult to explain to his own satisfaction. It was the right *kind* of attempt, perhaps, but it produced theories which were often unintelligible and were generally implausible, clouds of smoke rather than pillars of fire.

This view of Coleridge's situation is consistent with two characteristic later statements. The first of these is a marginal note on the Cambridge Platonist ("but more truly Plotinist") Henry More:

> There are three principle causes to which the imperfections and errors in the theological schemes and works of our elder Divines . . . may, I think, be reasonably attributed. . . . These Causes are,—1st and foremost, the want of that logical προπαιδεία docimastica, that Critique of the human intellect, which, previous to the weighing and measuring of this or that, begins by assaying the weights, measures, and scales themselves. . . . 2. The ignorance of Natural Science, their Physiography embrangled with an inapplicable Logic and a misgrowth of . . . substantiated Abstractions; and their Physiogony a Blank, or Dreams of Tradition & such 'intentional Colors' as occupy space but cannot fill it. Yet . . . a scheme of the Christian Faith which does not arise out of, and shoot it's beams downward into, the scheme of Nature . . . must be false or distorted in all it's particulars.[28]

The second is from the Philosophical Lectures of 1818:

> During the whole of the middle ages, and almost down to the time of the Restoration of Charles the Second we discover everywhere metaphysics, always acute and frequently profound, but throughout estranged from, not merely experimental physics generally, but from its most intimate connective, experimental psychology; while from the Restoration we have the opposite extreme, namely experimental physics and a truly enlightened though empirical and mechanical psychology estranged from and in utter contempt of all metaphysics.[29]

Both of these describe the shortcomings which Coleridge found in many of the earlier writers who interested him. The balanced judgment of the distinction between 'metaphysics' on the one hand and science and psychology on the other reflects also his development in the early nineteenth century when he had begun to find in modern science—not only in the speculations of the Germans but nearer home in the experiments and theories of Davy—acceptable equivalents for what had seemed inadequate and eccentric formulations. A discussion of this development belongs to the next chapter, but some illustration of the change which took place is relevant here for what it reveals of Coleridge's earlier attitudes.

We may see something of what was a pillar of fire and what in 1801 was still a cloud of smoke in Coleridge's reactions to Bruno's *De monade* and *De innumerabili immenso* which he read together and for the first time in the spring of that year. In a notebook, he copied out, with expressions of approval, several passages, the longest of which he translated in *The Friend* (1809–10):

A wise spirit does not fear death, nay sometimes—as in cases of voluntary martyrdom—seeks and goes forth to meet it, of its own accord. For there awaits all actual beings, for duration an eternity, for place immensity, for action omniformity. We pursue, therefore, a species of contemplation not light or futile, but the weightiest and most worthy of an accomplished man, while we examine and seek for splendor, the interfusion and communication of the Divinity and of Nature, not in meats or drink, or any yet ignobler matter, with the race of the thunder-stricken; but in the august palace of the Omnipotent, in the illimitable etherial space, in the infinite power, that creates all things, and is the abiding *being* of all things.

There we may contemplate the Host of Stars, of Worlds and their guardian Deities, numbers without number, each in its appointed sphere, singing together, and dancing in adoration of the One Most High. Thus from the perpetual, immense, and innumerable goings on of the visible world, that sempiternal and absolutely infinite Majesty is intellectually beheld, and is glorified according to his glory, by the attendance and choral symphonies of innumerable gods, who utter forth the glory of their ineffable Creator in the expressive language of Vision! To HIM illimitable, a limited temple will not correspond—to the acknowledgment and due worship of the Plenitude of *his* Majesty there would be no proportion in any numerable army of ministrant spirits. Let us then cast our eyes upon the omniform image of the Attributes of the all-creating Supreme, nor admit any representation of his Excellency but the living Universe, which he has created!—Thence was man entitled by Trismegistus, "the great Miracle," inasmuch as he has been made capable of entering into union with God, as if he were himself a divine nature; tries to *become* all things, even as in God all things *are;* and in limitless progression of limited States of Being, urges onward to the ultimate aim, even as God is simultaneously infinite, and everywhere ALL![30]

This "very sublime ennunciation of the dignity of the human Soul" [31] presents, "with some intermixture of error," [32] the kind of vision of man and the universe which Coleridge found and noted in various writers, and which, though it might be seen "as the fancies of an enthusiast, by such as

> ————deem themselves most free,
> When they within this gross and visible sphere
> Chain down the winged soul, scoffing ascent,
> Proud in their meanness,————

by such as pronounce every man out of his senses who has not lost his reason";[33] was nevertheless intelligible to those who had taken "the first step to knowledge . . . [which] is to dare to commune with our very and permanent self." [34] This was the pillar of fire. But in 1801, much remained a cloud of smoke. In his notebook, he also wrote:

If the 5 books de Minimo, &c to which . . . [*De monade*] is consequent, are of the same character, I lost nothing in not having it. The work . . . was far too numeral, lineal, & pythagorean for my Comprehension—it read very much like Thomas

Taylor & Proclus &c. I by no means think it certain that there is no meaning in these works, nor do I presume even to suppose, that the meaning is of no value—/ but it is ⟨till I understand a man's Ignorance, I presume myself ignorant of his understanding⟩ for others, at present, not for me—Sir. P. Sidney, & Fulk Greville shut the doors at their philos. conferences with Bruno—if his Conversation resembled this Book, I should have thought he would [have] talked with a trumpet.[35]

During the next few years, he began to think himself able to "understand the ignorance" of such a "vigorous mind struggling after truth, amid many prejudices"[36] and to explain those "numeral, lineal, and pythagorean" theories which he found in Bruno and in others. In fact he frequently adopted a numeral, lineal, and pythagorean language himself. But not yet.

Still more revealing because more fully documented is the record of Coleridge's study of the German mystic and theosopher Jacob Boehme. Not only are there numerous references to Boehme in the later notebooks and letters as well as in the published writings, but we now have Coleridge's four volumes of Boehme's *Works* which are among the most heavily annotated of the several hundred volumes containing Coleridge marginalia. While these marginalia were not begun until 1807–1808 when he received the books from De Quincey,[37] the detailed account which they contain of the evolution of his interpretation of Boehme implies much about the nature of his attitudes at an earlier period with respect not only to Boehme but to other writers as well.

Moreover, Boehme provides a useful example in that he is one of those authors whom a number of scholars have discussed as a specific and significant early influence. In *Strange Seas of Thought*, first published in 1945 and recently reissued, Newton P. Stallknecht devoted considerable space to a discussion of Coleridge and Boehme in an attempt to show that Coleridge provided a channel through which Boehme reached Wordsworth. From the fact that "Mr. Shawcross tells us [in a note to *Biographia Literaria*] that Coleridge was probably acquainted with Boehme's thought as early as 1795," Stallknecht concludes that it was "Boehme who transcendentalized Hartley in Coleridge's mind" and that "from Boehme, via Coleridge, comes the pantheistic theory of imagination that is so characteristic of Wordsworth." [38] Later, to "indicate the extent of Coleridge's debt to Boehme more definitely," he tries to demonstrate the kinship between Boehme's *De Signatura Rerum* and the speculative lines in "The Eolian Harp." [39] While no scholar, so far as I am aware, has completely accepted Stallknecht's view of the pervasiveness of Boehme's influence, most seem to agree with his basic assumption that such an influence did exist at least as early as 1795 and a number of further analogues and parallels have been adduced in evidence of it. [40]

During the early years, as I have mentioned, direct evidence of an early reading of Boehme is scanty. Before 1798, there is only the single mention of the name in a notebook, [41] and, if Beer's conjecture is correct, [42] an echo of *Aurora* in a few phrases in another notebook entry about a year later:

> throned angels—upboyling anguish
> Leader of a Kingdom of Angels.
> Love-fires—a gentle bitterness—
> Well-spring—*total God* [.] [43]

There are two more notebook entries before the commencement of the marginalia. In a note of 1801–1802, Coleridge recorded from Henry More's *A Brief Discourse of Enthusiasm* the notion "That all is God's self—that a man's self is God if he live holily—that the Waters of this World are mad" and identified it, as More did not, as "Behmen's opinion." [44] In a long note on language written in January of 1804, he spoke of "the all too often useless nomenclature in the philosophical writings of all men of originality—some quite overlayed by it, as poor Boehmen." [45] There are no mentions of Boehme in letters before 1810, [46] none in published works before 1817, [47] and none in recorded conversation before 1808. [48]

There are in addition a number of later occasions when Coleridge speaks of his obligation to Boehme. In nearly all cases, however, the period to which he refers is uncertain. In discussing, in *Biographia Literaria,* the "coincidence" between his own ideas and those of

Schelling, he mentions their mutual obligations to Kant and Bruno, and then continues: "Schelling has lately, and, as of recent acquisition, avowed the same affectionate reverence for the labours of Behmen, and other mystics, which I had formed at a much earlier period."[49] In a letter to his disciple Tulk in 1817, he concludes a long discussion of *Naturphilosophie* by saying:

> Accept this very rude sketch of the very rudiments of '*Heraclitus redivivus*'—One little presumption of their truth is, that as Wordsworth, Southey, and indeed all my intelligent Friends well know & attest, I had formed it during the study of Plato, and the Scholars of Ammonius [i.e. the early Neoplatonists], and in later times of Scotus (Joan. Erigina), Giordano Bruno, Behmen, and the much calumniated Spinoza . . . long before Schelling had published his first and imperfect view—.[50]

It is uncertain that Coleridge, whose study of Schelling seems to have begun not long before 1810 and whose first source for Schelling's *Naturphilosophie* was probably the *Darlegung* of 1806 which he mentions in *Biographia Literaria*, was aware that the "first and imperfect view" had appeared as early as 1797. The reference to "later times" and the grouping of Boehme with Kant and Bruno in the first instance and with Bruno, Scotus, and Spinoza in the second, all of whom he studied after his return from Germany,[51] suggests the later period. Certainly these remarks cannot be taken to *ex*clude the intensive study of Boehme which took place after 1807, though he *may* have had an earlier reading in mind as well. The comments to Crabb Robinson in 1812 on Boehme and Schelling were made four or five years after the marginalia were begun and need not refer beyond them.

The one exception to such instances is a letter to Tieck, also from 1817, in which Coleridge wrote:

> Before my visit to Germany in September, 1798, I had adopted (probably from Behmen's Aurora, which I had *conjured over* at School) the idea, that Sound was = Light under the praepotence of Gravitation, and Color = Gravitation under the prae-

potence of Light; and I have never seen reason to change my faith in this respect.[52]

This does not, however, settle the matter. Coleridge does not say that he found such a theory in Boehme when he read him during his schooldays (before 1789). In 1817, when he has long been accustomed to seeing in Boehme anticipations of this and other theories, he suggests that he arrived at it *"probably"* as a result of having *"conjured over"* Aurora some years earlier. Moreover, as I have pointed out elsewhere,[53] there is no evidence that he did hold such a theory before 1798; not, that is, a theory formulated in these terms. That material phenomena may be explained in terms of immaterial force or 'powers' is a belief which appears in many writers with whom Coleridge was familiar, Boehme among them, and is almost a necessary concomitant of a visionary metaphysic. But to say this is a very different thing from saying that Boehme provided the source for a specific formulation. Coleridge, however, often felt that the germ of a theory, the insight from which it evolved, was as valuable as a specific formulation. It is not surprising that in 1817 those who years before had provided some confirmation and support for the germinal insight should seem in a loose sense sources of later theories, especially when in the interim they had come to be intimately connected in his mind with those theories. But we should be chary indeed of looking for sources in a stricter sense and of antedating to the earlier period ideas which appear only at a later date.

Comments after 1800 show that for a time Coleridge regarded Boehme as presenting the same problem which he described in relation to Bruno. I have already mentioned his description of Boehme in 1804 as "quite overlayed" by a useless nomenclature, and as late as January, 1810, some time after he had read and annotated large parts of both *Aurora* and *The Three Principles* and only two years before his remarks to Crabb Robinson, he wrote to Lady Beaumont:

Of Jacob Behmen I have myself been a commentator, from Plato, Plotinus, Proclus, & some Catholic Writers of the Vie Intérieure.—But for myself I must confess, I never brought away from his Works any thing I did not bring to them—It is a maxim with me, always *to suppose myself ignorant of a Writer's Understanding, until I understand his Ignorance.* This I have not yet decyphered to myself in the Teutonic Theosopher: yet I conjecture that being ignorant of Logic & not versed in the Laws of the Imagination, he rendered many *Intuitions* in his own mind, perhaps of very profound Truths, and, as it were, *translated* them into such *Images* and *bodily* feelings as *by accident* were co-present with his Intuitions. It is plain, that the words and phaenomena of certain chemical experiments with Quicksilver, and Sulphur (which he learnt from Fludd, or disciples of Fludd) were present to his fancy while he was delving into the possible state of *Being* prior to Consciousness. . . . If it please God, I shall shortly publish . . . a work . . . entitled, The Mysteries of Religion, grounded in or relative to the Mysteries of Human Nature: or the foundations of morality laid in the primary Faculties of Man.—Some parts of the Aurora, and of the Three Principles, may possibly become somewhat clearer to you, after the perusal of my work. Either in this or in some after Number of the Friend I shall give the character of Jacob Behmen & compare him with George Fox—and both with Giordano Bruno.—The most beautiful and orderly development of this philosophy, which endeavors to explain all things by an analysis of Consciousness, and builds up a world in the mind out of materials furnished by the mind itself, is to be found in the Platonic Theology by Proclus.[54]

The views expressed in this very interesting statement are reflected in the marginalia. These do not, as we might expect, form a continuation of a dialogue begun at an earlier date, nor is there in the twenty thousand words or so of commentary any allusion to an earlier reading. Rather we find Coleridge attempting to understand and explain the obscurities of Boehme's works, interpreting them in terms of the ideas which he was able to "bring to them." Though he "possessed in very truth the vision and the faculty divine," Boehme was "a poor unlearned man [who] contemplated Truth and the forms of Nature thro' a luminous mist, the vaporous darkness rising from his Ignorance and accidental peculiarities of fancy and sensation." Deprived of a "technical education" he "neglected the *art* of reasoning, by acts of abstraction." Having "but a scanty store of words," he was able to put down "not *all*, nor perhaps exactly *how* . . . [he] *saw;* but what, with his former associations he could reproduce in his Consciousness after the Vision had past away." [55]

But we can see quite clearly in the marginalia both the nature of the 'clouds of smoke' and the manner in which they began to dissolve. *Aurora* and *The Three Principles*, the only works which Coleridge read before 1818 though he read parts of these repeatedly,[56] are largely devoted to an attempt to derive the natural world, known by 'Reason,' from the supernatural world, known by 'Understanding'; and to show that to the 'Understanding' the essential qualities of material phenomena are spiritual qualities, or, in effect, the qualities of consciousness. Since Boehme sees the natural world not only with the eye of a mystic but also through the eyes of the alchemists, the result is obscure and often fantastic. It was this attempt that particularly interested Coleridge and that forms the subject of the bulk of the marginalia, in which he tries to explain Boehme's explanations and to separate the "profound truths" from 'accidental' associations.

Some of the earliest notes, as the letter to Lady Beaumont would suggest, are more concerned with the reason for the eccentricities than with the "profound truths" which they may conceal. One such is a note on this passage:

And so now when the Astringent grapples with the Bitter, then the Bitter *leaps* aside, and takes the Sun's Sap along with it, and then the Astringent everywhere presses hard after it, and would *fain* captivate it, then the Bitter rushes out from the Body and extends itself as far as it can.

Coleridge comments:

Imagine a Poet intensely watching a Tree in a storm of Wind, unconsciously imitating its motions with his body, and then transferring to the Tree those sensations and emotions that accompanied his own gestures; and then you may understand Behmen, and his mode of describing the acts of Nature by antedating the passions, of which yet those acts may be perhaps, the nascent state and fluxional quantities.[57]

A step towards interpretation appears in another early note which begins:

> I conjecture, that Behmen, in this strange picture-language confused with the language of sensations, meant to convey the state of the absolute Self, considered as pure unlimited Activity, anterior (in nature) to its self-consciousness—and then by a ὑστερον προτερον of the Fancy attributes to such a State of Self-action those feelings which it would have occasioned *after* self-consciousness. . . .[58]

At the same time or at least before 1812, however, Coleridge also began to see ways in which Boehme's "Nature Spirits" and their operation might be equated with some current scientific explanations of natural phenomena. On Boehme's statement:

> First there is in the Divine Power the astringent Quality, which is . . . a sharp Compaction or Penetration in the *Salitter* . . . which *generates* Hardness, and also Coldness,

Coleridge remarked:

> The translation here adds to the difficulties arising from Behmen's want of words equal to the holding fast of the specific Identity in such various operations under the various influences. But the intention is clear. In the first place he makes four Qualities, that may be called Physical—The first is clearly the Species of Fixity, or Attraction, as he himself says; but as no Power ever can subsist in nature, really, separate, and this power seems more akin to the 3rd, he takes in contraction, or anticipates it/ for so he saw it in his spirit. Now attraction modified by contraction is indeed Astringency, and the cause

of Hardness (or relative Cohesion) Coherence, crystallization, and vegetative forms—likewise of colors—as Oxyds of the elementary Carbon.[59]

In isolation, Coleridge's comment may seem as cryptic and as fanciful as Boehme's original. But he was in fact, as I shall explain in the next chapter, drawing on Davy's experiments and hypotheses and, later, on the theories of Schelling and of German scientists, especially Steffens, Ritter, and Oken. And it was this that enabled him not only to explain Boehme as he did, but to recreate in terms which might be acceptable to a Wedding Guest, the correlation which Boehme tried to present between the universe as known in visionary experience and the universe as known to scientific analysis. This in turn enabled him to see Boehme as a significant stage in the progress towards a wholly adequate metaphysical system. But, I repeat, he did not offer, nor was he prepared to offer, such an interpretation when he read Boehme during the earlier period.

The important issue here is not merely the evolution of the influence of Boehme or of another writer per se. What is important is the fact that if Coleridge did not, during the nineties, find, as he later did, a way of making such visionary philosophies scientifically intelligible, then this is of great significance in the consideration of his relation to contemporary thought, for it means, as I said at the outset of this chapter, that he was not confronted with two sets of theories between which he could choose, but that he was confronted on the one hand with visionary accounts, with Mariner's tales, coupled with statements about the physical world which he could not accept, and on the other with the theories and experimental evidence of modern science and psychology where, if at all, he had to find the means of examining the oasis by daylight, of showing that it involved more than "substantiated abstractions" and "dreams of tradition."

Coleridge's concern with a "positivist world of rationalist investigation" thus bears some analogy to that concern, as a poet, with discursive intelligibility which I mentioned in earlier chapters. In both cases, he was unable or unwilling simply to disregard the demands of what Maritain called "the realm of rationalized and socialized communicability." [60] But in neither case was he led, as was Wordsworth in "Peter Bell," to confine himself to existing notions of what rationalization could explain or common sense admit. The Mariner talks *to* the Wedding Guest. Wordsworth in this poem talks *with* the Squire, his Wedding Guest; attempts to remain within the narrow boundaries of his practical understanding. The result is that the "groves Elysian" are not produced by, but rather, as in "Intimations," "fade into the light of" common day, which reveals the mundane reality behind the extraordinary appearance. Coleridge also feels compelled to talk with as well as to the Squire, the rational man, but not to the extent of agreeing that what the Squire can see and understand is all there is to be seen and understood. He is not prepared to limit himself to the vision of the blind, of those

> Who deem themselves most free
> When they within this gross and visible sphere
> Chain down the wingéd thought, scoffing ascent,
> Proud in their meanness: and themselves they cheat
> With noisy emptiness of learnéd phrase,
> Their subtle fluids, impacts, essences,
> Self-working tools, uncaused effects, and all
> Those blind Omniscients, those Almighty Slaves,
> Untenanting creation of its God.[61]

But he is anxious to demonstrate, to the Squire and to himself, that rational principles do not exclude or disprove the visionary. And he turns to the "world of rationalist investigation" for evidence that visionary experience *is* possible and significant, that the "groves Elysian" need not fade in the light of common day, that the truth in the dream need not dissolve with the dream.

I have already mentioned one instance of such support: the comment "I am a Berkleian" which Coleridge used to substantiate a visionary passage in "This Lime-Tree Bower." It can be argued that the reference applies only to the expression "all doth seem / Less gross than bodily, a living Thing / That acts upon the mind, and with such hues / As cloathe the Almighty Spirit," and that this, and similar expressions elsewhere,[62] reflect Berkeley's 'influence.' But whether the expression reflects Berkeley or not, the allusion has a greater significance than this. A notion derived from Berkeley is not simply added on to an ordinary perception. The reference to Berkeley rather serves to give some rational authority to what purports to be a moment of transcendent experience. And while it is true that Berkeley was by no means universally accepted as an authority, it is not at all as if Coleridge had written "I am a Behmenist" or even "I am a Plotinist." Whatever the contemporary opinion of Berkeley's antimaterialism, his earlier writings—and it is these and not *Siris* that are in question here—are very much in the tradition of eighteenth-century empiricism, and their appeal to Coleridge lay precisely in the fact that Berkeley developed his conclusion that the substratum of all phenomena was mental or spiritual rather than material from the empirical premises and by empirical methods.

An earlier and somewhat different example is found in "The Destiny of Nations," which opens with a philosophic summary translated into rather dubious poetry. This passage has been cited as evidence of the influence of Erasmus Darwin and Priestley, which it may well be, and also of Berkeley.[63] But what may be noted here is its function, which is to provide a philosophic justification for the Vision of the Maid of Orleans which follows, as if before recounting the "wildly working visions" which are the subject of the poem, Coleridge were trying to forestall the Squire's "Hold . . . against the rules / Of common sense you're surely sinning."

A much clearer and more comprehensive illustration than either of these, however, is "Religious Musings," the poem on which, in 1796, Coleridge was prepared "to rest for all my poetical credit," [64] and which includes footnotes citing Berkeley and Hartley as authorities. The enthusiasm of contemporary reviewers, many of whom praised "Religious Musings" as the 'height of sublimity,' [65] is unlikely to be echoed by a modern reader. We are more apt to feel in agreement with Geoffrey Yarlott who writes that "orthodox Christian sentiments jostle uneasily with elements of Neo-Platonism, and with the 'fairy way' and tributes to the materialists. This poem exemplifies perfectly the confused and eclectic nature of Coleridge's intellectual development during these formative years." [66] But for all its shortcomings, its turgid pseudo-Miltonic language, its personified abstractions, its shrill descriptions of current affairs, the poem is not merely a hotchpotch of half assimilated ideas. Although an artistic failure, "Religious Musings" is a significant attempt to meet what Coleridge took to be the rational demands of his age. He is not here addressing himself to Lamb or Wordsworth or Sara as in the conversation poems, but *ad populam*. His object is to make his audience wiser if not sadder men, and he does not depend upon his glittering eye or the poet's strange power of speech alone to carry conviction. The Mariner, himself an alien figure in the world of the Wedding Guest, simply appears and asserts. The poet of "Religious Musings," having left his 'Place of Retirement,' his solitary meditation, to "go, and join head, heart, and hand, / Active and firm, to fight the bloodless fight / Of science, Freedom, and the Truth in Christ," is concerned to argue and demonstrate. Coleridge is carrying his private experience into the public world and is trying to show both its validity and its practical significance.

What saves the poem from being an ideological hotchpotch is that it depends not on formal philosophical consistency but on integrity of vision. The central figure of the poem is that of the inspired "Philosopher and Bard" who can see all things as "Parts and proportions of one wondrous whole!" The figure is obviously similar to the one we find in "The Destiny of Nations" and in "Ode to the Departing Year," but it is also, in spite of the difference in rhetoric, essentially the same as the one we have earlier seen in more muted poems such as "Reflections" and "The Eolian Harp." We may recognize the "good man in his lonely walk" who perceives "fragments wild / Sweet echoes of unearthly melodies, and odours snatched from beds of Amaranth," and the "eloquent men" visited by "bright visions,"

> when, the summer noon,
> Beneath some arched romantic rock reclined
> They felt the sea-breeze lift their youthful locks;
> Or in the month of blossoms, at mild eve,
> Wandering with desultory feet inhaled
> The wafted perfumes, and the flocks and woods

> And many-tinted streams and setting sun
> With all his gorgeous company of clouds
> Ecstatic gazed!

And there is some foreshadowing of "The Ancient Mariner" in the image which Coleridge uses to illustrate the process of 'regeneration':

> As when a shepherd on a vernal morn
> Through some thick fog creeps timorous with slow foot,
> Darkling he fixes on the immediate road
> His downward eye; all else of fairest kind
> Hid or deformed. But lo! the bursting Sun!
> Touched by the enchantment of that sudden beam
> Straight the black vapour melteth, and in globes
> Of dewy glitter gems each plant and tree;
> On every leaf, on every blade it hangs!
> Dance glad the new-born intermingling rays,
> And wide around the landscape streams with glory!

"Religious Musings," however, does not only, as in these lines, describe such moments of personal illumination. The same pattern of darkness and light, blindness and vision, confusion and harmony, is repeated in terms of traditional religious symbols, of human history, and of contemporary philosophy.

In some respects, the poem is almost Blakean in intent, though not, in spite of a few memorable lines, in execution. For Blake, the mental movement of the visionary from the prison of Ulro to the joys of Eden is repeated in the progress of humanity through history towards an apocalyptic rebirth, and his symbols are simultaneously psychological, ideological, and historical. Coleridge also sees human history moving towards the same enlightenment that crowns the experience of the individual 'elect,' and also equates the present historical moment with a stage in a mental and spiritual process. And his combinations of biblical, allegorical, and historical figures, if less developed and less effective, have some of the same functions as their counterparts in Blake insofar as they provide a means whereby religion, history, and individual experience may be fused in a single vision.

But apart from the question of artistic success, there is an essential difference between Blake and Coleridge here, and that is Coleridge's need to show that his vision is also rational sense. We are assured, as we are not in Blake, that the machinery *is* machinery, though machinery with a 'real' purpose and meaning. Blake assumes the ability of a Wedding Guest to *see* once he is shown; Coleridge is concerned to quiet the Wedding Guest's objections by a running series of footnotes. Where the poem is not meant to be taken literally, he carefully translates the poetic statement into more familiar language, performing himself the function which Blake left for modern explicators whose business it is to help Wedding Guests to understand poems.

When the poem was first published in 1796, these notes consisted for the most part of biblical citations providing, in effect, the traditional form of notions which Coleridge presents in less orthodox and supposedly more philosophic language. In 1797, these were nearly all dropped, and Coleridge added a series of rather pedantic notes which seem calculated to give the impression that the poem rests on a foundation of sensible theory and solid fact. Thus to the lines describing the sun bursting through the mist which I have just quoted, he appends the comment:

> Our evil Passions, under the influence of Religion, become innocent, and may be made to animate our virtue—in the same manner as the thick mist melted by the Sun, increases the light which it had before excluded. In the preceding paragraph, agreeably to this truth, we had allegorically narrated the transfiguration of Fear into holy Awe.

And he proceeds in later notes to offer a variety of other explanatory dissertations. He discusses the view of superstition supposed to be "convey'd in this and subsequent lines"; "the *uses* of [Evil] . . . in the great process of divine Benevolence"; the French Revolution and the "downfall of Religious Establishments"; and the nature of the millennium, "the state of pure intellect; when all Creation shall rest from its labours." He notes with names and dates historical events to which the poem applies. When he describes the serpent who

> plants his vast moon-glittering bulk,
> Caught in whose monstrous twine Behemoth yells,
> His bones loud-crashing!

he informs us that

> Behemoth, in Hebrew, signifies wild beast in general. Some believe it is the Elephant, some the Hippopotamus; some affirm it is the Wild Bull. Poetically, it designates any large Quadruped.

This constant muttering in the reader's ear here verges on the ludicrous, but the purpose is clear: we are not to think that these visions are merely poetical fantasies to be enjoyed but not believed. A more than 'poetic faith' is demanded, and it is to secure that more than poetic faith that Coleridge turns at the beginning of the poem to Hartley, and at the end to Berkeley:

> See this *demonstrated* by Hartley, vol. 1, p. 114, and vol. 2, p. 329. See it likewise proved, and freed from the charge of Mysticism, by Pistorius in his Notes and Additions to part second of Hartley on Man, Addition the 18th, the 653rd page of the third volume of Hartley, Octavo Edition.
>
> .   .   .   .
>
> This paragraph is intelligible to those, who, like the Author, believe and feel the sublime system of Berkeley; and the doctrine of the final Happiness of all men.

I have already commented on Coleridge's use of Berkeley, and I should like now to consider the significance of the citation of Hartley. This appeared only in 1797, being dropped, not surprisingly, from the 1803 and subsequent editions. This does not mean, however, that it represents only a temporary and perhaps unimportant concern. Although by 1803, Coleridge had rejected various of Hartley's principles and was no longer prepared to refer to him for 'demonstration' or 'proof,' he continued, as I have shown elsewhere[67] to regard him with respect. By 1794, Coleridge had made an "intense study"[68] of "the great master of *Christian Philosophy*"[69] for whom he named his oldest child. In 1801, he could still write to Wedgwood that "we should give the name of Newton a more worthy associate—& instead of Locke & Newton, we should say, BACON & NEWTON, or still better perhaps, Newton and Hartley,"[70] and include Hartley with Berkeley and Butler as one of "the three greatest, nay, only three *great* Metaphysicians which this country *has* produced."[71] A few months later he mentioned Hartley along with "Zeno, St Paul, Spinoza . . . Kant, and Fichte" as a "*deep* metaphysician."[72] And even in 1803, he was proposing to write "an Essay containing the whole substance of the first Volume of Hartley, entirely defecated from all the corpuscular hypotheses—with new illustrations—& give my name to the Essay."[73] All this indicates something more than what has been described as "a brief flirtation"[74] with a philosophy "abhorrent to his deeper self."[75] I do not mean that Coleridge remained a 'Hartleyan'; I doubt that he ever regarded Hartley's philosophy as adequate.[76] But Hartley was trying to do something which seemed to Coleridge to need to be done. And it is this which is important.

Hartley's *Observations on Man* is in part an attempt to treat mind as a scientific 'object,' to explain mental events in terms of principles or 'laws' analogous to those which appear to be operative in physical events. In trying to demonstrate that thoughts were, like the motions of the planets, the effects of 'natural' causes and subject to 'natural' laws, Hartley was not, however, proposing a philosophy of materialism or skepticism. On the contrary, the purpose of his physiological and psychological theories was to provide a scientific 'proof' of the validity of religious and ethical ideas. In beginning with a physiological account of mental processes, and thus including these processes within the realm of natural laws, and by then deriving not only moral impulses but the experience of "self-annihilation and the pure love of God,"[77] Hartley was in effect trying to show a correspondence between 'inner' and 'outer,' between what is subjectively experienced and what is scientifically established, that bears some analogy to the Coleridgean position which I described earlier.

Hartley's starting point is in the conceptions of the mind and the physical universe put forward by Newton and Locke. The mind is an immaterial entity accessible only through the senses; the physical universe is a mechanical system of matter in motion. In order to explain the relationship between these two, Hartley adopts the notion that the mind is somehow so connected with the brain that physical events in the brain are necessarily accompanied by mental events in the mind. These physical events in the brain, Hartley suggests, are 'vibrations' which, in the case of sense perception, are transmitted through the nerve fibers and which correspond to the 'motions' (light waves, sound waves, and so forth) impinging on the organs of sense. A specific frequency of light, for example, thus produces a specific vibration in the brain which, in turn, is invariably accompanied by the sensation of red in the mind.

The advantage of this hypothesis for Hartley is that it enables him to assert a necessary connection between mental events and physical events without denying the existence of mind as a separate "immaterial substance"[78] and without becoming involved in the question of how such an immaterial substance can be affected by or affect the physical brain.[79] It does not matter for his purposes what the exact nature of the association of brain and mind is, or whether the doctrine of vibrations is literally true.[80] All that matters is that something like this must take place, that the mind functions as if its sensations were causally determined by physical stimuli, stimuli, that is, which belong to the shared, ordered, 'external' world. It is therefore possible not only to see how one more concerned with Hartley's ends than with his means could reject the doctrine of vibrations without rejecting Hartley *in toto*, but also to see how such a one could simultaneously accept Hartley, Berkeley, and Priestley, since the last two while denying in their different ways the distinction between mind and matter, affirmed that the mental and material were subject to the same laws.[81]

From this foundation, Hartley proceeds to elaborate a theory of association, insisting that not only perceptions but also "passions" and "affections" are "aggregates of simple ideas"[82] or sense images.

If certain sense images are repeatedly experienced together, an habitual response is set up so that a single one of the original stimuli will produce the whole complex response in the brain and also in the mind. And by such repetition, "clusters" of "simple ideas" will "by degrees, coalesce into one complex idea." [83] There exists, in other words, an 'attraction' between sensations and ideas experienced together analogous to the force of gravity supposed to exist between physical bodies.

This associative process does not stop simply with the production of complex images. Simple sensations include the sensations of pleasure and pain, and the desire for pleasure and aversion from pain form for Hartley a fundamental psychological principle. Since we desire pleasure and shun pain, our 'feelings' about different things and our actions with regard to them will depend upon the pleasure or pain which we have learned to associate with them. Feeling and will as well as perception, memory, and imagination, therefore, are determined by natural principles. "The will appears to be nothing but a desire or aversion sufficiently strong to produce an action that is not automatic primarily or secondarily. . . . Since therefore all love and hatred, all desire and aversion are factitious, and generated by association, i.e. mechanically; it follows that the will is mechanical also." [84]

It is this theory of the mind and character as wholly determined by its environment in accordance with fixed psychological laws which has seemed particularly unsatisfactory to critics looking forward to later doctrines of the creative imagination. But Hartley's purpose, as I have said, was not so much to demonstrate the material origins of ideas as to show the validity of Christian idealism, and it was this which a mechanistic psychology seemed to enable him to do.

In considering the problems of morality and religion, Hartley begins with what is essentially the old cosmological argument for the existence of God, but he turns that argument from a sequence of logical steps into a series of necessary 'associations.' From our experience, he says, we necessarily acquire the notion of cause, and this leads inevitably to the idea of a first cause, or God, an "infinite Being endowed with infinite Power and Knowledge." [86] Since we supposedly find in experience that the sum of happiness is greater than the sum of misery, our idea of God becomes that of one who is also "infinitely benevolent." [86] Since experience leads us to associate pleasures with their causes, we must ultimately come to associate all pleasure with the ultimate cause, the idea of God. "Since God is the source of all Good, and consequently must at last appear to be so, i.e. be associated with all our Pleasures, it seems to follow . . . that the idea of God, and of the ways by which his Goodness and Happiness are made manifest, must at last take the place of, and absorb other Ideas, and He himself become . . . All in All." [87]

As we come to associate greater pleasure with God than with anything connected with ourselves, our will, that is, our desire for pleasure, becomes wholly directed towards God:

> Our fears enhance our hopes, and nascent love; and altogether mortify our love for the world . . . till at last we arrive at an entire annihilation of ourselves, and an absolute acquiescence and complacence in the will of God, which affords the only answer to all our doubts, and the only radical cure for all our evils and perplexities. [88]

. . . .

> The virtuous dispositions of benevolence, piety, and the moral sense, and particularly that of the love of God, check all the foregoing ones, and seem sufficient utterly to extinguish them at last. This would be perfect self-annihilation, and resting in God as our centre. . . . We ought never to be satisfied with ourselves till we arrive at perfect self-annihilation, and the pure love of God. [89]

Historically, the realization of this process is still in the future; obviously mankind as a whole has reached no such peak of enlightenment. But individually, a proper, that is a 'natural' environment will produce such an ideal end. The world, Hartley argues, reveals the qualities of God, and through the operation of psychological laws, experience of the world undistorted by man-made evils will necessarily culminate in the religious experience of "perfect self-annihilation, and the pure love of God."

It was to this argument that Coleridge looked for support in

"Religious Musings." The opening section of the poem describes a Christmas Eve vision when

> high upborne,
> Yea, mingling with the Choir, I seem to view
> The vision of the heavenly multitude,
> Who hymned the song of Peace o'er Bethlehem's fields!

The thought of Christ, the most perfect image of "the Great Invisible (by symbols only seen)," leads to an account that moves through ascending stages of visionary intensity:

> Fair the vernal mead,
> Fair the high grove, the sea, the sun, the stars;
> True impress each of their creating Sire!
> Yet nor high grove, nor many-colour'd mead,
> Nor the green ocean with his thousand isles,
> Nor the starred azure, nor the sovran sun,
> E'er with such majesty of portraiture
> Imaged the supreme beauty uncreate,
> As thou, meek Saviour! at the fearful hour
> When thy insulted anguish winged the prayer
> Harped by Archangels, when they sing of mercy!
> Which when the Almighty heard from forth his throne
> Diviner light filled Heaven with ecstasy!
> Heaven's hymnings paused: and Hell her yawning mouth
> Closed a brief moment.

This opening passage is, in spite of some 'Socinian' implications, couched in relatively traditional terms. In the second section of the poem, Coleridge again describes a visionary ascent but this time in the language of Hartley:

> Lovely was the death
> Of Him whose life was Love! Holy with power
> He on the thought-benighted Sceptic beamed
> Manifest Godhead, melting into day

> What floating mists of dark idolatry
> Broke and misshaped the omnipresent Sire:
> And first by Fear uncharmed the drowsed Soul.
> Till of its nobler nature it 'gan feel
> Dim recollections; and thence soared to Hope,
> Strong to believe whate'er of mystic good
> The Eternal dooms for His immortal sons.
> From Hope and firmer Faith to perfect Love
> Attracted and absorbed: and centered there
> God only to behold, and know, and feel,
> Till by exclusive consciousness of God
> All self-annihilated it shall make
> God its Identity: God all in all!
> We and our Father one!

Not only does Coleridge here follow Hartley's steps from fear to hope to "perfect love" and echo his phrases ("absorbed," "centered," "self-annihilated"), but it is here that he adds the note which I quoted earlier exhorting the reader to "see this *demonstrated . . . proved, and freed from the charge of Mysticism.*"

Coleridge thus establishes at the outset the frame of reference in which the remainder of the poem is to be read. The two opening passages do not present us with traditional Christian images of cherubs and heavenly choirs 'jostling' with contemporary 'materialism.' The possibility of religious vision is central to the poem, and Coleridge's object is to show that what may be poetically described in traditional symbols may also be presented in terms of a 'scientific' analysis of the human mind. Hartley provides an essential part of the rational foundation of the poem, of the ground on which Coleridge hopes to meet and to convince his reader. The view of morality and history which follows is validated not by an appeal to doctrinal authority or assumed religious convictions but by an appeal to experience and to a rational psychology. There is hereafter a good deal of the language and machinery of traditional doctrine as well as Coleridge's own rather conventional and clumsy personifications, but these remain secondary. The machinery is not used to win the reader's assent to the possibility of an experience of "self-annihilation" and its concomitant moral and historical implications. The psychologically plausible experience rather prepares the reader to accept the machinery as a figurative language. We do not have to believe literally in "Cherubs and rapture-trembling Seraphim" in order to understand the vision of those "who in this fleshly World . . ./Adore with steadfast unpresuming gaze/Him Nature's essence, mind, and energy!"

In thus insisting on Hartley's importance after having tried to minimize the early influence of some other authors, it will I hope be clear that I do not mean to suggest that Hartley should take over the role of 'source' for Coleridge's philosophical position at this time. There is obviously a great deal in "Religious Musings" that cannot be 'found' in Hartley. And Coleridge demands of him more than he can really give. Hartley's 'self-annihilation' does not mean all that Coleridge would have it mean. In Hartley, it is essentially the equivalent in terms of associationist psychology of the traditional doctrine of perfect charity. Given Hartley's psychological premises, it does not and really cannot involve the kind of visionary apprehension which Coleridge suggests.

But as I have said earlier much that was essential to the visionary side of Coleridge did not need to be 'found': the Mariner's voyage is not speculative theory but psychological fact. Hartley was important because he seemed to provide a means of dealing with it as fact. And however much Coleridge may have diverged from Hartley's particular theories, he remained convinced of the value of "experimental physics and . . . experimental psychology," convinced that such physics and psychology could and would support and confirm the visionary experience.

During the nineties, Coleridge read, of course, not only the authors I have mentioned but many others as well, and he met in some of them ideas which at least in retrospect seemed to fit into the patterns of his maturer speculations. But I believe that those speculations derive not from any specific author or group of authors whom he read so much as from the character of the position which I have outlined. Coleridge came to see himself as helping to revive and hopefully to 'complete' a philosophy, a view of man and the universe, found in earlier writers, in Plato and the Neoplatonists, and continued by a variety of mystics, visionaries, and enthusiasts, in whom could be found "twilight Glimpses of awful Truths misapprehended by the unequal Intellect of the Beholder, & strangely mixed with the shapings of his own fancy." [90] What I am suggesting is that he 'derived' from this tradition only what in a sense he already knew. Certainly he was not like Thomas Taylor merely repeating to a rationalist age the words of visionary philosophers of the past.

In a notebook, Coleridge wrote:

> One excellence of the Doctrine of Plato, or of the Plotino-platonic Philosophy, is that it never suffers, much less causes or even occasions, its Disciples to forget themselves, lost and scattered in sensible Objects disjoined or *as* disjoined from themselves. It is impossible to understand the Elements of this Philosophy without an appeal, at every step & round of the Ladder, to the fact within, to the mind's Consciousness—and in addition to this, instead of lulling the Soul into an indolence of mere attention . . . rouses it to acts and energies of creative Thought, & Recognition—of conscious re-production of states of Being. I was not originally led to the study of this Philosophy by Taylor's Translations; but in consequence of early, half-accidental, prepossession in favor of it sent in early manhood for Taylor's Translations & Commentaries—& this, I will say, that no man worthy the name of man can read the many extracts from Proclus, Porphyry, Plotinus, &c . . . without an ahndung, an inward omening, of a system congruous with his nature, & thence attracting it—/ The boast therefore of the modern Philosophy is to me a decisive proof of its being an Anti-philosophy . . . that it calls the mere understanding into exertion without exciting or awakening any interest, any tremulous feeling of the heart, as if it heard or began to *glimpse* something which had once belonged to it, its Lord or its Beloved . . . . But yet it must not be denied or even withheld, that Taylor could not have understood the System, he teaches —for had he done so, he must have understood the difficulties that oppose its reception, the objections which immediately occur to men formed under notions so alien from it—Whereas

he no where prepares the mind, no where shews himself in a state of Sympathy with the hesitating Examiner—[91]

By 1798, Coleridge had developed a poetic language capable of expressing "the fact within" and of leading the reader to the "conscious re-production of states of Being." But though he "understood the difficulties . . . the objections which immediately occur" to the "hesitating Examiner," he had not as yet an adequate philosophical language. However confident he sometimes sounded ("see this demonstrated"; "I am a Berkleian"), he could only point to authorities who seemed not wholly to deny what he affirmed. Nevertheless, it is already clear what kind of a philosophic language he required: one that would enable him to state in terms intelligible to a "hesitant Examiner," to one "formed under notions so alien from" a "Plotino-platonic Philosophy" the substance of what he had been able to embody in poetic language. And it was such a language that he found in the next decade.

Chapter 4

The notion that Coleridge left for Germany a poet and returned a philosopher has long been accepted as at best no more than a half-truth. Some vision of an all-embracing philosophy was his before he left England, and some of his best poetry was written after his return. But even if the causes of his loss of poetic power and increasing devotion to metaphysics are found less in what happened while he was in Germany than in what happened after his return, in domestic discord, frustrated love, and chronic ill-health accentuated by drug addiction, the year 1798 still seems to mark a dividing line between the author of "Religious Musings" or "The Ancient Mariner" and the author of *The Friend*, *Biographia Literaria*, and *Aids to Reflection*. This is not only because the bulk of Coleridge's speculative and critical writing comes after that date and nearly all of his published poetry before it. It is also because the trip to Germany marks the *terminus ab quo* of his study of a school of philosophy with which he was hitherto unfamiliar and which appears increasingly to dominate his thought during the next twenty years.

According to Muirhead, Coleridge's philosophical studies in the first years of the nineteenth century opened up to him "a new view of the world" which required a "complete reorientation of the shaping spirit of imagination within him."[1] Herbert Read writes that "there is no doubt that the year in Germany was a decisive watershed in his intellectual development. The impact of the systematic atmosphere of a German university—and, one might say, the impact of a nation in a state of vivid intellectual awareness—all this sufficed to make him realize that in his previous studies he had merely floundered—that his head was stored with 'crude notions.'"[2] And J. B. Beer says:

> Coleridge soon discovered that, so far from fulfilling his vision, his researches were in danger of destroying his own visionary powers . . . . The process began in Germany . . . where in his physiological and New Testament studies he had been brought up against a form of scientific analysis more penetrating and destructive than anything which existed in England. There he must have learnt how little basis existed in history for his visionary world.[3]

There can be no doubt of the importance of Coleridge's German studies. His philosophical work is shot through with their terminology and arguments, especially those of Kant and the post-Kantian idealists. But it may be doubted whether those studies gave him a "new view of the world"; whether, even, they produced fundamental changes in his metaphysical position. I would suggest that what is involved is not so much a "new view of the world" as a different way of talking about it; that Coleridge's philosophy as it developed after 1798 was, like his poetry, a way of dealing with his own experience; that the real difference between the early and the later Coleridge is not so much the difference between different philosophies as it is the difference between poetry and metaphysics. Between "The Ancient Mariner" and *The Friend*, Coleridge ceased to regard himself primarily as a poet and came to regard himself primarily as a philosopher. As he lost faith in his ability to embody his apprehension of reality in poetry, he turned to the attempt to embody that same apprehension in the rather different formulations of philosophy. As philosophy in any formal sense, the result was, as I said in the Introduction, a failure. But I wish to consider not its value as philosophy but its function as language; to consider it not as a logical system nor as a description of reality but as a means of expression.

While during the years before 1798 Coleridge read widely and variously in philosophy, though perhaps not quite so widely and variously as has sometimes been supposed, I find no evidence that he seriously contemplated the writing of a major philosophical work, as distinct, that is, from a philosophical poem. He did have grandiose schemes for study. As early as 1796 he described to Poole a 'plan' to go to Jena to "study Chemistry and Anatomy, [and] bring back with me all the works of Semler and Michaelis, the German theologians, & of Kant, the great German metaphysician" in order that he might open a school whose proposed curriculum reads like the outline for a sort of 'Magnum Opus':

> 1. Man as Animal: including the complete knowledge of Anatomy, Chemistry, Mechanics & Optics.—2. Man as an Intellectual Being: including the ancient Metaphysics, the systems of Locke & Hartley,—of the Scotch Philosophers—& the Kantean S[ystem]—3. Man as a Religious Being: including an historic summary of all Religions & the arguments for and against Natural & Revealed Religion. Then proceeding from the individual to the aggregate of Individuals & disregarding all chronology except that of mind I should perfect them 1. in the History of Savage Tribes. 2. of semi-barbarous nations. 3 of nations emerging from semi-barbarism. 4. of civilized states. 5 of luxurious states. 6 of revolutionary states.—7.—of Colonies. During these studies I should intermix the knowledge of languages and instruct my scholars in Belles Lettres & the principles of composition . . .[4]

The course of study proposed for Charles Lloyd[5] and that laid down as the proper preliminary for writing an epic poem[6] were similarly ambitious and comprehensive. Even at this time, Coleridge had some notion of a 'Summa Philosophica' which would put all human knowledge in its proper place. But as the last instance would indicate, philosophy was for him subordinate to poetry. Apart from a remark to Thelwall that "in some form or other, & by some channel or other, I shall publish my critique on the New Philosophy,"[7] and some Hartleyan essays in *The Watchman*, there is no suggestion of his writing a philosophical work.

When at last he went to Germany in 1798, Coleridge followed a plan not unlike the one he had outlined to Poole two years before.

He learned the language, attended lectures in the natural sciences at Göttingen, and purchased a large number of philosophical works for future study. Although he must have become to some extent aware of recent developments in German philosophy, he does not seem to have made any study of it at the time. The books which he borrowed from the Göttingen library were all concerned with literature and history.[8] The notebooks for the period show an extensive study of Lessing, whose life he was planning to write, and considerable interest in the German reputation of the Scottish doctor John Brown,[9] but no evidence of new philosophical ideas or interests. He indulged his fondness for metaphysical discussion, but he seems to have been advocating his own ideas rather than acquiring new ones. "His fervour is particularly agreeable," wrote his companion Carlyon, "when contrasted with the chilling speculations of the German philosophers. I have had occasion to see these successively abandon all their strongholds when he brought to the attack his arguments and his philosophy . . . . They do not universally approve the mysticism of his metaphysics."[10] Both at Göttingen and on their Hartz tour, Coleridge discoursed at great length to Carlyon and his other companions on metaphysics, but according to Carlyon, who was admittedly often both bored and baffled, his subjects were the old ones of Hartley, Berkeley, Jeremy Taylor, Butler, Burnet, and Thomas Browne.[11] He spent a good deal of time, too, "Day after day, Day after day" discussing "The Ancient Mariner" and "the mysteries of the Albatross," a subject which to the weary Carlyon was unfortunately only "bewildering metaphysics."[12]

On his return to England in 1799, Coleridge found himself under various pressures. Financial pressure led him to suggest a number of money-making projects: a school book, a volume of his travels, a translation of Schiller, another of Blumenbach. Beyond this, he felt the need of justifying his annuity in general and his trip to Germany in particular by producing a "Life" of Lessing which would be worthy of the Wedgwoods' faith in him. He did not abandon poetry. He wrote or revived and revised a number of poems during 1799 and 1800, including "Love" and the second part of "Christabel."[13] And a number of his projects were poetic ones. He started to write a long poem "Mohammed" with Southey.[14] He planned to finish

"Christabel" and to write the poem to which "Love" is an introduction. But poetry did not come easily. In September, 1799, he rejected the idea of publishing a new volume of poems as he was "not in a poetical mood."[15] And in December, busy with contributions for the *Morning Post* and the translation of *Wallenstein*, he wrote, "I am afraid I have scarce poetic Enthusiasm enough to finish Christabel."[16]

It might have been expected that Coleridge's move to the north to settle near Wordsworth in July of 1800 would provide the necessary stimulus to his "poetic enthusiasm," and for a time and to some extent this seemed to be the case. He quickly finished the translation of *Wallenstein*, and devoted himself to assisting Wordsworth in the preparation of a second edition of *Lyrical Ballads*, which was to include the completed "Christabel" and some other new poems as well. With extraordinary devotion, Coleridge performed most of the hack work in the preparation of the new edition,[17] and found time also for a revision of "The Ancient Mariner" and the continuation, though not the completion, of "Christabel."

Wordsworth's company, however, did not long continue to stimulate Coleridge to new creative work. Coleridge received from his friend no such devotion and encouragement as he gave. Wordsworth was highly critical of "The Ancient Mariner," and in his preface to the new edition of *Lyrical Ballads* went out of his way to damn it with faint praise. Although at first "exceedingly delighted with the second part of 'Christabel,'"[18] he had, almost immediately, "determined not to print [it] with the L.B."[19] Only two months later, Coleridge wrote to Thelwall that he had "altogether abandoned" poetry, "being convinced that I never had the essentials of poetic Genius, & that I mistook a strong desire for original power."[20] Two days later he wrote, "As to our literary occupations they are still more distant than our residences—He [Wordsworth] is a great, a true Poet—I am only a kind of Metaphysician.—He has even now sent off the last sheet of a second Volume of his Lyrical Ballads"[21] —without "Christabel." Some months later, he wrote to Godwin, "If I die, and the Booksellers will give you anything for my life, be sure to say—Wordsworth descended on him like the Γνῶθι σεαυτόν from Heaven; by shewing him what true Poetry was, he made him know that he himself was no Poet." [22]

It would be unjust to conclude that Wordsworth's egotism and lack of critical understanding and encouragement were the cause of Coleridge's poetic decline. As the notebooks make painfully clear, deteriorating relations with his wife, the frustrated and agonizing love for Sara Hutchinson which obsessed him for years, increasing opium addiction, and wretched health made worse by opium and psychological turmoil, were at least as much to blame. There were in his life during the next few years too many of those "circumstances that have forced a man in upon his little unthinking contemptible self, [and] lessened his power of existing universally." [23] But as I have said before, the direction in which Coleridge seems to have been moving as a poet brought him increasingly into conflict with contemporary literary expectations. "The Ancient Mariner" and indeed all that he had published of what we would now consider his best and most characteristic work, met with critical indifference or incomprehension and hostility.[24] One may be forgiven for thinking that on top of all this the unsympathetic attitude of the friend and poet whom he most admired did much to destroy Coleridge's confidence in his own ability, to turn his hopes and his plans from poetry to prose. "I abandon Poetry altogether," he wrote even in September, 1800. "I leave the higher & deeper Kinds to Wordsworth, the delightful popular & simply dignified to Southey; & reserve for myself the honorable attempt to make others feel and understand their writings, as they deserve to be felt & understood." [25]

There were times, it is true, when his poetic confidence at least partly returned. In February, 1801, he wrote to Poole, "I hope that shortly I shall look back on my long & painful Illness only as a Storehouse of wild Dreams for Poems, or intellectual Facts for metaphysical Speculation. Davy . . . calls me the Poet-philosopher —I hope, Philosophy & Poetry will not neutralize each other, & leave me an inert mass." [26] And in July of 1802, perhaps encouraged, ironically, by the composition of "Dejection," he wrote to Sotheby, "I believe that by nature I have more of the Poet in me [than of the philosopher] . . . Thank Heaven! my better mind has returned to me—and I trust, I shall go on rejoicing." [27] Such moments, however, were transient. Only ten days later, he told Southey that "all my poetic Genius, if ever I really possessed any *Genius* . . . is gone." [28] He continued sometimes to write poems. There is a quantity of relatively light verse; there are many notes for poems; and there are the 'fragments' which I have spoken of earlier. But increasingly, he saw himself not as a poet-philosopher, but as a philosopher who had, perhaps, once been a poet.

As Coleridge's poetical hopes declined, his dreams of a great philosophical work grew. It is impossible to say exactly when he began to consider devoting himself to the composition of a major philosophical treatise. An unexplained remark to Southey in September, 1799, that "I am . . . resolved to publish nothing with my name till my Great Work" [29] may refer only to the "Life of Lessing" which is the only suitable project mentioned elsewhere at the time. But it is clear that as he relinquished the vision of himself as a poet, he replaced it with the vision of himself as a philosopher and critic. At about the same time that he first announced his intention to "abandon poetry" and confine himself to the role of interpreter, he wrote to Davy that "the [Essay on Poetry] is still more at my heart than the . . . [Life of Lessing]—it's Title would be an Essay on the Elements of Poetry/ it would in reality be a *disguised* System of Morals & Politics." [30]

The scope and significance of such a work grew rapidly in Coleridge's mind. A few months later, in February, 1801, he wrote, again to Davy, that "what my heart within me *burns* to do . . . is [to] concenter my free mind to the affinities of the Feelings with Words & Ideas under the title of 'Concerning Poetry & the nature of the Pleasures derived from it.'—I have faith that I do understand this subject/ and I am sure, that if I write what I ought to do on it, the Work would supersede all the books of Metaphysics hitherto written/ and all the Books of Morals too." [31] A month later, he mentioned to Poole a plan to publish "as a *Pioneer* to my greater work" a "work on the originality & merits of Locke, Hobbes, & Hume" [32] presumably based on the long philosophical letters which he had recently written to the Wedgwoods. The idea of both the historical preliminary and the work itself expanded greatly during the next two years. By February, 1803, he was proposing a "History of Metaphysics in England from Lord Bacon to Mr. Hume, inclusive." [33] And in June, in a letter to Godwin, the work appeared for the first time in its full glory as a critical history of logic from the beginning to Descartes and Condillac, to be followed by "my own Organum vere Organum . . . a Σύστημα of all *possible* modes of true, probable, & false reasoning." [34] When, a year later, Coleridge sailed for Malta in a vain search for health and peace of mind, Davy wrote, "You are to be the historian of the Philosophy of Feeling." [35] From this time on, nearly everything that Coleridge wrote or studied had a place in the ever-growing outline of his 'Magnum Opus.'

All this is important not simply with reference to the old question of whether an increasing preoccupation with metaphysics helped to destroy Coleridge's poetic powers or whether it served as a palliative for the loss of those powers and for other personal problems. It is important with respect to the point which I made at the beginning of this chapter concerning the new role that metaphysics was called upon to play in Coleridge's mind. During his early years, he required, as I have said, a philosophical rationalization of the kind of experience which in his poetry he tried to express. He turned to Hartley and others to support and justify his vision, to 'demonstrate and prove' that the acceptance of such a vision was reasonable. But he did not use philosophy as a means of expressing that vision. It provided footnotes, not text.

As Coleridge turned from poetry to philosophy, however, philosophy rather than poetry became his medium of expression. Instead of serving as a rationalization of poetic experience, philosophy became a substitute for it. This meant that what was apprehended by "the Vision and the Faculty Divine" had to be not only allowed for but included in the formulations of philosophy. And it is this, I believe, rather than any "new view of the world" that characterizes Coleridge's 'new' philosophical concerns.

In other words, his philosophy, as I see it, remained fundamentally an attempt to find a language, a set of symbols in terms of which he could describe and make intelligible his own experience of himself in the universe. Those relations between the whole and the part, between the essential and the existential, between the intuitive

Reason and the conceptual Understanding which we find variously formulated in his theology, in his psychology, in his philosophy of nature, are in essence the same as the relations between self and universe and between different states of mind and different modes of being which we find earlier, as experience rather than theory, in the poetry. It was these relations, this structure immediately apprehended in experience rather than deduced from experience, that throughout distinguished Coleridge's "view of the world" and provided the essentials of his philosophy.

It is true that Coleridge found a good deal of the language that he required in German philosophy, from which he borrowed more heavily than he often cared to admit. To the historian of philosophy, this is of primary importance. But I am more interested in the function that these borrowings were made to serve, in the degree to which they were subordinate to Coleridge's own needs and purposes. To consider this may not enhance Coleridge's philosophical status, but it may help to understand him better. He had, I think, something to say. He used Kant and Schelling and others in trying to say it. But he did not 'mean' merely the works from which he borrowed; they do not constitute the substance of what he said.

In the discussion of "The Ancient Mariner" in an earlier chapter, I said that the Mariner's voyage might be seen as the record of the evolution of a self, and that it presents us with a kind of spectrum of consciousness whose extremes are alienation and communion, with 'normal' consciousness of the self in the world lying somewhere between the extremes. While none of the other poems which I considered present the whole of this spectrum, they do reveal parts of it, particularly the movement from the 'normal' to communion, from discursive consciousness to what might be called 'unitive' consciousness. And I added later that this spectrum provided the underlying pattern for Coleridge's metaphysics.

In a passage which I quoted earlier from *The Friend*, Coleridge wrote:

> The groundwork, therefore, of all pure speculation is the full apprehension of the difference between the contemplation of reason, namely, that intuition of things which arises when we

possess ourselves, as one with the whole, which is substantial knowledge, and that which presents itself when, transferring reality to the negations of reality, to the ever-varying framework of the uniform life, we think of ourselves as separated beings, and place nature in antithesis to mind, as object to subject, thing to thought, death to life. This is abstract knowledge, or the science of the mere understanding.[36]

If such different ways of contemplation, of experience, are possible, then this raises questions about the nature of the mind and of the object or objects of its contemplation. For if the whole spectrum of consciousness is taken to be cognitively significant, then neither the mind nor its object, neither the self nor the not-self, is a fixed and definable entity. They become fixed, become 'mind' and 'object' as we move towards one end of the spectrum. As we move towards the other, distinctions fade, and qualitative harmony takes the place of quantitative differentiation. Moreover, if 'unitive' consciousness is taken, as Coleridge takes it, to be a religious experience, then the nature of 'God' must also be such as to permit such a relationship.

A thorough examination of the development of Coleridge's ideas of mind, of nature, and of God (of, that is, his psychology, his natural philosophy, and his theology) is an undertaking beyond the purposes or pretensions of this essay. But I should like to consider what seems to me the basis of his thought in each of these three areas, and the manner in which the languages which he found enabled him to give philosophic expression to his inward vision.

First I should like to turn not indeed to theology but to one element in Coleridge's theology, the question of the nature of God. Theology was, of course, a subject to which after 1800 Coleridge devoted an increasing proportion of his attention, and for a time during the nineteenth century he perhaps aroused more interest and exercised more influence as a theologian than in any other capacity. Many of the theological issues that seemed vital to him, however, especially during his later years, need not concern us here. He was anxious to show that the Bible and what he took to be the essential doctrines of Christianity were consistent with his philosophy, or vice versa. But the issue most involved in the other two areas of mind and nature, and the one which I wish to consider, is the conception of God as an archetype of human consciousness which was explicit by 1806 and not significantly altered thereafter.

During the earlier years, the problem of the formulation of the nature of God was not urgent. As a poet, Coleridge gave articulate form to religious experience, but this does not necessarily require a theology, certainly not a consistent one, and he did not, as we have seen, depend upon doctrinal language or authority. His Unitarianism enabled him without difficulty to believe in God and science, in the transcendent and the rational, and this was sufficient. In a revealing comment, he later wrote:

> I dare avow—& hope, I shall give no offence to serious Believers—that it appears to me scarcely possible, that a young man of ingenuous dispositions, warm sensibility, and an enquiring mind should avoid Socinianism—educated as we all are—1 The grounds are—the application of common Logic, i.e. the law of incongruity (regula contradictionis) to premises abstracted from Matter, & falsely applied to Spirit—. Thus in the word *one*—Logic in short applied without any previous analysis of the faculties of the mind, and the seat or source of different notions . . . . . 2. The custom so inveterate of disputing a Religion by Texts . . . the consequence of which must necessarily be, that one class of Texts appearing to contradict the other, the preference will—& indeed ought to be given to that sense which is the most congruous with Reason—3. Young men ignorant of the corruption & weakness of their own hearts, & therefore always prone to substitute the glorious *Ideal* of human nature for the existing reality . . . .—4. a subtler & abstruser ground—why young men are inclined to necessitarianism, in addition to the pleasure from clear & distinct notions, which those must needs be which are but in truth material Images by a sophism of metathesis passed off for operations of mind—in addition to this, strange as it may appear, yet it is true, that we least value & think of that which we enjoy in the highest degree—this free-agency, the unsettled state of Habit

not yet Tyranny—we begin to think of, & intellectually to know, our freedom when we have been made to feel its imperfections, & its loss . . . .[37]

As this suggests, and as many other notes confirm, Coleridge's dissatisfaction with Unitarianism, which to the later irritation of some of his erstwhile coreligionists he identified with what he called Socinianism,[38] and his movement towards trinitarianism, had more than one cause, some of them involving the personal problems I have spoken of in this chapter. But one reason was the realization of the inadequacy of the "application of common Logic . . . to premises abstracted from Matter, & falsely applied to Spirit," and of "material Images . . . passed off for operations of mind" to express the complexity that he felt in the relation of the natural and the transcendent.

As early as 1801, Coleridge wrote in a notebook that "as we recede from anthropomorphitism, we must go either to the Trinity or to Pantheism. The Fathers who were Unitarians, were Anthropomorphites." [39] The note appears in the midst of several that are at least by implication critical of a mechanical psychology. One of these mentions that "Materialists unwilling to admit the mysterious of our nature make it all mysterious— . . . ." [40] And it is suggestive that the note immediately preceding this on anthropomorphism is the comment on Wordsworth's "We see into the Life of Things" which I discussed earlier and which concludes, "the Idea becomes dim whatever it be—so dim that I know not what it is—but the Feeling is deep & steady—and this I call *I*—identifying the Percipient & the Perceived—." [41]

One might expect, perhaps, that Coleridge would be drawn by pantheism rather than trinitarianism. In many of the poems, finite nature appears as a limitation within which man may be imprisoned, but it also provides the way of liberation. Given a favorable environment, the experience of God seems to come easily. But Coleridge was aware, as "The Ancient Mariner" shows, that one may experience a 'universe of horror' as well as a 'universe of bliss,' and that it may not always be true that "Nature ne'er deserts the wise and pure." Something more than the presence of natural beauty was required for the experience of transcendence. Pantheism, we might say, is adequate only to the 'unitive' end of the spectrum; it does not allow for the failure of vision. And such failures became of increasing concern. I have already mentioned the "Lines written in the album at Elbingerode," in which the "surging scene" produces only a "low and languid mood." Two months earlier, Coleridge had written to his wife that

> my Imagination is tired, down, flat and powerless; and I languish after Home, for hours together, in vacancy; my *feelings* almost wholly unqualified by *Thoughts*. I have, at times, experienced such an extinction of *Light* in my mind, I have been so forsaken by all the *forms* and *colourings* of Existence, as if the *organs* of Life had been dried up; as if only simple BEING remained, blind and stagnant!—After I have recovered from this strange state, & reflected upon it, I have thought of a man who should lose his companion in a desart of sand where his weary Halloos drop down in the air without an Echo.[42]

And the problem increased in the years following his return from Germany. Although he could write to Wedgwood in 1803 that "I do not think it possible, that any bodily pains could eat out the love & joy, that is so substantial a part of me, towards hills, & rocks, & steep waters! And I have had some trial,"[43] he had found, as "Dejection" shows, that he could contemplate the beauty of nature and feel only numbness. He found too as time went on a growing sense of personal inadequacy and personal guilt. He never approached the extreme of asceticism, but it was at least in part an increasing sense of the shortcomings as well as the limitations of the finite world and the finite self that led in later years to his rigorous rejection of pantheism as involving the perfection of God in the imperfection, as he came to see it, of man and nature.

It is thus not surprising that we find Coleridge moving towards what he saw as the other alternative, trinitarianism. This was not, as it used sometimes to be thought, merely a return to the comforts of orthodoxy. The conception of trinity as a paradigm for the relation of the finite and the infinite is by no means confined to Christianity, but is a means, even a fairly obvious means, by which the visionary and the mystic has formulated the distinction and the relation which he finds between the extremes of his own experience. Coleridge had long been familiar with many such formulations, though he had not earlier felt the need to adapt them to his own situation. He did feel such a need after his return from Germany. And during the next few years, he devoted a good deal of time to the study and restudy of such fathers of the church as Scotus and Aquinas,[44] and, as we have seen, to the study or restudy of both Christian and non-Christian Neoplatonists including Plotinus, Proclus, Ficino, and Bruno, in all of whom he found a cosmology involving a trinitarian deity.

The results of his meditation and study appear in a long letter written to Thomas Clarkson in October, 1806, shortly after his return from Malta. This is the letter from which I have quoted before his statement that God could be known but not conceived, and that a concept of God could be only a "congruous notion." [45] He continued:

> God is the sole self-comprehending Being, i.e. he has an Idea of himself, and that Idea is consummately adequate, & superlatively real—or as great men have said in the throes and strivings of deep and holy meditation, not only substantial or essential, but super-substantial, super-essential. This Idea therefore from all eternity co-existing with, & yet filiated, by the absolute Being . . . is the same, as the Father in all things, but the impossible one, of self-origination. He is the substantial Image of God, in whom the Father beholds well pleased his whole Being —and . . . he . . . as delightedly & with as intense LOVE contemplates the Father in the Father, and the Father in himself, and himself in the Father. But all the actions of the Deity are intensely real or substantial/ therefore the action of Love, by which the Father contemplates the Son, and the Son the Father, is equally real with the Father and the Son; & proceeds co-eternally both from the Father and the Son—& neither of these Three *can* be conceived *apart*, nor *confusedly*—so that the Idea of God involves that of a Tri-unity.[46]

Like some of those earlier writers whose influence seems apparent in this extract, Coleridge has here conceived of God as an archetypal consciousness, and presented the persons or elements of the Trinity as aspects of that consciousness. In his poetry, he presented the relation between the worlds of natural perception and supernatural vision as a relation between two states of mind, and it is essentially this relation which his conception of trinity attempts to define. God is on the one hand pure 'Being,' the essence of all 'reality,' a kind of spiritual energy unlimited and undifferentiated. On the other hand, God is conscious of himself, and his 'Idea,' his *concept* of himself, is the second element in his nature, the 'Logos.' These two are interdependent, and between them exists, as a third aspect of reality, a kind of dynamic tension, "the action of Love." Illimitable 'Being,' which would by itself be "blind and stagnant," is forever conscious of, and in love with, the infinite forms which it might take, while it forever evades definition by any particular form.

Coleridge was fond of illustrating this notion of God as self-conscious 'Being' by the apt analogy of a circle. In a note of 1808–12, he wrote:

The Son is the omnipresent center of that infinite Circle, whose only Circumference is in its own Self-comprehension, the eternal Act of which for ever constitutes that Center. The immanent Energy of the divine Consciousness is, and is the cause of, the co-eternal Filiation of the Logos, the essential Symbol of the Deity, the substantial, infinite, sole adequate, Idea in God, of God; in and by whom the Father, thus *necessarily* self-manifested, doth freely in the ineffable overflowing of Goodness create . . . But the second Energy—in order (for time attributed to the Infinite Eternal is a contradiction in thought) of the Father in and through the Son, and of the Son in and from the Father, and in and from Himself, as in and from the Father, is, and is the co-ternal Procession and Procedence of, the Holy Spirit—[47]

In the consciousness that is God, then, unitive and discursive are known as essentially identical. There can be no sense of alienation.

God's consciousness of self is all-inclusive rather than all-exclusive. His contemplation is always the "contemplation of reason" since, being the whole, he cannot "possess himself" other than "as one with the whole." While this makes intelligible the notion of a God in whom we may "live and move and have our being," it also permits those states of mind in which "we think of ourselves as separated beings," in which the finite is seen not as the focusing of reality into a specific form, but as a distinct self-existing entity.

> In the Logos, or adequate Idea of the Divine Being, . . . in the Son, I say, are contained all possible Ideas *eminenter*. But in him all are as one—yet even as the divine act of Self-consciousness gave substantial Essence to his great Idea, even so all the included Ideas produced existing Images of themselves in the power and thro' the free goodness of Deity, for it was better that they should be, than not be. But yet by existence, i.e. *stare extra*, they of necessity became *finite*, & therefore *inadequate*, Images of their Prototypes in the divine mind; and as finite derived their distinguishing and separate Natures from *not-Being:* as Plato has set forth almost inspiredly. Hence the chasm infinitely infinite between Deity and the Creature . . . [which can be bridged only by] the reduction of Soul to Spirit, of the Image to it's Idea, which could only be effected by producing in them the condition of their Ideas, namely, the being all, as one, in one—and thereby putting off the evils of separation and finiteness. . . . Then will the Spirit drink in perfection in an eternal growth by the beatific vision of the Unutterable, in whose Image it was created—[48]

The alienation of the finite self is the result of separative self-consciousness, of the definition of self which necessarily excludes its dissolution in the 'All,' and which therefore isolates it from the 'reality' of 'Being.' "He that lusteth for himself . . . he lusteth after a lie, and a false imaginary center." [49] In taking the finite self as the defining center of consciousness, one loses consciousness of the unitive, the "contemplation of reason," and sees only a world of "phantoms and false life," [50] of 'Death.'

A somewhat different, more cryptic, but thoroughly Coleridgean exposition appears in a note of 1806 and is worth repeating for what it reveals of the way in which Coleridge's mind was working at this time.

Σωμα ψυχοπλαστον Ψυχη σωμαπλαττουσα Reo = reor probably an obsolete Latin word, and res the second person singular of the Present Indicative—If so, it is the Iliad of Spinozo-Kantian, Kanto-Fichtian, Fichto-Schellingian Revival of Plato-Plotino-Proclian Idealism in a Nutshell *from* a Lilliput Hazel. Res = thou art thinking.—Even so our "Thing": id est, thinking or think'd. Think, Thank, Tank = Reservoir of what has been *thinged*—Denken, Danken—I forget the German for Tank/ The, them, This, These, Thence, Thick, Thing, Thong, Thou, may all be Hocus-pocused by metaphysical Etymology into Brothers and Sisters—with many a Cousin-German/ All little Miss Thetas, the ⊙ being a Circle, with the Kentron [*Kentrum*], or central Point, creating the circumference & both together the infinite Radii/—the Central point is primary Consciousness = living Action; the circumference = secondary Consciousness (or Consc: in the common sense of the word) and the passing to and fro from the one to the other Thought, Things, necessary Possibilities, contingent Realities/ = Father, Son, Holy Ghost/ the Το ον, Ο Λογος, η Σοφια/—The · is I which is the articulated Breath drawn inward, the ○ is the same sent outward, the ⊙ or Theta expresses the synthesis and coinstantaneous reciprocation of the two Acts, the Dualism of *Thought* by *Distinctions*, the Unity of *Thing* by Indivisibility/ and then the Radii, Ακτῖνες = Res in Theta (or perhaps Delta) = Αγω (acta) εν Θητα (or Tau)—(O Lord! What thousands of Threads in how large a Web may not a Metaphysical Spider spin out of the Dirt of his own Guts/ but alas! it is a net for his own super-ingenious Spidership alone! It is so thin that the most microscopical Minitude of Midge or Sand-flea—so far from being detained in it—passes thro' without seeing it.—) These Words within the Crotchets—are Truth for the Worldlings, all without are Crotchets with a Vengeance to them but to me those Words are the Crotchets, the capapee Masquerade Domino of my own Convictions in the Opinions of the men of supposed gesunder Menschenverstand/ the former are the naked Flesh & Blood, Bone and Muscle of my own individual Faith/ [51]

Like many of his speculations on natural philosophy, which I shall discuss later, this may well at first seem like the work of a "Metaphysical Spider" gone mad, an instance of the same kind of fanciful excess which we find, and which Coleridge often criticized, in some of the Neoplatonists and alchemists. But there is, as Miss Coburn's explanatory note makes clear,[52] an intelligible meaning behind the fancy. And what is significant and characteristic, I think, is the manner in which Coleridge grasps at whatever terms he can find to illustrate and give articulate form to "the naked Flesh & Blood, Bone and Muscle of my own individual Faith." The etymology of *res* and the shape of *theta* are not the basis for what he is arguing, not information from which he is drawing conclusions, but are 'objects' which because of the pattern which he sees in them may be "Hocus-pocused" into symbols of the systolic rhythm of consciousness. We may remember the remark that "Language & all *symbols* give *outness* to Thoughts/ & this the philosophical essence and purpose of Language." [53] Fanciful etymology, the shapes of letters, and puns may seem to provide a frivolous language for the expression of serious thought, but as Coleridge once said of puns, it is "the buffoon Brutus concealing Brutus, the Consul." [54]

That such 'hocus-pocus' is not mere play but is part of the attempt to find symbols to "give *outness* to Thoughts" is apparent in another note written in 1807:

The Sky, o rather say, the Æther, at Malta, with the Sun apparently suspended in it, the Eye seeming to pierce beyond, & as it were, behind it—and below the aetherial Sea, so blue, so a zerflossenes Eins, the substantial Image, and fixed real Reflection of the Sky—O I could annihilate in a deep moment all possibility of the needlepoint pinshead System of the *Atomists* by one submissive Gaze! Λογος ab *Ente*—at once the existent

Reflexion, and the Reflex Act—at once actual and real & therefore, filiation not creation/ Thought *formed not fixed*—the molten *Being* never cooled into a *Thing*, tho' begotten into the vast adequate Thought. Est, Idea, Ideatio—*Id*—inde, ʜᴏᴄ et *illud*. Idea—*atio*, seu *actio* = Id: iterum, Hoc + Id, & then Id + Ea (i.e. Coadunatio Individui cum Universo per Amorem) = Idea: Idea + actio = Ideatio, seu αγιον πνευμα, which being transelemented into we are mystically united with the *Am—* Ειμι—.[55]

The latter part of this is, as Miss Coburn says, "scarcely intended as a serious etymological exercise but is a use of etymology as a 'suggestive analogy' which will provide him with a vivid series of word-symbols." [56] While he was in Malta, Coleridge concluded a description of the night sky with the observation that "deep Sky is of all visual impressions the nearest akin to a Feeling/ it is more a Feeling than a Sight/ or rather it is the melting away and entire union of Feeling & Sight." [57] Now remembering that occasion or one like it, he is trying to formulate something of the relation of "Feeling & Sight," or "Being" and "Thing," of thinking and thought, which the experience suggested. Miss Coburn's detailed and perceptive gloss of this note concludes:

> This seems to show in highly condensed form five modes of transition in thought:
> (a) From existence to creative Word . . . ;
> (b) From thing to symbol to Idea;
> (c) From thing to person;
> (d) From contemplation of a thing or symbol to contemplation of Idea and then to transelementation into spirit;
> (e) From scrutiny of the world to mystical union with God.[58]

The value to Coleridge of this "highly condensed form" is, of course, that to him these five modes are 'really' the same, and are all implicit in his contemplation of the sky of Malta. The etymological hocus-pocus provides him with a language, a set of symbols, in which to state that "principle that was derived from experience, but of which all other knowledge should be but so many repetitions under various limitations, even as squares, triangles, etc., etc., are but so many positions of space." [59]

The key phrase here is "derived from experience." However gnomic Coleridge may become, in these as in innumerable other instances his formulations are ultimately descriptions of *human* consciousness, or the processes of perception and conceptualization. He is not simply attempting a logical reconciliation of the notions of finite man and infinite God, but is rather attempting to state the relations implied in the *experience* of being, of finiteness and infinity, alienation and union. 'God' is human consciousness raised to an absolute, converted into the principle in terms of which "all other knowledge" will "be but so many repetitions under various limitations." And the principle will 'work' since all knowledge is human knowledge and will therefore reveal characteristics of human consciousness.

Coleridge's search for a language in which to state the nature of 'God' often shows the influence of earlier writers, as is apparent in the first two of the extracts which I have cited. But I think that here as elsewhere the question of influence can easily be misleading. He had not just discovered their language for the first time. He had come to need it and found how he could use it. He knew, in a sense, what he was looking for. He found languages which he could adapt to his purposes in Plotinus, in Proclus, in St. John, in Bruno, in Boehme, and in "many a Cousin-German." He could have found them in many another writer whom he did not know, of whom he had never heard. More important than where he found them is the question of why he needed them and how he used them.

As 'God' meant for Coleridge ultimate reality, so theology was the proper end of all science and philosophy, and his conception of the nature of God is closely related to his speculations about the philosophy of nature and about human psychology. In the letter to Clarkson, he wrote that

> The Idea of God involves that of a Tri-unity; and as that
> Unity or Indivisibility is the intensest, and the Archetype, yea,
> the very substance and element of all other Unity and Union,
> so is that Distinction the most manifest, and indestructible of

all distinctions—and Being, Intellect, and Action, which in their absoluteness are the Father, the Word, and the Spirit will and must forever be and remain the 'genera generalissima' of all knowledge.[60]

If for the "Idea of God" we substitute some such phrase as 'the Idea of consciousness,' or, since strictly speaking 'the Father,' 'Being,' is preconsciousness, 'the Idea of the emergence of consciousness,' then we may say that Coleridge's philosophy of nature was, fundamentally, an elaboration of this statement.

It is common enough knowledge that Coleridge regarded specific phenomena as concrete manifestations of universal 'Ideas,' and the notion that the particular is somehow or other symbolic of the universal is such a very old one and is so very familiar in poetry as well as in theology and philosophy, that we are apt, especially when discussing poets, even poet-philosophers, to accept it or at least to suspend disbelief without any very careful examination of what is meant in a particular instance. But Coleridge was not simply following in a vaguely Platonic tradition. He was, as I have said, very much aware of the fact that earlier Neoplatonic and mystical philosophies had been routed by a mechanistic world view partly because they were less able to provide satisfactory explanations of the phenomena of scientific observation. If he was to be able to take the directly intuited patterns of consciousness, rather than the mechanical patterns of eighteenth-century science, as the basis of reality, then he had to be able to define finite phenomena in terms of consciousness without contradicting the 'facts' of scientific observation and experiment.

Newtonian science postulated an inferred reality in terms of the structure of the phenomenal world as known to discursive consciousness. For Newton, the universe at any moment was a particular order of diverse bodies in space. Newton's laws were mathematical descriptions of the relation between the particular order in space at one moment and the particular order in space at another moment. Such a system proved far more useful in the explanation of natural phenomena than had the teleological assumptions of an earlier age, and seemed to many to have been proved beyond the shadow of a doubt. If the Mariner's experience was a "dream of truth," however, if the visionary experience of phenomena as the changing forms of a universal radiance is cognitively valid, then finite phenomena cannot be adequately described solely in terms of an order in time and space. Such a description could define phenomena as they exist in a discursive order but not as they dissolve in the unity of transcendence. If the relation between finite concept and infinite consciousness is the archetype, then an analogous relation should be revealed in physical nature. And it seemed to Coleridge that some of the most recent developments in science and especially in chemistry did reveal precisely such an analogous relation.

This conviction was not derived from an ordinary layman's cursory acquaintance with scientific theory. While Coleridge was no scientist, his interest in natural science was a long-standing one, going back to his days at Christ's Hospital when he read his brother Luke's medical books and had a transient interest in himself becoming a doctor. And his letters, notebooks, and marginalia show that throughout his life he read widely and critically in scientific books and journals. He may have put his faith in theories which were later discarded, and he may have erred in extending their inferences beyond the point that caution or scientific accuracy could allow, but he was not ill informed.

We should remember moreover that during the late eighteenth and early nineteenth centuries, some areas of natural science were almost in their infancy. Mathematics, mechanics, and astronomy were, it is true, highly developed, but chemistry, the biological sciences, and the study of magnetic and electrical phenomena were only beginning to become established. Many of the fundamental discoveries from which modern science developed had been made, but many of these had not yet won general acceptance. During the 1790's, Priestley, one of Coleridge's early heroes and the discoverer of oxygen, was vigorously upholding his theory of phlogiston against the new, and correct, suggestion that combustion was oxidation, and was arguing that water was not composed of oxygen and hydrogen, as Lavoisier believed, but was rather a component of all gases. Both static electricity and the phenomenon of galvanism, or current electricity produced by chemical action, were known, but the connection between them was not understood. Dalton's atomic theory, which Coleridge strenuously opposed, was, in the first decade of the nineteenth century, just coming to be accepted by competent scientists.

It is quite understandable, therefore, that Coleridge, seeing hints of developments which would confirm his expectations, should have seized those hints in confidence that the developments would surely follow. The confidence, of course, was not borne out, and the acceptance of Dalton meant, for a long time to come, once again a universe composed of discrete bodies in space, however minute those bodies might be thought to be. It is indicative of Coleridge's attitudes that it was over the acceptance of Dalton that he parted ways with his scientist friend Davy. Davy accepted Dalton because he offered a better explanation of experimentally verified facts. Coleridge rejected Dalton because his theory was incompatible with the 'reality' which Coleridge wished to describe. After Davy's 'conversion,' Coleridge wrote as a postscript to a long chemical note, "Alas! Since I wrote the preceding note, H. Davy is become Sir Humphry Davy and an *Atomist!*"[61] And in a notebook, he added, "You have combined arsenic with your gold, Sir Humphry! You are brittle, and I will rather dine with Duke Humphry than with you."[62] But Coleridge and Davy were not looking for the same things.

The development of Coleridge's natural philosophy has never been the subject of a thorough study,[63] perhaps partly because more than any other area of his speculation it appears to us now to have been a dead end, and partly because so much of it seems obviously derived from German *Naturphilosophie*. Certainly after about 1809–10, the language and ideas which we find in Coleridge's writing on the subject are very close to those of Schelling and his friends and disciples. And it is easy to see why their work should have attracted him. Like alchemy, of which it is in effect an updated version, early nineteenth-century *Naturphilosophie* saw the physical world in terms of what are essentially psychological patterns, and up to a point it provided precisely the kind of language which Coleridge required, authenticated by its apparent consistency with current scientific investigations and by the fact that some of its proponents—Steffens, Ritter, and later Oken—were themselves scientists.

Were it only a matter of Coleridge having discovered and adopted the theories and language of *Naturphilosophie*, the situation would be simple enough. But he did not apparently make a study of Schelling before 1809–10, though he knew enough of him to write the note in 1806 which I have quoted above. He may possibly have heard something of Schelling, who began lecturing at Jena in 1798, while he was in Germany, though he says nothing of him at the time and there is no clear indication of familiarity for at least ten years thereafter. In 1799, however, he met Humphry Davy, and in the next few years, before Davy became an "*Atomist*" and an apostate, his value to Coleridge was undeniable. "Humphrey Davy," Coleridge wrote, "in his Laboratory is probably doing more for the Science of Mind, than all the Metaphysicians have done from Aristotle to Hartley inclusive."[64] What Davy was doing in his laboratory led him to conclusions sufficiently close to some theories of the *Naturphilosophen*—on whom he in fact had some influence—that it is extremely difficult to untangle the origins of specific formulations in Coleridge. But Coleridge's notes clearly show Davy's influence before they show Schelling's. Whether before 1809–10 Coleridge had any detailed knowledge of Schelling's theories or not, it would seem that what he learned from Davy was an important intermediate step to bring him to a position from which the relevance of the formulations of *Naturphilosophie* would appear.

Even before he met Coleridge, Davy had published a rather brash essay in which he sought to show the fundamental role of light in the production of physical phenomena and in which he suggests that "the laws of gravitation, as well as the chemical laws, [will] be considered as subservient to one grand end, *Perception*."[65] The essay was criticized, and justifiably so, for its scientific shortcomings, but it shows the kind of theoretical bent which helped to attract Coleridge. Davy was suggesting that the principles governing the production of physical phenomena had something in common with the principles governing the processes by which phenomena are perceived, and more important, since this could be said also of Hartley and Priestley, he at least hints at a central characteristic of "the transcendent or genetic philosophy,"[66] the notion that 'things' should be analyzed not as mechanical configurations of matter but as the products of elemental forces, thus providing an analogy to the process in which "Feelings die by flowing into the mould of the Intellect, & becoming Ideas." [67] As Coleridge wrote in an undated note:

> Even so as Thoughts, from Images even up to Ideas, are distinct but not divided Existents of the Mind, quasi proles semper in utero, so are the Products of Nature, which we call Things or *Fixes* (res fixae, intellectiones coagulatae) are never really producta jam et vere fixa; but themselves portions of the act of producing.[68]

As a result of his work at Beddoes' Pneumatic Institute at Bristol, Davy was, in 1801, appointed lecturer in chemistry to the Royal Institution, and his lectures there, some of which Coleridge attended and others of which he read,[69] continued to provide material for a "genetic philosophy." Davy looked for elemental dynamic principles in the phenomena which he examined experimentally. He was interested in reproductivity, irritability, and sensibility as characteristics of organic bodies;[70] in the relation of the characteristics of length (associated with magnetism) and surface (associated with static electricity) with galvanic phenomena;[71] and most importantly with the role of electricity in chemical phenomena. All of these are important in the theories of *Naturphilosophie* and all appear in Coleridge's notes and in the later *Theory of Life*. And it is important that he was familiar with them not only as terms in German theory but also in Davy's explanations of his experimental investigations.

The results of Davy's work during his first few years at the Royal Institution were set forth in a series of papers beginning with his Bakerian Lecture in 1806. It was the arguments put forth in this and subsequent papers that led Coleridge to credit Davy with "doing more for the Science of Mind, than all the Metaphysicians have done," and in January, 1809, he wrote to Davy that "a brief account of your first Lecture of this Season"

> furnished to my Understanding & Conscience proofs more convincing than the dim Analogies of natural organization to hu-

man Mechanism, both of the Supreme Reason as superessential to the World of the Senses; of an analogous Mind in Man not resulting from it's perishable Machine, nor even from the general Spirit of Life, it's inclosed stream or perfluent water-force; and of the moral connection between the finite and the infinite Reason, and the aweful majesty of the former as both the Revelation and the exponent Voice of the Latter, immortal Timepiece [of] an eternal Sun.[72]

The basis for this enthusiasm was Davy's suggestion that in various cases the difference between apparently distinct substances might be due solely to differences in electrical properties, that "matter of the same kind, possessed of different electrical powers, may exhibit different chemical forms."[73] Davy had not yet committed himself to the new atomic theory and it seemed possible to him that oxygen, hydrogen, nitrogen, and water might all be different forms of a single unknown, and that combustion, the oxidation of metals, and various characteristics of the 'fixed alkalis' and 'rare earths' might be explained in a similar manner.[74] It seemed to Coleridge that Davy would in time be able to demonstrate that all substances were in reality constituted by certain elementary forces that could themselves be resolved into a single force. In November, 1807, he wrote that Davy,

by the aid and application of his own great discovery, of the identity of electricity and chemical attractions, . . . has placed all the elements and all their inanimate combinations in the power of man; having decomposed both the Alkalies, and three of the Earths, discovered as the base of the Alkalies a new metal, the lightest, most malleable, and most inflammable substance in nature . . . He has proved too, that by a practicable increase of electric energy all *ponderable* compounds (in opposition to *Light & Heat*, magnetic fluid, &c) may be decomposed, & presented simple—& recomposed thro' an infinity of new combinations. . . . Davy supposes that there is only one power in the world of the senses; which in particles acts as chemical attractions, in specific masses as electricity, & on matter in general, as planetary Gravitation. Jupiter est, quodcumque vides; when this has been proved, it will then only remain to resolve this into some Law of vital Intellect—and all human Knowledge will be Science and Metaphysics the only Science.[75]

And a year or so later, he wrote:

> O how gladly would I resign my Life, even were I happy, even were it not sickly and like a Sheep with the *Rot* . . . were it even worthy of W., yet resign it I would, to procure for mankind such health and longevity to H. Davy, as should enable him to discover the Element of the metals, of Sulphur and of Carbon. O! he will do it! Yea, and perhaps reveal the *synthetic* Idea of the Antithets, Attraction and Repulsion.[76]

The idea that material phenomena are produced by immaterial 'powers' was of course not new. It was assumed in Plotinus' notion of ideas as formative forces rather than simply archetypal images, in Bruno's 'polar logic' which found in the physical universe a movement towards finite individuality always balanced by a movement back to formlessness, in Boehme's 'nature spirits,' to name but three instances familiar to Coleridge. But Davy provided more than a theory. He provided the authority of a reputable scientific analyst backed by scientific experiment. Davy, we might say, could 'demonstrate and prove and free from the charge of mysticism' the kind of conception of the material world which Coleridge felt must be true.

Coleridge's use of Davy is particularly well illustrated by his marginalia on Boehme which I discussed in the previous chapter, and I should like to take one example from that marginalia because it also shows something of the relation between the material which Coleridge drew from Davy and ideas which he found in *Naturphilosophie*. A little preliminary information is necessary. Boehme described the evolution of the finite universe from undifferentiated energy or 'will,' and he explains in a manner similar to what we saw in some of Coleridge's discussions of the trinity but in much more obscure language, how 'will' evolves through self-limitation into a trinity which is God and which is also the underlying 'reality' of all finite minds and all finite objects. As in God a 'will' or energy by its nature infinite generates a counteracting will, a desire for self-comprehension, which limits it, and as these two interact in an harmonious whole, so all finite substances are composed by a specific balance of opposing energies, of 'contraction' or 'hardness,' expansion or 'water' (fluidity), and motion or mobility. Much of Boehme's terminology is drawn from Alchemy, and for "the Divine Powers, out of which the Body or Corporeity is," he uses the alchemical term *Salitter*. In his Bakerian Lecture for 1807, Davy suggested that,

> a modification of a phlogistic chemical theory might be defended on the idea, that the metals and inflammable solids usually called simple, were compounds of the same matter as that existing in hidrogen with peculiar unknown bases; and that the oxides, alkalis, and acids, were compounds of the same bases with water; and that the phaenomena presented by the metals of the fixed alkalis might be explained on this hypothesis.[77]

The "fixed alkalis" included Soda, Potash, Lime, Strontian, and Barytes. Davy had been interested in these substances for some time and Coleridge attended his lecture on them in February 1802. One of Coleridge's notes on that lecture mentions that when "muriatic acid Gas [combines with] the Volatile Alkali—the 2 aeriform substances become a white solid—(Volatile Alkali = Ammoniacal Gas)."[78] Carbon was an obvious and standard example of "inflammable solids usually called simple." Alternative names for hydrogen and oxygen were 'inflammable air' and 'combustive air.'

All this provides the basis for a note which Coleridge wrote about 1808 to explain Boehme's term *Salitter*:

> By the Salitter we should understand that general Element, which whether it be an etherial Metal Terrific, or an earth metallific, is the centripetal Principle, that by its accersive power over the repulsional or centrifugal elements furnishes the conditional cause of all the Forms of sense, visible, tangible, etc. By this Archeus of the omne tangibile the two airs of am-

monia and volatile Alkali, on blending pass at once into a solid form, and it may be conjectured, that the same will be discovered in the inflammable air, and is the principle of this combustible becoming water when combined with the Combustive air. It may possibly be the same in essence with the diamond or carbon and differ from Soda, Potash, Lime, Strontian, Barytes, by combined Waterstuff, in addition to the Combustive or Oxalkalarch Air.[79]

Coleridge has added the notion of centrifugal and centripetal forces, which are suggestive of the 'systolic' pattern found in Boehme as well as throughout Coleridge but which also, like attraction and repulsion, have a long history as elemental 'powers.' He has also included Paracelsus' term *Archeus*, the primal essence, and his own coinage "oxalkalarch."[80] But it is Davy who provides the substance that gives the whole some semblance, at least, of scientific validity; that makes it, hopefully, palatable to a Wedding Guest; and that makes it possible for Coleridge to argue that the truth in Boehme's dream can be reformulated by the true philosopher in terms of 'modern' knowledge.

While Coleridge, as I have said, knew something of Schelling at the time this note was written, there is nothing, except a similarity of purpose for which he did not need Schelling as a 'source,' to show any influence. A little later, however, but still before 1812, Coleridge added this postscript:

The Salitter is Gravitation or the power of Depth, therefore truly the Powers each in the other, as the synthesis of Attraction and Repulsion, yet truly a third power, in which both the former are co-inherent and one: but it is gravitation as in the Sun, at once the center of *gravity* and the fountain of Light—. The metals are in substance Carbon + azote, some *primarily* oxydated, others hydrogenized—but beyond the powers of the Laboratorium microchemicum for that very reason. Quartz &c = N + E, Sulphur, Phosphorus, Potassium, S + W. Oxygen itself, more aptly named Zoote, is Carbon + neg. Electricity, and Azoote but the zoomet (allon) or zöium + W. or pos.

Electricity.—So instead of Carbon, or Diamond, or Quartz, I should prefer inventing a name for the north polar Metal—either phytomet (met for metallon) or Phytium.[81]

While there is perhaps no single point in this postscript which could not have been derived from Davy or some other alternative source, it unquestionably shows as a whole the influence of Schelling and, directly or indirectly, Steffens. Davy's suggestion that hydrogen and oxygen were the simplest substances exhibiting, respectively, a positive and a negative electrical charge may have been sufficient basis for the notion that hydrogen was the material symbol and manifestation of a positive force and oxygen the material symbol and manifestation of a negative force. But the identification of gravity as the "power of Depth"; its relation to light; the notion that the prototype of all metals is the magnet whose poles correspond to carbon and nitrogen (azote); and the references to what Coleridge later called the 'material tetractys,' in which the four elements of earlier times, representing the elemental 'powers' of nature, are transformed into North, South, East, and West; attraction, repulsion, contraction, dilation; carbon, nitrogen, oxygen, and hydrogen—all these are found together in Schelling,[82] whom we know Coleridge was studying by 1810. But if there can be no doubt that he was adopting parts of Schelling's system and terminology, it is also apparent that the effect of Schelling is to supplement and extend rather than to revolutionize Coleridge's position.

So much of "Heraclitus redivivus" may already have tested my reader's patience, and I shall not pursue the elaborations of *Naturphilosophie* further. But this was an important, I may say an essential, segment of Coleridge's thought. If it seems at times too much to resemble the problem of angels on the head of a pin, our impatience may be lessened if we remember the purpose that informs the complexity of detail. All this detail is an attempt to explore and substantiate the notion that things are forms of perception, a mode of knowing reality, "*Fixes* . . . intellectiones coagulatae . . . portions of the act of producing." As time went on, Coleridge became inclined in his natural philosophy, as also, I think, in his theology, to lose himself in the manipulation of terms, to let the elaboration of the language outrun, like a reindeer's horns, its purpose. Nevertheless, the original impetus was an understandable one, a valid need to overcome the apparent opposition between the visionary and the 'real,' the poet and the practical man, the Mariner and the Wedding Guest. And the *Naturphilosophie* is only another, if less attractive, facet of what is expressed in this note:

> The soil that fell from the Hawk poised at the extreme boundary of Sight thro' a column of sunshine—a falling star, ~~of a chrystal~~ gem, the fixation, & chrystal, of substantial Light, again dissolving & elongating like a liquid Drop—how altogether lovely this to the Eye, and to the Mind too while it remained its own self, ~~an~~ all & only its very Self—. What a wretched Frenchman would not he be, who could shout out—charming Hawk's Turd. . . . What seest thou yonder? A.—The lovely countenance of a lovely Maiden. . . . Y—*A Bit of Flesh.* Z. That which cannot be seen unless by him whose very seeing is more than an act of mere sight—that which refuses all *words* because words being perforce ~~meaningless~~ generalities, tho' some less than others, do not only awake but really involve associations of other words as well as other Thoughts—but that, which I see, must be felt, be possessed, in and by its sole self! [83]

To see the world in a grain of sand, to find the lovable and the beautiful in the form of a watersnake or the liquid droppings of a hawk, to see all as "hues that veil the Almighty Spirit"—all this is part of the same vision that sees the *Salitter* revealed in the combination of gases and the characteristics of the 'fixed alkalis.'

When, lastly, we turn from the nature of the finite world to the structure of the finite mind, we discover similar responses to similar problems. The essential distinction between the God-centered and the self-centered consciousness, and between the living and the dead, the joyous and the numb worlds apprehended in those states of consciousness goes back to some of Coleridge's early poems and to the heyday of his enthusiasm for Hartley. But as a mechanical science proved inadequate for the description of a world in which an object may exist both as a distinct entity and as part of an undifferentiated whole, so did a mechanical psychology prove inadequate for the description of the experience of both distinction and unity.

As in the philosophy of nature, the central problem is the spatio-temporal order of discursive experience. By taking sense perception as the source of all consciousness, and by taking both the content and the structure of sense experience to be determined *ab extra*, the empirical psychologists included all consciousness within the spatio-temporal order of the Newtonian universe. On his own premises, Hartley's 'Theopathy' could never be more than an aggregate of discursive ideas; it could never be an experience of unity. Nor could consciousness, itself a product of external stimuli, include those depths of being which Coleridge insisted were the initial source of the true philosopher's knowledge. "All metaphysical philosophy," Coleridge wrote, "indeed is at last but an examination of our power of knowledge—and the different systems are best distinguished by their different accounts of these powers."[84] Empirical descriptions of our power of knowledge could not include the kinds of knowledge which Mariners bring back.

There is, of course, a good deal of early criticism, some of which I have mentioned, of the limitations of materialism, of those who "within this gross and visible sphere/ Chain down the wingéd thought." In a long note on these lines in the 1796 *Joan of Arc*, for instance, Coleridge concludes a complaint about Newton's theory of 'aether,' and, in passing, Hartley's doctrine of vibrations, with a comment on the atheistic consequences of Newton's philosophy and the inadequacy of philosophies which are "received not for their Truth, but in proportion as they attribute to Causes a susceptibility of being *seen*."[85] But antimaterialism alone did not provide a solution, and Coleridge did not immediately find an adequate examination or account of what, he thought, we do in fact know. In a revealing note for a poem on Spinoza, to whom for a time he looked for assistance, he wrote in 1799:

> I would make a pilgrimage to the burning sands of Arabia, or &c &c to find the Man who could explain to me there can be *oneness*, there being infinite Perceptions—yet there must be a *one*ness, not an intense union but an Absolute Unity, for &c[86]

When, a few years later, he copied this in another notebook, he added:

> Eternal universal mystery! It seems as if it were impossible; yet it *is*—& it is everywhere!—It is indeed a contradiction *in Terms:* and only in Terms!—It is the co presence of Feeling & Life, limitless by their very essence, with Form, by its very essence limited—determinate—definite.[87]

Coleridge's escape from descriptions of mind involving such contradictions was clearly bound up in some manner with his study of Kant. In March, 1801, following some months of study and reflection, he wrote to Poole:

> The interval since my last letter has been filled up by me in the most intense Study. If I do not greatly delude myself, I have not only completely extricated the notions of Time and Space; but have overthrown the doctrine of Association, as taught by Hartley, and with it all the irreligious metaphysics of modern Infidels—especially the doctrine of Necessity—This I have *done; . . . .*[88]

Exactly a week later, he wrote again to Poole:

> Newton was a mere materialist. *Mind,* in his system, is always *passive,*—a lazy *looker-on* on an external world. If the mind be *not passive,* if it be indeed made in God's Image, and that, too, in the sublimest sense, the *Image of the Creator,* there is ground for suspicion that any system built on the passiveness of the mind must be false, as a system.[89]

These letters, cryptic as they are, clearly indicate the rejection of a psychology dominated by the spatio-temporal order of the physical world. And during the months of study which preceded them, Coleridge for the first time read Kant with care.

Kant's quarrel with empiricism sprang not from a concern with spiritual intuition or with the unitive and aesthetic qualities of experience, but from his realization of the fact that an empirical sensationalism, especially as carried to its logical extreme in Hume, was unable to account for scientific knowledge. Neither the uniform time and space of Newtonian physics nor the necessary causation presumed by scientific theory could possibly be given in sense experience. We relate events which we experience to events which we do not experience by referring both to a single 'public' time and space and to a principle of causation which extend beyond the limits of any individual consciousness. It follows, according to Kant, that there is an element in knowledge not given *ab extra* in sense perception and which must therefore have its source in the knowing mind itself. Time and space, he argues, are not properties of an externally given physical reality, but are universally necessary 'forms of sensibility' which the mind applies to sense data in order to make perception possible. Similarly, he argues that the concepts in terms of which we interpret the events which we perceive in space and time—causality, relation, etc.—are also a priori 'categories of the understanding.'

This, roughly, was the argument with which Coleridge became familiar during the winter of 1800–1801, which, as he said in *Biographia Literaria*, seized him as with a "giant's hand," and which influenced him in many ways thereafter. The question which we must consider, however, is again whether Coleridge found in this a new philosophical starting point so that his later epistemology was a modification and interpretation of Kant's, or whether, as is my contention, he saw in it a new way to support and explain that relation between discursive and unitive consciousness which had been his concern from the first.

There is no question but that Coleridge was familiar with Kant's treatment of time and space when he wrote to Poole. About a month earlier, Poole had written concerning Tom Wedgwood's philosophical speculations, "The subjects he has cleared are no less than *Time, Space, and Motion*." [90] In reply, Coleridge wrote on February 13:

> I take T. Wedgewood's own opinion, his own convictions, as STRONG presumptions that he has fallen on some very valuable Truths—some he stated but only in short hints to me/ & I *guess* from these, that they have been noticed before, & set forth by

Kant in part & in part by Lambert . . . . I have been myself *thinking* with the most intense energy on similar subjects/ I shall shortly communicate the result of my Thoughts to the Wedgewoods/"[91]

Having suggested that Wedgwood might have noticed the "very valuable truths" concerning time and space which had "been noticed before, & set forth by Kant," it would be odd indeed that Coleridge should, a month later and to the same correspondent, say that in the interval between the two letters, "*I* have not only completely extricated the notions of Time and Space; but have overthrown the doctrine of Association, as taught by Hartley," if what he meant was simply, 'I have adopted Kant's treatment of time and space to which I referred in my last letter.' That Coleridge was referring to an analysis of the concepts of time and space which had nothing to do with Kant would seem extremely unlikely, especially in view of his later use of parts of Kant's argument. But it does seem probable in view of Coleridge's own speculations both before and after this time, that what he had come to see was the relevance of Kant's analysis to his own situation, and that the accomplishment which he announced to Poole involved not simply the understanding of Kant, but the application of what he had learned and was learning to problems other than those with which Kant was primarily concerned.

Kant's initial concern was, as we have seen, with knowledge of the world of physics, the 'public' world of time and space, of scientific entities and the relations between them. His purpose was the extrication of the knowing mind from the limitations of knowledge imposed by empirical sensationalism. To this end, he argued for the necessity of intuitive a priori knowledge of theoretical, formal, ideas. These a priori intuitions did not, however, for Kant, involve knowledge of Absolute Reality, nor were they intuitions of a structure other than the logical order of time and space. For Coleridge, the value of intuition lay not only in the knowledge of the abstract, formal, logical order of the Pure Reason, nor, though this was important to him, in the ethical concepts of the Practical Reason, but in its penetration to that preconceptual, prelogical reality which for Kant was forever beyond experience.[92] As empirical sensationalism in Hume precluded the possibility of what was to Kant, the mathematical physicist, the most certain kind of knowledge, so Kant, in fact, precluded the possibility of what was to Coleridge, the intuitive poet, the most certain kind of knowledge, that "substantial knowledge" of existence as "an eternal and infinite self-rejoicing, self-loving, with a joy unfathomable, with a love all comprehensive." [93] Whereas Kant argued that there was an a priori theoretical factor in experience which was the foundation of, in the first *Kritik*, science, and in the second, ethics, it was Coleridge's conviction that there was what may be called an aesthetic factor which was the foundation of religion and art. And I may add that this was *not* the subject of Kant's third *Kritik*, on aesthetic *Judgment*.

This difference is not only implicit in Coleridge's work both before and after his first study of Kant; it is clearly reflected in various comments and speculative fragments of the same period as that study. For some time, he had devoted a good deal of his attention to a re-examination of the nature of human consciousness. In January, 1800, he suggested to Davy that he and Beddoes should "give a compact compressed history of the Human Mind for the last century." [94] And in June, he asked Davy to "state your metaphysical system of Impressions, Ideas, Pleasures, & Pains, [and] the laws that govern them . . . . As soon as I settle, I shall read Spinoza and Leibnitz— and I particularly wish to know wherein they agree with, & wherein differ from, you. If you will do this, I promise you to send you the result—& with it my own creed." [95] In September, still suggesting that other people carry out his plans for him, he urged Godwin, a not very happy choice, to "write a book on the power of words, and the processes by which the human feelings form affinities with them." [96] The letters on Locke and Descartes criticizing "some *errors* . . . in the generally received *History* of metaphysical opinions" which he sent to Wedgwood and Poole during February of 1801 were presented as introductory to later letters, never written, containing "the result of *my* meditations on the relations of Thoughts to Things." [97] In the same month, February, 1801, he expressed to Davy his hope of producing a book on "the affinities of the Feelings with Words & Ideas under the title of 'Concerning Poetry & the nature of the Pleasures derived from it,'" a book which would "supersede all the Books of Metaphysics hitherto written/ and all the Books of Morals too."[98]

Although the only extended philosophical discussions of this time, the Wedgwood letters, are concerned with the examination of the development of empiricism after Descartes, we do have some indication of what this work concerning feelings, words, and ideas might have contained. It would seem, in fact, to be much the same work as the one which Coleridge proposed to Godwin, and in that letter there is a summary of the argument to be followed:

> I wish you to write a book on the power of words, and the processes by which human feelings form affinities with them —in short, I wish you to *philosophize* Horn Tooke's System, and to solve the great Questions—whether there be reason to hold, that an action bearing all the *semblance* of pre-designing Consciousness may yet be simply organic, & whether a *series* of such actions are possible—and close on the heels of this question would follow the old 'Is Logic the *Essence* of Thinking?' in other words—is *thinking* impossible without arbitrary signs? &—how far is the word 'arbitrary' a misnomer? Are not words &c germinations of the Plant? And what is the Law of their Growth?—In something of this order I would endeavor to destroy the old antithesis of *Words* & *Things*, elevating, as it were, words into Things, & living Things too. All the nonsense of vibrations etc you would of course dismiss.[99]

This is a highly significant series of questions. Coleridge is proposing that an examination of the relation between *feelings* and *words* will lead to the conclusion that thought cannot be explained in physiological terms, as Hartley tried to do, and that instead of thought consisting in the arrangement of 'signs' (which represent concepts), signs are an integral outgrowth of the processes of thought.

We may see a connection here with three rather widely separated notebook entries. The first was written in the spring of 1799:

> The elder Languages fitter for Poetry because they expressed only prominent ideas with clearness, others but darkly—There-

fore the French wholly unfit for Poetry; because is *clear* in their Language—i.e.—Feelings created by obscure ideas associate themselves with one *clear* idea. When no criticism is pretended to, & the Mind in its simplicity gives itself up to a Poem as to a work of nature, Poetry gives most pleasure when only generally & not perfectly understood.[100]

In a very similar vein, in November, 1801, Coleridge questioned:

Whether or no the too great definiteness of Terms in any language may not consume too much of the vital & idea-creating force in distinct, clear, full made Images & so prevent originality—*original* thought as distinguished from positive thought—[.] [101]

Between these two, in the spring of 1801 at about the time of the letter to Poole he wrote a note which I have included before but which, because of its relevance here, I shall repeat:

—and the deep power of Joy
We see into the *Life* of Things—
i.e. By deep feeling we make our Ideas dim—& this is what we mean by our Life—ourselves. I think of the Wall—it is before me, a distinct Image—here. I necessarily think of the Idea & the Thinking I as two distinct & opposite Things. Now let me think of myself—of the thinking Being—the Idea becomes dim whatever it be—so dim that I know not what it is—but the Feeling is deep & steady—and this I call *I*—identifying the Percipient & the Perceived—.[102]

The relationship between indefinable 'feelings' and defined concepts ('Images,' 'Ideas') suggested here seems to underlie several comments in the letters, some of which we have also seen before. In the letter to Poole in which he spoke of the 'extrication of time and space,' Coleridge added, "I trust . . . that I shall be able to evolve all the five senses, that is, to deduce them from *one sense*, & to state their growth, & the causes of their difference—& in this evolvement to solve the process of Life & Consciousness." [103] Some time later, in January, 1803, was his suggestion to Wedgwood that "Death exists only because Ideas exist/ that life is limitless Sensation; that Death is a child of the organic senses, chiefly of the Sight; that Feelings die by flowing into the mould of the Intellect & becoming Ideas." [104] And a few months later, he wrote to Southey:

> I used to be compounding . . . half-verbal, half-visual metaphors. It argues, I am persuaded, a particular state of general feeling and I hold that association depends in a much greater degree on the recurrence of resembling states of feeling than on trains of ideas, . . . and if this be true, Hartley's system totters. . . . I almost think that ideas *never* recall ideas as far as they are ideas, any more than leaves in a forest create each other's motion. The breeze it is that runs through them—it is the soul, the state of feeling. If I had said no *one* idea ever recalls another, I am confident that I could support the assertion. [105]

Taken all together, these remarks fill in the outline proposed to Godwin. 'Feelings,' Coleridge suggests, are not contingent on the images of sense preception, nor is the structure of consciousness contingent on a spatio-temporal order of sensuous stimuli. Conceptual consciousness, rather, evolves from unconceptualized 'feelings' which are defined and 'fixed,' which become part of a logical order by "flowing into the mould of the intellect & becoming Ideas."

What Kant contributed to this was the demonstration on scientific and logical rather than religious or mystical grounds that time, space, and logical relationships were not observed properties of reality but necessary properties of the way in which the human mind conceives reality. The important word here is *demonstration*. The mere idea that time and space are the limitations of sublunar intellects rather than 'real' properties is an ancient one and is a common correlative of the ineffability of mystical experience. For Coleridge, Kant's virtue was that he drew his conclusions not from undemonstrable private intuitions but logically from the undeniable evidence of science and common sense.

I would suggest, then, that Coleridge's use of Kant has something in common with his use of Davy. In both cases, his ultimate purpose was other than theirs. But both seemed to him to provide proof that the spatio-temporal structure of discursive experience is not the ultimate structure of reality. Taken together, they seemed to show that the most advanced scientific analysis of nature and the most advanced logical analysis of the problems of epistemology both pointed towards the conclusion that the experienced relationship between unitive and discursive experience corresponded to an actual relationship between essential unity and existential diversity. And it was the demonstration of such a correspondence that Coleridge required.

In the last circle of Paradise, Dante sees, "legato con amore in un volume, / cio che per l'universo si squaderna." Coleridge's intention, as the outlines of that impossible and Olympian work the *Magnum Opus* show, was, like Dante's, the explanation of all things, all knowledge, all experience, in the unity of love, of the mystic's vision of the heart of light. As he wrote in the margins of Occam:

There is, it is admitted, a Reason, to which the Understanding must convert itself in order to obtain from within what it would in vain seek for without, the knowledge of necessary and universal conclusion—of that which is because it must be, and not because it had been seen. May there not be a yet higher or deeper Presence, the source of Ideas, to which even the Reason must convert itself? Or rather is not this more truly the Reason, and the universal Principles but the Gleam of Light from the distant and undistinguished community of Ideas—or the Light in the Cloud that hides the Luminary? O! let these questions be once fully answered, and the affirmative made sure and evident—then we shall have a Philosophy, that will unite in itself the warmth of the mystics, the definiteness of the Dialectician, and the sunny clearness of the Naturalist, the productivity of the Experimenter and the Evidence of the Mathematician . . . .

> Where'er I find the Good, the True, the Fair,
> I ask no names. God's Spirit dwelleth there!

> The unconfounded, undivided Three.
> Each for itself, and all in each, to see
> In Man, and Nature is Philosophy.[106]

Coleridge saw in the history of the development of theology, of philosophy, of science, and of psychology, a progressive if often erratic approach to the discovery that that structure of unitive and discursive consciousness which was for him embodied in the Trinity was in very fact the "Archetype . . . of all knowledge." Wherever he found a glimpse or a fragment of this 'truth,' there he felt at home. And it is this which accounts for most of his philosophical enthusiasms from Plotinus to Schelling.

It would be a mistake to minimize the effects of Coleridge's philosophical studies on his own formulations or to argue that he anticipated to any significant degree the systematic reasoning of the various German philosophers whom he has been accused both of copying and, in many instances, misunderstanding. It was not in the creation of abstract system that his genius lay. But it would be equally a mistake to read his speculations as nothing more than derivations. I have argued that the fact that he adopted and adapted the formulations of other writers, and especially of Kant and later of Schelling and the *Naturphilosophen* is of less importance than the purpose for which he used them. Whatever and whose-ever language he employed, he was from the first consistently trying to explore and explain not theories which he read about but his own experience of a universe which could be known by union as well as by analysis and of a self which was more than a percipient of passing objects and events.

It was Coleridge's dream that in his projected 'great work' the 'truth' which he contemplated would at last appear with perfect clarity as "the principle that was derived from experience, but of which all other knowledge should be but so many repetitions under limitations." In this, he failed. He left only fragments, and there are few people now who would find in those fragments the foundations of an acceptable explanation of the complexities of the universe in which we live. But if I am correct in my conception of Coleridge's purpose, then his speculations have another significance and another value. The universe which he tried to define as philosopher was the universe which he experienced as poet. The formulations which he adopted as philosopher provided him with a language in which he could talk about his experience as poet. And it is to this that I shall now turn.

Chapter 5

ONE OF COLERIDGE'S FREQUENTLY REITERATED complaints concerns those who mistake the "dead letter" for reality, who take literally what is properly figurative, who mistake "congruous notions" for statements of absolute fact. Convinced as he was that concepts do not mirror reality but evolve from the preconceptual, as things evolve from 'spirit,' ideas from 'feeling,' that "the whole universe must be represented as a single transparent Drop—a divine Chaos, not as the confused commixture of all Distincts, but as the identity of them all," and that the true philosopher "begins with Qualities, & maketh Quantity one of the Results . . . for Quantity is image and symbol,"[1] he saw words and theories composed of words as in themselves partial and inadequate. "It is," he wrote, "the instinct of the Letter to bring into subjection to itself the Spirit.—The latter cannot dispute—nor can it be disputed for, but with a certainty of defeat. For words express generalities that can be made *so* clear— they have neither the play of colors, nor the untranslatable meanings of the eye, nor any one of the thousand indescribable things that form the whole reality of the living fuel—[.]"[2] He therefore required of a reader that he take words not merely as signs of definitions, verbal concepts, but as symbols of what he can know only by reference to his own experience, his own 'Reason.' Thus he once said that "a defence of mystical feelings" might be "drawn from the pleasure all good minds receive from descriptions of material Objects, Landscapes, Trees &c they have never seen/ Assuredly, the impressions received by the words are very faint compared with the actual impression—it is but a dim abstract at best—and most often a sort of *tentative process* now by this analogy, now by that, to recall the reader to some experiences, he must have, tho' he had not attended to them." [3] And something similar applies in philosophy:

> One and perhaps the greatest obstacle to the apprehension of the transcendent or genetic philosophy arises in the tendency to look abroad, *out* of the thing in question, in order by means of some *other* thing analogous to understand the former. But this is impossible—for the thing in question *is* the act, we are describing—Cohesion, for instance—& by this all coherents & all particular forms of cohesion are to be rendered intelligible, not it by them . . . . [4]

And "the thing in question . . . the act" is found within, rather than without, the mind. In a note that reveals something of how he himself thought and read, he wrote:

> O that I had but Boscovich's works! I do fervently wish to make myself master of his Ideas on the oneness of Attraction & Repulsion! Yet why should I not myself abstract myself into *power* & try to conceive a mode of its possibility—nay, if at all of its necessity—and what will Attraction + Repulsion be translated into acts of Consciousness? [5]

The implications of such remarks become of primary importance when we turn from other areas of Coleridge's metaphysics to his aesthetics. In common with most Romantic critics, Coleridge considered a work of art in terms of the mind of the artist who produced it and of the mind of the audience on whom it had an effect. But he talks about art in terms of the assumptions and theories about the world, about the human mind, and about language which constitute his metaphysics. If his discussions of art, and more specifically of poetry, are to be truly meaningful, the metaphysics in terms of which they are presented must be taken as symbolic, as a system of "congruous notions." For if we understand Coleridge's statements concerning imagination, form, and symbol simply in relation to his metaphysical statements, especially when, as in Chapter XII of *Biographia Literaria,* these are adaptations of Schelling; if we rest satisfied with the idea that imagination is 'creative' and that the form of art like the forms of nature evolves 'from within,' we are in effect taking the metaphysics not as a 'propaideutic device' but as a literal description of reality. And we are making the validity and value of the aesthetics depend upon the acceptability of the metaphysics as a statement of fact. Since, I assume, we do not accept Coleridge's, or Schelling's, metaphysics as such a statement, this is, in effect, to divorce the aesthetics from the reality of art and to make it nothing more than an intellectual curiosity, intricate and intriguing, perhaps, but ultimately meaningless. This is the reason why some critics, notably Raysor, have felt Coleridge's aesthetic theories to be an unfortunate intrusion in his criticism.

But if, as I have argued, Coleridge's metaphysics is "an elaborated transformed symbol" of his own experience of human consciousness, then we may understand it not as a literal description of inferred facts outside the range of our experience, but as a figurative description of facts within the range of our experience. Whether or not we accept the view of the visionary and the mystic that the experienced relation between the sense of unity and the perception of things corresponds to the relation between 'God' and the 'world' and reveals the essential pattern of reality, the experience remains a psychological fact. And Coleridge's notions of the nature of art and artistic creation should, therefore, be referred not simply *to* the notions of his metaphysics, but *through* them to the facts of consciousness from which the metaphysics derive.

In what should, I think, be considered a key statement in his aesthetics, Coleridge wrote:

> What the Globe is to Geography, *miniaturing* in order to *manifest* the Truth, such is a Poem to that Image of God, which we were created with, and which still seeks that Unity or Revelation of the *One* in and by the *Many*, which reminds it, that tho' in order to be an individual Being it must go forth *from* God, yet as the *rec*eding from *him* is to *pro*ceed towards Nothingness and Privation, it must still at every step turn back toward him in order to *be* at all.[6]

The "Image of God, which we were created with" is, I take it, the human mind, or more specifically that structure of consciousness which is the foundation of Coleridge's conception of God. The poem, the work of art, is then an embodiment of that structure, a 'manifestation' of the systolic movement between 'Being' and 'thing,' 'Life' and 'image,' which is variously formulated in Coleridge's metaphysics. As the "Image of God" is not static but dynamic, a reflection of the archetype of all creative processes, whether in the natural world or in the human mind, so is the poem dynamic, a manifestation of that same creative process, or, we may say, the psychological process from which the conception of the others originates.

Coleridge's statement seems to be obviously applicable to the poems which I discussed in earlier chapters, and it could almost serve as a statement of what the Mariner learns, insofar as that learning can be reduced to abstract terms. It also provides a context in which we may consider the meaning of some of the central notions which Coleridge elsewhere uses in discussing the nature of poetry. For these may be seen as attempts to define aspects of the process here described and to explain how this process can in fact be made manifest in a poem.

The most frequent and the most familiar term in Coleridge's aesthetics is, of course, *imagination*. The earliest version of the famous distinction between imagination and fancy appears in a letter of 1802,[7] by which time he was familiar with Kant, Fichte, and probably Maas. But imagination 'means' in Coleridge not only an element in an abstract logical system but an aspect of human experience with which he was concerned much earlier. The question here is not where he found or why he chose the word, but to what in his experience of poetry it refers.

Coleridge rarely used his own work to illustrate his aesthetic principles, and according to his account in *Biographia Literaria*, it was the reading of Wordsworth's "Guilt and Sorrow" in 1796 rather than the writing of his own poetry which first led him to think about the qualities which he later distinguished as fanciful and imaginative. The excellence, he wrote,

which in all Mr. Wordsworth's writings is more or less pre-
dominant, and which constitutes the character of his mind,
I no sooner felt, than I sought to understand. Repeated meditations led me first to suspect (and a more intimate analysis of
the human faculties, their appropriate marks, functions, and
effects matured my conjecture into full conviction,) that fancy
and imagination were two distinct and widely different faculties . . . .[8]

The excellence which he "felt" in Wordsworth was, he says,

the union of deep feeling with profound thought; the fine
balance of truth in observing, with the imaginative faculty in
modifying the objects observed; and above all the original gift
of spreading the tone, the *atmosphere*, and with it the depth and
height of the ideal world around forms, incidents, and situations, of which, for the common view, custom had bedimmed
all the lustre, had dried up the sparkle and the dew drops.[9]

In view of Coleridge's own poems at the time, it does not seem
probable that Wordsworth's poem deserves sole credit for stimu-
lating Coleridge's reflections. But the account is nevertheless valuable
for its description of the qualities which are singled out as con-
stituting at least one kind of poetic excellence, and which seem to
point to the conclusion that fancy and imagination are "two distinct
and widely different faculties." The distinction, it would appear,
is between fancying new appearances and seeing the familiar anew.
The question of seeing anew and of how "so to represent familiar
objects as to awaken in the minds of others a kindred feeling concerning them" which is, Coleridge goes on to say, the "most un-
equivocal mode of manifestation of genius" is reminiscent of the
passage concerning the droppings of the hawk which I cited in the
previous chapter.[10] In that passage, it may be remembered, Coleridge
speaks of a kind of seeing which "is more than an act of mere sight"
and which "refuses all *words* because words being perforce generalities . . . do not only awake but really involve associations of other
words as well as other Thoughts." Words interfere with the ability

to see, 'feel,' and 'possess' the object "in and by its sole self" because they give not the object but an abstraction in a discursive pattern of association. Wordsworth, Coleridge suggests, the poet of genius and imagination, somehow and to some extent, overcomes this difficulty. He restores "the lustre . . . the sparkle and the dew drops," evokes "feelings as fresh, as if all had then sprang forth at the first creative fiat," by "spreading" around what is described "the tone, the *atmosphere*, and with it the depth and height of the ideal world."

Seeing the object anew with its sparkle and dew drops would seem, then, to involve seeing it in relation to the "ideal world," to the "creative fiat." Knowing something of what Coleridge meant by "ideal world" and "creative fiat," we might say that seeing as "more than an act of mere sight," as feeling and possessing the "sole self" of what is seen, means seeing it as it 'goes forth from' and 'turns back towards' 'God.' And imagination would seem to have something to do with such a way of seeing and with the communication of it to others by means of a work of art.

Coleridge includes as part of Wordsworth's excellence "the fine balance of truth in observing, with the imaginative faculty in modifying the objects observed." What is meant by such imaginative modification is clarified by a typical statement in a lecture in which he defined imagination as "the power of modifying one image or feeling by the precedent or following ones . . . combining many circumstances into one moment of thought to produce that ultimate end of human thought and human feeling, unity, and thereby the reduction of the spirit to its principle and fountain, who alone is truly *One*." [11] The 'modification' of the image by the imagination is not, thus, an end or value in itself but a means of producing "unity, and thereby the reduction of the spirit to its principle and fountain," of producing, that is, an awareness of the "ideal world." This is the necessary condition for 'seeing' the image, as an evolving form rather than as merely a thing perceived. And in "fine balance" with "truth in observing," it gives us again the pattern of the "Image of God."

Taken literally, the definition of imagination which I have quoted would, like many of Coleridge's speculative statements, be less than illuminating. Few of us, I imagine, would be prepared to agree that the reading of a poem produces in us a "reduction of the spirit to its principle . . . who alone is truly *One*." But if we consider not the letter but the spirit, it is apparent that Coleridge is here talking about the same aspects of experience that I have discussed earlier: the relation he felt between the sense of 'Being' and the evolution of the sense of self and of percepts and concepts. We learn, normally, to perceive, think, and talk in terms of a world of discursive consciousness, of 'me' and 'not-me,' 'subject' and 'object.' It is the relations of this world that we analyse, and it is this world, this product of consciousness, if you will, that prosaic language expresses and communicates. But the poem, Coleridge suggests, conveys not only this product but the process by which it comes into being, by which we become conscious of 'things.' In distinguishing the materialist from the transcendentalist, he distinguished 'mechanical' from 'chemical' logic. With that no doubt in mind, he wrote, "Form is factitious *Being*, and Thinking is the Process, Imagination the *Laboratory*, in which Thought elaborates Essence into Existence." [12] The poem reproduces the laboratory.

The *locus classicus* for Coleridge's conception of imagination is, of course, the conclusion to Chapter XIII of *Biographia Literaria*. But this fascinating and somewhat cryptic passage is anticipated and illuminated by a notebook entry, undated but certainly earlier, in which he said:

> The image-forming or rather re-forming power, the imagination in it's passive sense, which I would rather call Fancy = Phantasy, . . . this, the Fetisch & Talisman of all modern Philosophers (the Germans excepted) may not inaptly be compared to the Gorgon Head, which *looked* death into every thing—and this not by accident, but from the nature of the faculty itself, the province of which is to give consciousness to the Subject by presenting to it its conceptions *objectively* but the Soul differences itself from any other Soul for the purposes of symbolical knowledge by *form* or body only—but all form as body, i.e. as shape, & not as formal efformans is dead— Life may be *inferred*, even as intelligence is from black marks on white paper—but the black marks themselves *are truly "the*

dead letter." Here then is the error—not in the faculty itself, without which there would be no *fixation,* consequently, no distinct perception or conception, but in the gross idolatry, of those who abuse it, & make that the goal & end which should be only a means of arriving at it. . . .

From the above deduce the worth & dignity of poetic Imagination, of the fusing power, that fixing unfixes & while it melts & bedims the Image, still leaves in the Soul its living meaning—[.] [13]

In *Biographia Literaria,* Coleridge makes a distinction between "the primary IMAGINATION . . . the living Power and prime Agent of all human Perception," the "secondary" or poetic imagination, and the fancy. The distinction between the first and last of these does not yet clearly appear in this passage, but it is perhaps therefore all the easier to see their character and the relation between them. As in another passage Coleridge spoke of the "Products of Nature" as "Things or *Fixes* (res fixae, intellectiones coagulatae)" which, however, are properly considered as "portions of the act of producing," [14] so he here speaks of perception and conception as involving a similar "fixation." Thoughts, images, things of which we are conscious are 'fixed' not because reality consists of fixed entities but because we 'fix' them by the act of thinking or seeing and at the same time 'fix' our individual selves. Perception and conception *are* acts of 'fixation' in what would otherwise be an undifferentiated continuum. As Coleridge wrote in Malta in 1804:

How opposite to nature & the fact to talk of the one *moment* of Hume; of our whole being an aggregate of successive single sensations. Who ever *felt* a *single* sensation? Is not every one at the same moment conscious that there co-exist a thousand others in a darker shade, or less light; even as when I fix my attention on a white House on a grey bare Hill or rather long ridge that runs out of sight each way . . . the pretended single sensation is it anything more than the *Light*-point in every picture either of nature or of a good painter [?] [15]

What Coleridge complains of is the failure to see "fixes" *as* "portions of the act of producing" by those who take the discursive order of multiplicity in time and space to be reality and concern themselves with its 'mechanical' relationships rather than with the 'chemical' or psychological processes from which it derives. To detach the 'fix' from the process is to "proceed towards Nothingness and Privation," towards the Mariner's world of alienated selves and things. And it is here that fancy operates with, as he says in *Biographia Literaria,* "counters" that are "fixities and definites," "objects . . . fixed and dead."

The difficulty in Coleridge's position arises, however, not with the distinction between imagination and fancy, but with that between the 'primary' and the poetic imagination. As the poem 'miniatures in order to manifest' the "Image of God," so the poetic imagination is an "echo" of the primary, "identical . . . in the *kind* of its agency, and differing only in *degree,* and in the *mode* of its operation." [16] We may understand the notions of fancy and of imagination as the prime agent of perception in terms of the relation between what Coleridge calls Reason and Understanding, or between what I have called unitive consciousness and discursive consciousness. But it is not so obvious what Coleridge refers to when he speaks of a process involving a "fusing power" which "fixing unfixes & . . . melts & bedims the Image," or which "dissolves, diffuses, dissipates, in order to recreate." [17] And it is even less obvious what qualities in a poem reveal such a process. For this reason, a number of critics have denied that any such process in fact takes place, or that the poetic imagination is other than a mode of 'fancy.'

But as I have said that Coleridge's conception of God derives from his experience of consciousness which he thereafter describes as the *image* of God, so I should argue that it is his experience of what he calls the poetic imagination that leads to the notions of the primary imagination and of fancy, and that it is therefore here most of all that we need to understand the experiential referent. No mode of fancy, as Coleridge describes it, could produce the kind of poem of which he speaks, or, for that matter, the kind of poem which he wrote. It is because such a fancy, and the kind of use of language which it implies, is inadequate to the explanation of what happens in some poems (and not merely of what he thinks *should* happen) that he is forced to this distinction of terms. And we may therefore look for explanation to the situation which he is attempting to describe.

The world of discursive consciousness is a world of experience ordered, conceptualized, made available to intellectual consideration. Insofar as the ordering of our various experiences is the same, we are able to describe our experiences to each other by means of language, in which that order is necessarily embodied. What is common to our experiences as so ordered provides us with objective 'facts,' with the 'public world' of time and space which is the center of reference for our communication. The tree in my experience which shades my house and which I cherish is not identical with the tree in my neighbor's experience which blocks his driveway and which he wishes to cut down. But our ordered experiences do share certain characteristics; they 'overlap,' so to speak, and that 'overlap' provides the single 'public' tree to which we both refer.

The problem arises when we wish to communicate our experience not of discursive but of unitive consciousness. I am forced by the structure of language to speak of the tree which moves me to tears of joy in the same words in which I speak of the tree which stands in the way. I am forced to separate into *me, tree,* and *emotion,* into separate concepts, that undifferentiated moment of me-tree-joy. However precise our language, however subtle and complex the structure of meaning which we present, we are still dealing with concepts, with what Coleridge called the fixed and definite counters of the fancy. We are manipulating the products of perception, and we cannot compose from concepts that flash of intuition in which experience is grasped as a vivid and living whole and which it is the function of the poetic imagination somehow to express.

The 'dissolving, dissipating, diffusing' activity of the imagination cannot, therefore, be simply characteristic of the poet's vision which is thereafter expressed in language. The result of a dissolution of 'fixes,' of percepts and concepts, could not be stated in words which mean percepts and concepts and patterns composed of them. The poetic imagination, Coleridge says, "dissolves . . . in order to re-create." But again, if recreation has taken place prior to the poem, it is difficult to see how the result would differ, at least for the reader, from the product of the primary imagination or of the fancy. It is the poet's object to bathe our eyes in the river of light, but he must meet us not in the highest sphere of paradise but on the common ground, and we cannot understand what transformation has already taken place for him unless he makes it happen thereafter to us. The poem, in other words, must produce in us, the readers, both the dissolution of that conceptual order in which 'normal' discursive apprehension is imprisoned and the recreation if it is to communicate the process which is imagination.

At this point, I find suggestive Ernst Cassirer's discussion of the origin and nature of myth developed at length in the second volume of *The Philosophy of Symbolic Forms* and partially and more briefly in the essay *Language and Myth*. In that essay, he writes:

> The mythical form of conception is not something superadded to certain definite elements of empirical existence; instead the primary 'experience' itself is steeped in the imagery of myth and saturated with its atmosphere. Man lives with objects only insofar as he lives with these forms; he reveals reality to himself, and himself to reality, in that he lets himself and the environment enter into this plastic medium, in which the two do not merely make contact, but fuse with each other. . . .[18]
>
> It seems only natural to us that the world should present itself to our inspection and observation as a pattern of definite forms, each with its own perfectly determinate spatial limits that give it its specific individuality. If we see it as a whole, this whole nevertheless consists of clearly distinguishable units which do not melt into each other, but preserve their identity that sets them definitely apart from the identity of all the others. But for the mythmaking consciousness these separate elements are not thus separately given, but have to be originally and gradually derived from the whole; the process of culling and sorting out individual forms has yet to be gone through.[19]

Whereas "the aim of theoretical thinking is primarily to deliver the contents of sensory or intuitive experience from the isolation in which they originally occur," mythical thinking "does not dispose freely over the data of intuition, in order to relate and compare them to each other, but is captivated and enthralled by the intuition which suddenly confronts it. It comes to rest in the immediate experience." [20] It is this concentration of the entire self in one moment of experience to the exclusion of all other considerations which, Cassirer argues, produces myth:

> This focusing of all forces on a single point is the prerequisite for all mythical thinking and mythical formulation. When, on the one hand, the entire self is given up to a single impression, is 'possessed' by it and, on the other hand, there is the utmost tension between the subject and its object, the outer world; when external reality is not merely viewed and contemplated, but overcomes a man in sheer immediacy, with emotions of fear or hope, terror or wish-fulfillment: then the spark jumps somehow across, the tension finds release as the subjective excitement becomes objectified, and confronts the mind as a god or daemon. [21]

I do not wish to argue for the validity of Cassirer's explanation of the origin of primitive myth, nor, certainly, that Coleridge's thinking was simply mythical in this sense. But I do think that the mode of consciousness which Cassirer describes is involved in what Coleridge refers to as 'poetic imagination' and that the problem of the poet as he presents it might be described as that of the transformation of ordinary language and ordinary perception into a kind of 'mythic' language and 'mythic' perception.

The process by which the mind moves from discursive to unitive consciousness involves, as I have said, the suppression of those orders in terms of which we normally organize and interpret experience, or which, in Cassirer's words, enable us "to deliver the contents of sensory or intuitive experience from the isolation in which they originally occur." What the imagination has to 'dissolve' is that normal patterning of experience which breaks it up into parts and 'fixes' those parts in relation to a larger discursive pattern, a pattern which is to some degree inherent in the structure of the language which the poet uses. [22] It is not a matter of breaking up old percepts or concepts in order to compose new ones; that is the work of the fancy. Nor is it a matter of constructing new and more elaborate patterns of meaning. The purpose of such dissolution is to make possible a different kind of apprehension of what had been so ordered, to communicate the world as possessed rather than as understood.

Cassirer's discussion of 'mythical' consciousness and Coleridge's notion of imagination as a process both imply a particular dramatic and intellectual situation, which we find in Coleridge's poems and which seems to underlie a number of his critical dicta. In many of the poems, the reader's own position and the images with which he is confronted are isolated from those 'normal' discursive intellectual connections which would interfere with exclusive possession by the moment of experience. The beautiful, he wrote, "excludes the distinct consciousness/ which, n.b. is what we mean by the conscious Presence of the forms of the Understanding—for these are determined by a logical necessity,"[23] and it is these forms which lead us to separate and discriminate in terms of a larger conceptual pattern. In a notebook, he remarked that,

> of all men I ever knew, Wordsworth himself not excepted, I have the faintest pleasure in things contingent and transitory. I never . . . ask in a stagecoach, Whose house is that? . . . I am not certain whether I should have seen with any emotion the mulberry tree of Shakspere. If it were a tree of no notice in itself, I am sure that I should feel by an effort . . . . If a striking tree, I fear that the pleasure would be diminished rather than increased, that I should have no unity of feeling, and find in the constant association of Shakspere having planted it an intrusion that prevented me from wholly (as a whole man) losing myself in the flexures of its branches and intertwining of its roots.[24]

Similarly, it is for Coleridge one of the characteristics of imaginative poetry that it does not make us think *about* a thing but makes the thing seem immediately present in experience. The poet must "make everything present by a series of images,"[25] since "it is only by sensuous images that we can elicit truth as at a flash." [26] He needs "the power of so carrying on the eye of the reader as to make him almost lose the consciousness of words—to make him *see* everything —and this without exciting any painful or laborious attention, without any anatomy of description." [27]

As the image must be present in its sensuous immediacy, free from the "contingent and transitory," from normal conceptual associations, so too must the subject, the perceiver, be free from interests and purposes which might lead outside the experience itself. "I must be alone," Coleridge said, "if either my Imagination or Heart are to be excited or enriched." [28] And in a comment on enthusiasm, "the absorption of the individual in the object contemplated," he noted that "the enthusiast . . . is a solitary." [29] In many of his poems, we are made to share this solitude. We are not addressed as an audience, as individuals with purposes and interests; we are rather permitted to overhear, and invited to enter the poem by identifying ourselves with the speaker. We are led away from our familiar context, from social and intellectual circumstances, up a hill or through a field or across an unknown ocean, where the familiar is seen as unfamiliar, as something new. We are persons, yet impersonal, and we see real trees, real landscapes, real watersnakes, yet ones which have no particular location in time and space, no history, no relevance to us except as forms which we possess in our immediate apprehension.

This same concern underlies the criticism in Chapter XXII of *Biographia Literaria* of the inclusion in poetry of characters who are unrepresentative of their circumstances. By such characters, Coleridge argues, the reader is made so conscious of the circumstances that he is faced with "delusion" rather than with that illusion "which simply permits the images presented to work by their own force." [30] Peculiarities of circumstances force those circumstances on our attention, entrap us in the contingent and transitory. And the same issue appears again in those comments on the relation of feelings to words which I discussed briefly in the preceding chapter.[31] Where there is "too great definiteness of terms," where language presents us only with "clear ideas" which are wholly "understood," the discursive order, the distinction between subject and objects, is made inescapable. In such circumstances, we "necessarily think of the

Idea & the Thinking I as two distinct & opposite Things" instead of being conscious only of the "feeling," the "life," and thus "identifying the Percipient & the Perceived."

By such means, then, we are brought to something like the point where, in Cassirer's words, the 'self' and the 'environment' may "not merely make contact, but fuse with each other," where "external reality is not merely viewed and contemplated, but overcomes a man in sheer immediacy," where we do not see a "charming hawk's turd" but possess and are possessed by "a falling star, gem, the fixation, & chrystal, of substantial Light, again dissolving & elongating like a liquid Drop . . . lovely . . . to the Eye, and to the Mind too while it remained its own self, all & only its very self," an experience which "refuses all *words*" because they "involve associations of other words as well as other Thoughts" and prevent the object, the image, from being "felt . . . possessed, in and by its sole self!"[32] If at such a moment the "spark jumps," the "subjective excitement becomes objectified," then the form which we 'see' has become not the form of something 'other,' but a form of our own consciousness, a form in which, for the moment, we contemplate our own being. The poem, in other words, miniatures in order to manifest the "Image of God" by such a manipulation of dramatic and verbal relationships that we are led from the understanding of words as 'meaning' percepts and concepts to a situation in which words 'mean' and objectify our own 'inner' substance. Instead of words defining relationships in an abstract, outer, public world, they define modes in which our 'essence' achieves 'existence.'

It will be obvious that the poems which I discussed in earlier chapters seem to me to reveal a progress towards the realization of such a conception of poetry, and I wish to turn to the question of Coleridge's practice as a poet in the light of what I take to be his theory. But before I do, I should like to consider briefly two other central notions in his aesthetics: the notion of 'organic form' and the notion of 'symbol.' Both of these again may easily lead to the problem of Coleridge's relations to his "cousins German," but here I wish rather to speak of them in relation to the matters which I have been discussing above.

Both the concept of organic form and the concept of symbol seem at first to refer to relations supposed to exist between different parts of the poem and between the poem and something 'beyond' it. The problem is apparent in this extract, partly translated from Schelling, from Coleridge's essay "On Poesy or Art":

> The artist must imitate that which is within the thing, that which is active through form and figure, and discourses to us by symbols—the Natur-geist, or spirit of nature, as we unconsciously imitate those whom we love; for so only can we hope to produce any work truly natural in the object and truly human in the effect. The idea which puts the form together cannot itself be the form. It is above form, and is its essence, the universal in the individual, or the individuality itself,—the glance and the exponent of the indwelling power.[33]

Similarly, he wrote in *The Statesman's Manual*:

> A symbol . . . is characterized by the translucence of the special in the individual, or of the general in the special, or of the universal in the general; above all by the translucence of the eternal through and in the temporal. It always partakes of the reality which it renders intelligible; and while it enunciates the whole, abides itself as a living part in that unity of which it is the representative.[34]

Both of these statements, and many others like them, suggest that the poem or work of art is valuable not as it presents us with the 'surface' of nature, but as it enables us to see *beyond* the surface to the 'essence,' the *Naturgeist*, the 'eternal.' These are metaphysical concepts. But if we remember to what aspects of the experience of nature and of poetry Coleridge has elsewhere taken these concepts to refer, we may see that it is still the characteristics of experience which are involved, and that the distinctions which he is trying to make are still distinctions not in *what* we see but in *how* we see. They are in fact essentially the same distinctions which were involved in the concepts of imagination and fancy.

As he often explained imagination in contradistinction to fancy, so Coleridge was fond of explaining the concept of 'symbol' in contradistinction to 'allegory.' In *The Statesman's Manual,* he wrote that "an allegory is but a translation of abstract notions into a picture-language, which is itself nothing but an abstraction from objects of the senses; the principle being more worthless even than its phantom proxy, both alike insubstantial, and the former shapeless to boot." [35] Similarly, in a lecture two years later, he said, "We may then safely define allegoric writing as the employment of one set of agents and images with actions and accompaniments correspondent, so as to convey, while in disguise, either moral qualities or conceptions of the mind that are not in themselves objects of the senses, or other images, agents, actions, fortunes, and circumstances . . . ." [36]

I have mentioned earlier that Coleridge himself often wrote in this way,[37] and such 'allegoric' writing may be admirably illustrated by his pair of poems "To an Unfortunate Woman at the Theatre" and "To an Unfortunate Woman whom the author had known in the days of her innocence," the latter being subtitled in manuscript "Allegorical Lines on the Same Subject." [38] The first of these is an explicit apostrophe to a 'fallen' woman. The second is a description of a

> Myrtle-leaf that, ill besped,
>> Pinest in the gladsome ray,
> Soil'd beneath the common tread
>> Far from thy protecting spray!

While this poem describes a natural object, it does not lead us to see and possess that object "in and by its sole self," but leads us rather to suppress the immediate sensuous image in favor of a more abstract concept. We are asked to make a series of relations between the images presented and a pattern of social ideas which is inferred, and it is the ideas inferred which are the substance and 'meaning' of the poem.

Coleridge was, however, in the series of poems which I discussed, moving away from this kind of writing towards the kind of writing which he came to describe as 'symbolic.' The distinction, while not expressed in these terms, is clear in that letter to Sotheby in 1802 in which he first mentioned the difference between imagination and fancy. In a criticism of Bowles's latest poems, he complained:

There reigns thro' all the blank verse poems such a perpetual trick of *moralizing* every thing—which is very well occasionally—but never to see or describe any interesting appearance in nature, without connecting it by dim analogies with the moral world, proves faintness of Impression. Nature has her proper interest; & he will know what it is, who believes & feels, that every Thing has a Life of it's own, & that we are all *one Life*. A Poet's *Heart* & *Intellect* should be *combined, intimately* combined & *unified*, with the great appearances in Nature—& not merely held in solution & loose mixture with them, in the shape of formal Similes. I do not mean to *exclude* these formal Similes—there are moods of mind, in which they are natural— pleasing moods of mind, & such as a Poet will often have, & sometimes express; but they are not his highest, & most appropriate moods. They are 'Sermoni propriora' which I once translated—'*Properer for a Sermon.*' [39]

This last remark may perhaps have some reference to "Reflections on Having Left a Place of Retirement" whose motto is "Sermoni propriora," but which I considered as an early stage in the development of the 'imaginative' or 'symbolic' poem. If, as is by no means certain, Coleridge did have this motto in mind six years later when he wrote this letter, it indicates only, I think, that he had become aware of that poem's shortcomings. Certainly it reveals something beyond "formal Similes," though it contains these as well, and in the poems which follow, the formal simile appears less and less as a possible verbal equivalent for the vision which is expressed.

Both formal similes and allegory lead us, as in "To an Unfortunate Woman," from the images presented to concepts which they are taken to represent. By a symbol, on the other hand, we are made to see "the translucence of the eternal through and in the temporal." The difference between this and the seeing of "dim analogies with the moral world" is clear when we realize that for Coleridge the apprehension of the 'eternal' or the 'universal' is not the apprehension of a concept of any sort. The symbolic relation is not, therefore, like the allegorical relation, an intellectual one between an image or group of images and a concept, however 'metaphysical.' The symbol is an image which *as image* may, and indeed must, be part of a discursive pattern, but which *as symbol* is 'imaginatively' experienced as melting into and evolving from a pre-conceptual unity of 'being.'

Much the same argument applies also to Coleridge's use of the notion of organic form. The word 'organic' itself obviously implies and is intended to imply that the growth of a work of art is somehow comparable to the growth of a living thing. This idea, which was commonplace in German Romanticism, seems to rest on a metaphysical assumption of a parallelism between the processes of mind and the processes of nature such as Coleridge and Schelling both elaborated. But before a poem was explained as being something like a tree, a tree was explained as being something like a poem. Coleridge's analysis of the processes of nature was, as I said in the previous chapter, essentially an attempt to show that the structure of nature corresponded to the structure of experience, that a 'real' relation between essence and existence answered to the experienced relation between unitive and discursive apprehension. And since we are concerned with poems and not with trees or chipmunks, the metaphysics of nature is relevant here only as it reflects characteristics of the apprehension of nature.

"The artist," Coleridge said in one of the passages quoted above, "must imitate that which is within the thing . . . the Natur-geist, or spirit of nature . . . which puts the form together." And in a lecture he spoke of beauty as involving not "a conspiration of component but of constituent Parts, not of parts *put* to each other, but of distinct but indivisible parts growing out of a common Antecedent Unity, or productive Life & Will." [40] As with the 'eternal' and 'universal' in the definition of symbol, so here the 'Natur-geist' and the 'Antecedent Unity' refer not to a metaphysical concept 'beyond' the image, to something which is, like the deist's 'first cause' *inferred* and logically understood rather than intuitively known, but to "something which the mind can know but which it cannot understand," [41] to a spirit and unity which are 'within' and prior to the image, as the unconscious is prior to the conscious.

If organic form involves such a relationship, it follows again that it must be characteristic not of the poem as object but of the poem as we experience it. 'Mechanical' form, in which 'parts' are "*put* to each other," can be objectively understood, for it involves objective relations between defined entities. Organic form, however, does not appear in an objective relation between parts, but in a relation between parts and that 'feeling' which is an identification "of the percipient and the perceived," of reader and image. If the reader is not thus involved in the poem, then it is not, for him, symbolic and its form is not, for him, organic.

Commenting on Raphael and Michaelangelo in his *Philosophical Lectures,* Coleridge said that they succeeded

> in reducing external form to a symbol of the inward and imaginable beauty. We feel it to this day. We feel it for this reason, because we look at the forms after we have long satisfied all curiosity concerning the mere outline; yet still we look and look and feel that these are but symbols. Full worthily have they expressed themselves. Why, having seen their outlines, why, having determined what they appeared to the eye, do we still continue to muse on them, but that there is a divine something corresponding to something within, which no image can exhaust but which we are reminded of when in the South of Europe we look at the deep blue sky? The same unwearied form presents itself, yet still we look on, sinking deeper and deeper, and therein offering homage to the infinity of our souls which no mere form can satisfy.[42]

This is a recurrent theme, and one which we have seen before in other extracts, as, for instance, when he wrote "in looking at objects of Nature . . . I seem to be seeking, as it were *asking* for, a symbolical language for something within me that already and forever exists, than observing anything new";[43] or "deep sky is, of all visual impressions, the nearest akin to a feeling. It is more a feeling than a sight, or, rather, it is the melting away and entire union of feeling and sight."[44]

It was the experience of such a "union of feeling and sight" without losing the awareness of either the 'feeling' or the 'sight' that to Coleridge was the 'image of God' and which poetry, as well as music and painting, aimed at its best to communicate. His notions of imagination, symbol, and organic form are attempts to formulate the distinctive character of such communication. We might say, roughly, that the notion of imagination looks to the philosophy of mind for its definition, that of symbol, to theology, and that of organic form, to the philosophy of nature. But all three refer ultimately to the problem of expressing in language an intuitively known structure of experience. All three, in other words, provide a means of talking about not so much the metaphysics as the psychology of art.

Coleridge's views of 'imagination,' 'allegory,' and 'symbol' as I have interpreted them have some obvious shortcomings as the basis for a general aesthetic or critical position. There are important kinds of poetry, particularly didactic poetry and satire, for which they make no adequate provision. They apply primarily to those forms of art which *are* attempts to give artistic form to nonverbal or nonconceptual experience, which includes most Romantic and much post-Romantic poetry. And they are, as might be expected, most obviously meaningful in terms of Wordsworth's poetry and Coleridge's Conversation Poems, in which, so to speak, the inner world is seen in a common grain of sand, and an image or pattern of images which exists for us, and is intelligible, as part of a discursive order is made to exist for us also as an 'objective correlative' for psychological conditions of which, perhaps, we only then become aware. This happens clearly in the transformation of "This Lime-Tree Bower," which I discussed in Chapter 2, and it happens continually in Wordsworth, though with some important differences.

This is not the place for any extended discussion of Wordsworth, but an example may lead to some further clarification of Coleridge. And it seems to me that a particularly apt example, and one which points to ways in which Wordsworth differs from Coleridge, is found in "Strange Fits of Passion." The central image in this poem is in the lines,

> When down behind the cottage roof,
> At once, the bright moon dropped.

And the function of the rest of the poem is to make this image work 'imaginatively,' to transform it into a 'symbol.' As in Coleridge's

Conversation Poems, we are first introduced into a simple and familiar situation, and are asked not for intellectual understanding, but for sympathetic participation as actual or potential 'lovers':

> Strange fits of passion have I known:
> And I will dare to tell,
> But in the Lover's ear alone,
> What once to me befell.

The description in the next five and one-half stanzas is of conventional details, and the language is simple, sometimes trite:

> When she I loved looked every day
> Fresh as a rose in June,
> I to her cottage bent my way,
> Beneath an evening-moon.
>
> Upon the moon I fixed my eye,
> All over the wide lea;
> With quickening pace my horse drew nigh
> Those paths so dear to me.
>
> And now we reached the orchard-plot;
> And, as we climbed the hill,
> The sinking moon to Lucy's cot
> Came near, and nearer still.
>
> In one of those sweet dreams I slept,
> Kind Nature's gentlest boon!
> And all the while my eyes I kept
> On the descending moon.
>
> My horse moved on; hoof after hoof
> He raised and never stopped:
> When down behind the cottage roof,
> At once, the bright moon dropped.
>
> What fond and wayward thoughts will slide
> Into a Lover's head!
> 'O mercy!' to myself I cried,
> 'If Lucy should be dead!'

In those middle stanzas (up to "never stopped"), several important effects are produced with great deftness. Insofar as it is conventional and trite, the description calls up no irrelevant associations, no 'intellectual encumbrances.' Like the speaker, we are lulled into a kind of trance, not unrelated to that of "A slumber did my spirit seal." We are aware only of the moving moon and the moving horse, whose hypnotic plodding is echoed in the rhythm of the lines. And we are thus prepared to respond, even though we may not 'know' why, as the speaker does not, to the image of the setting moon. To the speaker, the thought "If Lucy should be dead" is simply "fond and wayward," without any logical antecedent. But it is, of course, the sudden disappearance of the moon, of something that was securely present in his consciousness, that shocks him into an obscure awareness of mortality, as the smooth flow of the poem is broken by the emphatic "dropped." It is not an intellectual process, a train of thought that leads to an interpretation of the image, something to be expressed in "formal Similes." We do not have, as we might in another kind of poem, something like:

> The moving moon drops slowly down the sky;
> For she must set, and all of us must die.

The speaker is not *thinking* in this way, nor are we. What, with him, we become aware of is "something within [us] that already and forever exists." It was by such unanticipated erasures of something of which we were conscious, such sudden "fallings from us, vanishings," that we first became aware of mortality. The poem evokes that primordial reaction, not some later verbalized knowledge.

This is an instance of what Wordsworth called the 'language of Nature' as opposed to 'poetic diction,' and the distinction he was trying to make is related to that between 'fancy' and 'imagination.' Wordsworth's examples of poetic diction are instances of figurative language which, like many of Coleridge's examples of 'fancy,' is, or seems to him to be, purely verbal. In a passage from Cowper, for instance, Wordsworth singles out as "vicious poetic diction" the lines,

> But the sound of the church-going bell
> These valleys and rocks never heard,
> Ne'er sighed at the sound of a knell,
> Or smiled when a sabbath appeared.[45]

And his objection is, clearly, that the lines include *mere* figures of speech. There are states of mind in which valleys and rocks might seem to sigh or smile. But here *sighed* and *smiled* are suggested by *knell* and *sabbath*.

In "Strange Fits of Passion," however, we have not a figure of speech but, so to speak, a figure of experience. And when Wordsworth uses figures of speech, as he often does, it is, when he does not offend against his own principles, because they are demanded by and express the speaker's state of mind. In "Nutting," for example, the woods are described as, figuratively, a woman, and his action as, figuratively, a rape. But to him the woods were alive and virginal; the action *was* a rape. And the experienced quality preceded the verbal figure.

Wordsworth in such instances uses language, images, and patterns of images to convey complex psychological states. But he differs from what some of Coleridge's remarks might lead us to expect in the degree to which, we might say, he makes us aware only of the 'miniature,' of the relation between the poet's or speaker's individual unity of consciousness and the diverse images which become its symbols. While there is the assumption that the deepest human feelings are universal, and that there is in "what we half perceive and what create" the shaping spirit of an omnipresent 'Nature,' the focus, nevertheless, is in a strong sense of personal consciousness. And there is only rarely that further sense, common in Coleridge, of the pattern which the individual consciousness in turn 'images,' in which the individual consciousness is known as an aspect or 'symbol' of a larger 'unity' only rarely the kind of experience which, in my first chapter, I argued might still be called 'mystical' as well as 'visionary.'

This, I would suggest, may be one reason for the different role that time often seems to play in Wordsworth and in Coleridge.

Wordsworth's 'spots of time' are in *one* way *out of* time: the remembered images are always intensely present, are not only forms in the past but have become the permanent forms of his mind. But what Wordsworth gives us is the process of evolution of this mind in time, and if "all time is eternally present," it is because of the present unity of *his* consciousness. In Coleridge we do not find this process *in time*. The transformation from 'thing' to 'symbol' takes place in a moment. Except, for instance, for the remark near the beginning,

> I have lost
> Beauties and feelings, such as would have been
> Most sweet to my remembrance even when age
> Had dimm'd mine eyes to blindness,

there is nothing in "This Lime-Tree Bower" of Wordsworth's sense of a visionary moment acquiring significance and exercising influence through time. It is true that in fact it is a remembered vision that illuminates the present, and that there is a thought of the future ("Henceforth, I shall know . . ."), but the poem presents a mental movement that is essentially present, that involves no *significant* concern with past or future. Illumination is something that happens *now*, and either does, as in "This Lime-Tree Bower," or does not, as in "Dejection," take place. If it does, past and future are 'temporarily' irrelevant: the moment is out of time and timeless. If it does not, memories of past moments serve only for contrast and regret.

This does not mean, however, that Wordsworth falls outside Coleridge's theoretical discussion, for the relation of consciousness to poem still 'miniatures' the '*image* of God.' A more problematic situation than that involved in Wordsworth's differences from Coleridge may in fact seem to arise in Coleridge's differences from Wordsworth in those poems in which he does not draw his imagery from the familiar world, but resorts to the exotic, the legendary, and the supernatural. But while this difference is important so far as a comparison of Wordsworth and Coleridge is concerned, it is, in terms of the principles which I have been discussing, more apparent than real. It is, in fact, precisely the difference which Coleridge describes in *Biographia Literaria* in his account of the genesis of *Lyrical*

Ballads.[46] He there explained, it will be remembered, that he was to employ "persons and characters supernatural, or at least romantic; yet so as to transfer from our inward nature a human interest and a semblance of truth"; while Wordsworth was to "excite a feeling analogous to the supernatural, by awakening the mind's attention from the lethargy of custom, and directing it to the loveliness and wonders of the world before us." Both, that is, were to produce poems of psychological validity, true to our "inward nature," though one was to use the familiar images of our common experience and the other not.

As a figure of speech may be either 'fanciful' or 'imaginative,' so too may 'nonrealistic' imagery. In a note occasioned by a nightmare, Coleridge wrote:

> Night-mair is, I think, always . . . a state not of Sleep but of Stupor of the outward organs of Sense . . . . This Stupor seems occasioned by some painful sensation, of unknown locality, most often, I believe, in the lower Gut, tho' not seldom in the Stomach . . . . [In such a situation, a sensation may occur] to which the Imagination therefore, the true inward Creatrix, instantly out of the chaos of the elements or shattered fragments of Memory puts together some form to fit it— . . . . In short, this Night-mair is not properly a *Dream*, but a species of Reverie, akin to Sonambulism, during which the Understanding & Moral Sense are awake tho' more or less confused, and over the Terrors of which the Reason can exert no influence because it is not true Terror: i.e. apprehension of Danger, but a sensation as much as the Tooth-ache, a Cramp—I.e. the Terror does not *arise* out of a painful Sensation, but is itself a specific sensation . . . .[47]

While Coleridge is not here using 'imagination' in precisely the sense with which I have been concerned, but, as in a note which I have discussed above,[48] in a sense which includes "phantasy," and while we are not at the moment considering the effects of discomforts in "the lower Gut," this note may justifiably be, in Coleridge's words, "hocus-pocused" into relevance. For here again it seems to Coleridge that the nightmare image is produced "to fit" a pre-existing 'feeling' and does not, as he goes on to suggest in the same note, represent merely "the reflections & confused Echoes of our waking Thoughts & experiences." Since the image is produced "to fit" a "Terror" which is not the *result* of sensation and perception, but which is rather *like* a sensation, the image 'means' "Terror," bears the same relation to "Terror" that the symbols of which I have been speaking bear to the 'feeling,' the 'sensation,' if you will, of union or alienation.

'Supernatural' images might seem, and may be, the products of 'fancy' since they are, like the images of nightmare, composed of "shattered fragments of memory." Fancy too puts together forms, but as in the case of allegory or figures of speech, these are forms constructed in terms of the intelligible discursive order, rearrangements of concepts and parts of concepts which have already been and remain 'fixed.' What imagination "dissolves" is not the familiar *thing* but the familiar conceptual order in which it *is* a thing. And that order may be "dissolved" and replaced by an imaginative order whether the images are drawn from familiar landscapes or from strange seas and pleasure gardens which we never have, and never will, see with our "fleshly gaze." The symbolism of "The Ancient Mariner" is more complex, and produces a much greater intensity of response than that in "This Lime-Tree Bower," but the movement from the discursive to the symbolic order is not essentially different in kind.

This is true even of the 'fragment' "Kubla Khan," in which the movement is not dramatised within the poem. The poem presents us with both vision and visionary, but the visionary appears only afterwards, in the second section of the poem. We are not led to vision; we are simply presented with it. But we are presented with it in such a way that we are forced to read it symbolically. "Kubla Khan" can be, and has been, read as 'meaning' nothing but its surface. But so can any poem. It can be, and has been, read as 'allegory.' But so can any poem. It is possible to refuse what a poem demands. "Kubla Khan" 'dissolves' the normal discursive order, forces us to awareness of a symbolic order, not by leading us away from the familiar but by disregarding it. It would not be quite accurate to say that the poem has no discursive pattern. The gardens occupy twice five miles of fertile ground, and their construction follows upon the Emperor's decree. But the poem's space and time are dissociated from ours, and we cannot use them to connect it with any conceptualized world which we know. The patterns which we recognize, in which we discover "something within [us] that already and forever exists" are, like those in the Mariner's tale, psychic ones. We do not find out anything about the poem by looking up Kubla Khan in a history or by looking for his garden on a map any more than, as Coleridge once pointed out, we learn anything about *Comus* by being told that *haemony* is *spleenwort*.[49] We may translate the psychic patterns which we recognize or to which we respond into conceptual terms as we may those in "The Ancient Mariner." We may say, perhaps, that the river between its pulsing source and the caves in which it vanishes is 'life'; that the pleasure dome precariously poised between sun and ice, between birth and death, between the beginning and the end, is a work of art. But we are restating in another, and abstract, language—as Coleridge restates in his metaphysics—only something of what the poem symbolizes. A poet does not need to sail desolate seas alone or feed on honey dew and the milk of paradise to write an allegory.

Few intelligent readers of poetry would now read "Kubla Khan" either as a meaningless dream or as an allegory whose meaning could be stated with equal accuracy in abstract terms. And we now have various ways of talking about such poems. But as Coleridge did not inherit the poetic language of "Kubla Khan," neither did he inherit a language which could begin to explain it. For the first time in England, he developed, however imperfectly and with however much assistance, a language which could discuss the poetry he had written. It was not a slight achievement.

Postscript

In one of his many reminders to himself, Coleridge wrote, "Mem. —I am persuaded that the chemical technology, as far as it was borrowed from Life & Intelligence, half-metaphorically, half-mystically, may be brought back again . . . to the use of psychology in many instances—& above all in the philosophy of Language."[1] Much of the language and 'technology' by which Coleridge was attracted was, perhaps to a greater extent than he was entirely aware, so "borrowed from Life & Intelligence, half-metaphorically, half-mystically." Neoplatonism, and occult, alchemical, and visionary philosophies all had roots in the mythical and the mystical, in the depths as well as the surface of the human psyche. Boehme could find in alchemy both a confirmation of his mystical vision and a language for it precisely because alchemy was in part a transformation of psychological facts into objective facts of nature, and therefore made it appear that nature revealed the 'spiritual' truths which the mystic found in his own 'imaginative' experience. Even contemporary German metaphysics owed much to these same roots.

Eighteenth-century rationalism had discredited the mythical and symbolic languages which had traditionally answered to the need for a way to express such depths of consciousness and feeling, regarded them, as Wordsworth said, as

> A history only of departed things,
> Or a mere fiction of what never was [.][2]

"The mechanical system of philosophy," Coleridge wrote in *Bio-*

graphia Literaria, in a note on the propriety of classical mythology in poetry, "has needlessly infected our theological opinions, and teaching us to consider the world in its relation to God, as of a building to its mason, leaves the idea of omnipresence a mere abstract notion in the stateroom of our reason." [3] And the break-through of the Romantics, in which Coleridge played a part, was as much as anything an attempt to reconstitute a language for nondiscursive experience.

I have in the preceding pages been concerned chiefly with the relation of Coleridge's poetic and speculative languages to what I believe to be their underlying psychological pattern, since it is this more than their position in intellectual history which, I think, gives them now interest and validity, and furthermore constitutes Coleridge's real originality. I have mentioned at various points the question of his indebtedness to other writers, a subject which has received extensive though not yet exhaustive study. The debts, the borrowings, are inescapable. Yet I do not think it can be denied by anyone who has read the notebooks with care that he thought that he was pursuing his own ends, that he saw what he read as grist for his own mill and not as flour ready-ground. There may have been, especially as he grew older, some self-deception, and certainly he did not produce, as he hoped, an original system of philosophy. But nevertheless, his belief that the position he was trying to enunciate and the problems he was trying to solve were his and not someone else's was justified.

But if an essential part of Coleridge's meaning is to be found in his own experience, his own self-exploration, it is still obviously true that particular problems involved in finding a language, either poetic or speculative, were largely determined by the artistic and intellectual climate of the time. For this reason, as Coleridge can easily be seen as continuing an older tradition, or as turning to what seemed to be its revival in Germany, so he can equally well be seen as continuing principles of the Enlightenment. He accepted both, and if his concern with a psychic cosmology allies him with earlier writers, his desire for empirical demonstration allies him with the Enlightenment.

In this desire to combine an inward looking symbolism with an outward looking empiricism, Coleridge was indulging in a kind of optimism that has not often survived the Romantics and some of their immediate successors. He still hoped for a reintegration of knowledge and experience, for a world and a society where 'inner' and 'outer' would not seem divergent or conflicting. In the fourth of his *Philosophical Lectures* of 1818, after a discussion of music as "the best symbol ⟨of the Idea⟩ perhaps, for it is, as far as sight is concerned, formless, and yet contains the principles of form," Coleridge wrote:

> We feel therefore that our being is nobler than its senses and the man of genius devotes himself to produce by all other means, whether a statesman, a poet, a painter, a statuary, or a man of science, this same sort of a something which the mind can know but which it cannot understand, of which understanding can be no more than the symbol and is only excellent as being the symbol.[4]

Not only the artist and the scientist, as we might expect, but even the statesman is to see and help to make available to others the visionary universe. And in *The Statesman's Manual*, we find his dream of a society guided by a "clerisy" not of religious instructors in any limited sense but of teachers who, like emissaries of Plato's philosopher-kings, can lead all men towards the realization of the Good, the Beautiful, and the True.

Coleridge seems in this to come at the end rather than the beginning of an era. The world he wanted was that suggested by the conclusion of "This Lime-Tree Bower," pervaded by a spiritual radiance, the world dreamed of by Wordsworth, and, in spite of their differences, by Shelley in *Prometheus Unbound*. But the outer world was resistant. Wordsworth, who was a great psychological poet though not, as Coleridge hoped, a great philosophical one, could render with extraordinary subtlety the modulations of his own consciousness, but he could not, in *The Excursion* or elsewhere, successfully transform his experience into a language for dealing with the world 'without.' His retreat from involvement in France to seclusion in Grasmere may have preserved the integrity of his soul, but it finally led him to a crotchety conservatism which, as the inevitable railroad came, could only complain,

> Is then no nook of English ground secure
> From rash assault?

Keats never solved, even in *Hyperion*, the problem which he raised in "Sleep and Poetry," of reconciling the world of poetic vision with that of "human strife." And what we have of Shelley's unfinished *Triumph of Life* seems to most readers to preclude an optimistic conclusion. Coleridge, the Sage of Highgate, surrounded by disciples, seems increasingly remote and irrelevant. And it appears like at least a momentary admission of failure when we read his often quoted but memorably eloquent letter to Gillman in 1825:

In youth and early manhood the mind and nature are, as it were, two rival artists both potent magicians, and engaged, like the King's daughter and the rebel genii in the Arabian Nights' Entertainments, in sharp conflict of conjuration, each having for its object to turn the other into canvas to paint on, clay to mould, or cabinet to contain. For a while the mind seems to have the better in the contest, and makes of Nature what it likes, takes her lichens and weather-stains for types and printer's ink, and prints maps and facsimiles of Arabic and Sanscrit MSS, on her rocks; composes country dances on her moonshiny ripples, fandangos on her waves, and waltzes on her eddy-pools, transforms her summer gales into harps and harpers, lovers; sighs and sighing lovers, and her winter blasts into Pindaric Odes, Christabels, and Ancient Mariners set to music by Beethoven, and in the insolence of triumph conjures her clouds into whales, and walruses with palanquins on their backs, and chases the dodging stars in a sky-hunt! But alas! alas! that Nature is a wary wily long-breathed old witch, tough-lived as a turtle and divisible as the polyp, repullulative in a thousand snips and cuttings, *integra et in toto*. She is sure to get the better of Lady *Mind* in the long run and to take her revenge too; transforms our to-day into a canvas dead-coloured to receive the dull, featureless portrait of yesterday; not alone turns the ci-divant sculptress with all her kaleidoscopic freaks and symmetries! into clay, but *leaves* it such a *clay* as to cast dumps or bullets in; and lastly (to end with that which suggested the beginning) she mocks the mind with its own metaphor, meta-morphosing the memory into a *lignum vitae* escritoire to keep unpaid bills and dun's letters in, with outlines that had never been filled up, MSS. that never went further than the title-pages, and proof-sheets, and foul copies of Watchmen, Friends, Aids to Reflection, and other *stationary* wares that have kissed the publishers' shelf with all the tender intimacy of inosculation! [5]

But Coleridge did foreshadow the future even though it was to be a future which in many ways he would not have liked. To the degree that he remained, as he did, faithful to his own intuitions, he antici-pated much that is characteristic of modern poetry and criticism. The figure of the Mariner and of the poet-prophet of "Kubla Khan" is still valid in a way that Wordsworth's Recluse is not. While Cole-ridge was not, like Blake, prepared to accept the role of 'greybeard loon' but struggled throughout his life to explain the rationality of his lunacy, he nevertheless had followed, as a poet, the dictates of his inner being, and those poetic fragments which I have mentioned tantalize us with the notions of what might have been the result had there been more Charles Lambs to encourage him.

And yet whatever we may regret, and whatever we may think of the inadequacies of his philosophical efforts, he did continually turn that philosophic language back to the concerns and insights that formed the basis of his poetry. I said in my Introduction that Cole-ridge had survived by virtue of a few great poems, and that his philosophy as philosophy had little value today. But because of what those few great poems reveal, it is possible to learn from his less successful efforts a great deal about the problems of the human mind and the worlds it creates, about the nature of different kinds of language, the purposes which they serve, and the substance which they reveal.

Coleridge was much concerned, and especially as he grew older, with solutions and with systems. But he was and remained much more alive than many 'better' philosophers to the elusive questions which experience poses. In *Urn Burial*, Browne asked "what song the Syrens sang, or what name Achilles assumed when he hid himself among women." The question led Coleridge to write in his notebook:

> Can'st tell what Song the Syrens sang?
> What names perchance
> The unslit Girl with robe-protruding Lance,
> Achilles, bore, whose arm-enamoured Eye
> Betrayed the Hero to Ulysses sly? [6]

Coleridge remained one who heard the sirens, who saw the meaning in the eye. Both the question and the poem still recommend him to our attention.

Notes

*See the Bibliography for an explanation of the
short titles used for primary sources in the Notes.*

Introduction (pages 1–17)

1. *Statesman's Manual*, Shedd, I, 462.
2. *Inquiring Spirit*, pp. 33–34.
3. *Collected Letters*, II, 279.
4. *Philosophical Lectures*, p. 186.
5. [It was, as I have mentioned in the Preface, only after this book had been sent to the printer that I read R. A. Durr's article " 'This Lime-Tree Bower My Prison' and a Recurrent Action in Coleridge" (*ELH*, XXVI [1959], 514–530), which provides an important exception to the following note. Durr suggests that the "action" which he sees in "This Lime-Tree Bower" recurs in "other writings early and late" and that "this action expresses concretely, symbolically, what was perhaps his central concern throughout his life."] There have of course been any number of studies in which some kind of psychological analysis is involved, but only Burke's fragmentary discussion (see pp. 6–7) suggests extending this to the consideration of recurrent patterns in Coleridge's nonpoetic work. There would seem to be fairly widespread agreement that Coleridge's experience as a poet did play a part in his rejection of mechanical psychology and his insistence on the creative activity of the mind, a view particularly well presented by Dorothy Emmet in "Coleridge on the Growth of the Mind," but this involves a correlation of experience and formulation only in the most general terms, and studies which attempt to deal with the wider range of Coleridge's work have, for the most part, been concerned with the history and explication of ideas or with external influences. While there have been in recent years a number of distinguished and important works, such as those by R. H. Fogle (*The Idea of Coleridge's Criticism*), J. A. Appleyard (*Coleridge's Philosophy of Literature*), and James D. Boulger (*Coleridge as Religious Thinker*), in which Coleridge's intellectual development is considered both extensively and intensively, they do not involve the kind of examination which I propose. Discussions of the relation of Coleridge's experi-

ence to his writing have usually belonged to the tradition of biographical criticism or have been concerned with his particular psychological problems. Many of these provide valuable illumination of experiential qualities in individual works (see, for example, George Whalley, "The Mariner and the Albatross," and D. W. Harding, "The Theme of 'The Ancient Mariner'"), but without attempting to consider what I should regard as their more general relevance. Maude Bodkin (*Archetypal Patterns in English Poetry*) discusses universal 'archetypes' in "The Ancient Mariner" and "Kubla Khan" but is not concerned with Coleridge's other work. Albert Gérard has examined the experiential structure of the 'conversation poems' in two important essays ("Counterfeiting Infinity" and "The Systolic Rhythm"), but again limits himself to particular poems. With the exception of Burke, whose promise remains unfulfilled as of this writing, neither these nor other critics, so far as I know, have considered experiential patterns as a basis for Coleridge's more abstract formulations.

6. Erich Neumann, *The Origins and History of Consciousness*, I, 263.

7. Herbert Read, *The Forms of Things Unknown*, pp. 26–27.

8. Kenneth Burke, *The Philosophy of Literary Form*, p. 19.

9. *Philosophical Lectures*, p. 186.

10. R. D. Laing, *The Politics of Experience*, p. 99.

11. For example by Harold Bloom in *The Visionary Company* and by J. B. Beer in *Coleridge the Visionary*.

12. Northrop Frye, *Fearful Symmetry*, p. 8.

13. Frye, p. 8.

14. Mark Schorer, *The Politics of Vision*, p. 45.

15. Frye, p. 8.

16. René Wellek, "Coleridge's Philosophy and Criticism," p. 114

17. See Jacques and Raissa Maritain, *The Situation of Poetry*, for an interesting discussion of the relation and distinction between mysticism and poetry. Dorothy Sayers in "The Beatrician Vision in Dante and other Poets" argues that experiences described in Dante, Blake, Wordsworth and others "are in the proper and technical sense mystical" though distinguished from "mystical experiences of the classical type" in that "every one has a basis in the world of physical phenomena." The identity of mystical and psychotic experience has been frequently affirmed both by those who consider mystical experience psychotic and by those who consider some psychotic experience genuinely mystical. Among the former, a classic work is J. H. Leuba, *The Psychology of Religious Mysticism*; among the latter John Custance's *Wisdom, Madness and Folly* is of particular interest. Among those who have believed that mystical experience may be produced by drugs, Aldous Huxley's *The Doors of Perception* remains valuable because of his knowledge of traditional mysticism. The recent 'psychedelic' cults have produced a voluminous

literature of which selections may be found in David Solomon's *LSD*. The identity of 'genuine' mystical experience with 'nature mysticism,' psychosis, or the experiences produced by drugs is denied by R. C. Zaehner in *Mysticism, Sacred and Profane*, who is in turn answered by Walter T. Stace in *Mysticism and Philosophy*.

18. See pp. 37–38.

19. Boehme, I, i, 248.

20. William James, *The Varieties of Religious Experience*, p. 414.

21. Apart from works by and about individual mystics, there are a number of more general studies and collections including Evelyn Underhill, *Mysticism*; Rudolf Otto, *Mysticism East and West*; W. R. Inge, *Studies of English Mystics*; Aldous Huxley, *The Perennial Philosophy*; and the works mentioned above by James, Stace, and Zaehner.

22. Basil Willey, *The Seventeenth Century Background*, pp. 99–100.

23. *Collected Letters*, II, 961

24. *Notebooks*, I, #1758.

25. I. A. Richards, *Coleridge on Imagination*, p. 10.

26. *Collected Letters*, I, 479.

27. *Collected Letters*, II, 916.

28. *Collected Letters*, II, 709.

29. *Notebooks*, I, #1834.

30. *Notebooks*, I, #1387

31. *Collected Letters*, II, 1193–1194.

32. Boehme, I, ii, [2].

33. Manuscript fragment printed in J. H. Muirhead, *Coleridge as Philosopher*, p. 282.

34. *Notebooks*, I, #1717.

35. This difference was first clearly, and sympathetically, discussed by F. J. A. Hort in *Cambridge Essays*, pp. 292–351. The best modern account, but an unsympathetic one, is probably still René Wellek's in *Immanuel Kant in England*.

36. Boehme, III, i, 33.

37. *Statesman's Manual*, Shedd, I, 460, note.

38. Boehme, I, ii, [2].

39. *The Friend*, Shedd, II, 469.

40. *Literary Remains*, II, 405. The Greek passage but with a very different translation is found in John Smith's *Select Discourses*, pp. 164–165.

41. Underhill, p. 95.

42. *Biographia*, I, 99.

43. *Notebooks*, I, #1710.

44. From an unpublished note dated "Messina, 9 October 1805" in the British Museum copy of Ficino's *Platonic Theology*. Coleridge gives this as the explanation of the "present attitude" towards Platonism.

Chapter 1 (pages 18–42)

1. *Notebooks*, I, #1504 note. Since this chapter was written, Geoffrey Yarlott has discussed in some detail relations between the poem and later notebook entries (*Coleridge and the Abyssinian Maid*, pp. 155–175).

2. Leslie Stephen, *Hours in a Library*.

3. Humphry House, *Coleridge*, p. 113.

4. Robert Penn Warren, "A Poem of Pure Imagination," pp. 114–115.

5. Irene Chayes, "A Coleridgean Reading of 'The Ancient Mariner,'" pp. 87, 99.

6. *Biographia*, II, 20.

7. E. E. Stoll, "Symbolism in Coleridge," p. 221.

8. C. G. Jung, *The Interpretation of Nature and the Psyche*, p. 31.

9. For example, *Clavis*, ii: 132.

10. John Custance, *Wisdom, Madness, and Folly*, p. 46.

11. Custance, p. 64.

12. Custance, p. 29.

13. Custance, p. 76.

14. R. D. Laing, *The Politics of Experience*, pp. 42–43.

15. *Notebooks*, II, #2546.

16. The comment was made, I believe, during a talk at Princeton University in 1951, and I have not found it in print. The function of rain imagery "as a transcendent translation of release (as physiologically conceived in terms of urination)" is, however, mentioned, though without any reference to Coleridge, in *A Grammar of Motives*, p. 302.

17. John Livingston Lowes, *The Road to Xanadu*, p. 498 note 67.

18. *Notebooks*, I, #1725.

19. There is some similarity here to Wordsworth's lines in *The Borderers*:

> Action is transitory—a step, a blow,
> The motion of a muscle—this way or that—
> 'Tis done, and in the after-vacancy
> We wonder at ourselves like men betrayed.

Parts of my view of the Mariner's crime have, I find, been anticipated by Geoffrey Hartman in a very interesting discussion of the relation of "The Ancient Mariner" to *The Borderers* in his *Wordsworth's Poetry*, pp. 131–135.

20. *Notebooks*, II, #2090.

21. *Aids to Reflection*, pp. 353–356.

22. Chayes, pp. 85–86.

23. *Aids to Reflection*, Shedd, I, 356.

24. *Collected Letters*, II, 814.

25. Southey's judgment (in his review of *Lyrical Ballads* in the *Critical Review*, XXIV [1798], 197–204) that "The Ancient Mariner" was "absurd and unintelligible" was in agreement with that of most reviewers. "Kubla Khan" was, of course, not published until 1816, but the reviews which it then received justified Coleridge's hesitations. Most found the poem unintelligible and uninteresting. Coleridge's early and generally conventional poems received high praise, but it was not until Lockhart's 1819 essay in *Blackwoods* (VI, 3–12) that a serious discussion of "The Ancient Mariner" appeared in print, and not until an anonymous article in 1829 (*Westminster Review*, XII, 1–31, variously and doubtfully attributed to Bowring and to Mill) that we find any understanding of Coleridge's experiential structure.

26. Jacques Maritain, *Creative Intuition in Art and Poetry*, pp. 319–320.

27. In "Late Autumn's Amaranth: Coleridge's Late Poems," George Whalley writes: "What he was looking for—as many uncanny notes, drafts, titles, and hints written in the Notebooks show—was what Yeats, Eliot, Pound and Joyce were to discover almost a hundred years later. The late poems seem to me to give clear if intermittent evidence of this."

28. *Notebooks*, II, #2086.

Chapter 2 (pages 43–77)

1. G. M. Harper, "Coleridge's Conversation Poems," pp. 3–27.

2. Marshall Suther, *Visions of Xanadu*.

3. Max Schulz, *The Poetic Voices of Coleridge*, p. 7.

4. Schulz, p. 7.

5. Schulz, p. 51.

6. *Notebooks*, III, #4046.

7. W. K. Wimsatt, *The Verbal Icon*, pp. 103–118.

8. In *From Sensibility to Romanticism*, ed. F. W. Hilles and H. Bloom, pp. 527–560.

9. Albert Gérard, "The Systolic Rhythm: The Structure of Coleridge's Conversation Poems," pp. 307–319.

10. Geoffrey Hartman, *Wordsworth's Poetry*, pp. 11–12.

11. Hartman, pp. 17–18.

12. *Poetical Works*, I, 11. The poem was sent to George Coleridge in a letter dated June, 1791 (*Collected Letters*, I, 14).

13. *Collected Letters*, I, 103.

14. *Collected Letters*, I, 104 note.

15. *Collected Letters*, II, 864.

16. Elisabeth Schneider, *Coleridge, Opium and Kubla Khan*.

17. Both poems were first published in 1796, but the subtitle of "The Eolian Harp" gives the date of composition as August, 1795. There is no known manuscript of "Reflections" but there is an early version of "The Eolian Harp" in the Cottle MSS (*Poetical Works*, II, 1021). Since, however, this is a much abbreviated and as it stands essentially different poem, the earlier date may be misleading.

18. Geoffrey Yarlott, *Coleridge and the Abyssinian Maid*, p. 97.

19. *Notebooks*, II, #2453 (1805).

20. *Collected Letters*, I, 916 (1803).

21. At the end of the eighteenth century, the term *sublime* did, of course, have fairly definite implications which Coleridge may have intended here. See Marjorie Nicolson, *Mountain Gloom and Mountain Glory*. Even so, the application of the term to the mountain itself is a return to a more conventional use of language.

22. See p. 165.

23. See p. 171. If the use of the phrase "Sermoni propriora" as the subtitle of the poem is meant to convict these particular lines of being an instance of "loose mixture . . . in the shape of formal Similes," then I should argue that it applies, if at all, only to the last lines of the passage, in which Coleridge might be said to fall back on a conventional verbal form which was perhaps not adequate to his purpose.

24. This has become almost a commonplace, but the first critic to observe something of this pattern was the anonymous reviewer mentioned in Chapter 1, note 25.

25. See p. 51

26. Herbert Lindenberger, *On Wordsworth's Prelude*.

27. See note 17 above.

28. *Poetical Works*, II, 1021.

29. The date of the first draft is about six weeks before Coleridge's marriage.

30. The 1796 text given here differs in a few minor respects from the variants printed by E. H. Coleridge in *Poetical Works*.

31. *Notebooks*, I, #51.

32. See p. 12.

33. Humphry House, *Coleridge*, p. 76.

34. Yarlott, p. 96.

35. *Collected Letters*, I, 334–335.

36. *Collected Letters*, I, 334.

37. *Collected Letters*, I, 350.

38. The first revision appeared in a version sent to Charles Lloyd, also in 1797 and otherwise nearly identical with that in the letter to Southey. The manuscript of the Lloyd copy is lost, but the first part of it was printed by J. D. Campbell in the notes to his edition of the poems.

39. *Shakespearean Criticism*, II, 138.
40. *Notebooks*, I, #921.
41. *Collected Letters*, II, 458–459.

Chapter 3 (pages 78–111)

1. J. B. Beer, *Coleridge the Visionary*, p. 287.
2. Printed in the Preface to *The Excursion*.
3. *Biographia*, I, 59.
4. *Collected Letters*, I, 260.
5. Letter to Dr. Trusler, August, 1799. *The Complete Writings of William Blake*, p. 793.
6. See p. 65.
7. *Collected Letters*, II, 810 (1802).
8. There are far more discussions of this subject than can be listed here. Among them are: Claude Howard, *Coleridge's Idealism* and A. E. Powell, *The Romantic Theory of Poetry* both concerned with Neoplatonism and Cambridge Platonism; R. L. Brett, "Coleridge's Theory of the Imagination," on Cudworth; Newton P. Stallknecht, *Strange Seas of Thought*, on Boehme.
9. "Christ's Hospital Five and Thirty Years Ago."
10. See p. 79.
11. Morley, I, 70.
12. Morley, I, 88.
13. *Biographia*, I, 94.
14. *Biographia*, I, 95, 98.
15. *Biographia*, I, 98.
16. *Collected Letters*, I, 264.
17. George Whalley, "The Bristol Library Borrowings of Southey and Coleridge, 1793–1798."
18. *Notebooks*, I, #201. This is one of several instances where notebook entries which at first seem to point to the reading of various authors have in fact a common secondary source. See Miss Coburn's note to this entry and to #180. Such evidence suggests that Coleridge's acquaintance with complete and original works, especially during his early years, may have been less extensive than has sometimes been assumed.
19. J. B. Beer, "Coleridge and Boehme's *Aurora*," p. 182.
20. *Notebooks*, I, #174.
21. *Notebooks*, I, #927–929.
22. *Notebooks*, I, #1626.
23. See "Coleridge and Opium Eating," *Collected Writings of Thomas De Quincey*, ed. Masson (Edinburgh, 1890), V, 183 note.

24. *Notebooks*, I, #1678.

25. *Collected Letters*, II, 866.

26. *Biographia*, I, 97–98.

27. Beer, *Coleridge the Visionary*, p. 60.

28. Brinkley, p. 332.

29. *Philosophical Lectures*, p. 318.

30. *Notebooks*, I, #928 and note; *The Friend*, Shedd, II, 110.

31. *Notebooks*, I, #928.

32. *The Friend*, Shedd, II, 109–110.

33. *The Friend*, Shedd, II, 110.

34. *The Friend*, Shedd, II, 108.

35. *Notebooks*, I, #928.

36. *The Friend*, Shedd, II, 110.

37. See note 23 above. De Quincey reports that he saw at least one volume "overflowing" with marginalia a few months after he had given the books to Coleridge.

38. Newton P. Stallknecht, *Strange Seas of Thought*, p. 43.

39. Stallknecht, p. 106.

40. See, for example, Dorothy Mercer, "The Symbolism of *Kubla Khan*"; Irene Chayes, "A Coleridgean Reading of 'The Ancient Mariner'"; Beer, *Coleridge the Visionary*, passim.

41. *Notebooks*, I, #174. See p. 84.

42. See note 19 above.

43. *Notebooks*, I, #272. Miss Coburn points out in her note that most of the phrases in the entry of which this is a part are from Jeremy Taylor and that all may be. But she has no particular source for these lines, and Beer's conjecture is persuasive.

44. *Notebooks*, I, #1000E and note.

45. *Notebooks*, I, #1835.

46. *Collected Letters*, III, 278.

47. *Biographia*, I, 95, 103.

48. John W. Robberds, *Memoir of . . . William Taylor of Norwich*, I, 25.

49. *Biographia*, I, 103.

50. *Collected Letters*, IV, 775.

51. He wrote to Southey in September, 1799, that he was "sunk in Spinoza" (*Collected Letters*, I, 534). He read Bruno in 1801 (see p. 87), and Erigena in 1803 (*Collected Letters*, II, 949).

52. *Collected Letters*, IV, 750–751.

53. "Coleridge and Jacob Boehme."

54. *Collected Letters*, III, 278–279.

55. Boehme, I, i, 22.

56. According to a note on *Mysterium Magnum* (III, i, 11) dated November, 1819, Coleridge had read only the first volume, containing

Aurora and *The Three Principles* before that date, though a dated note in Vol. II shows that he had read the first few pages in October, 1818. The notes in Vol. I show several readings, but the distribution of the notes and sections of unopened pages indicate that *Aurora* was the only one of Boehme's works which he ever read in its entirety.

57. Boehme, *Aurora*, xxi:95 (I, i, 214).

58. Boehme, I, ii, 28. The note is a comment on *The Three Principles* iv:47. Coleridge later cancelled it, adding "The above note was written, while I was but in the dim dawn of knowledge—& wholly in the *subjective* Thinking—of course incapable of coming near Behmen."

59. Boehme, *Aurora,* viii:21 (I, i, 62).

60. See p. 41.

61. "The Destiny of Nations" lines 27–35. I hope I need not add that my remarks on "Peter Bell" are not intended as a general judgment of Wordsworth.

62. For example in "The Destiny of Nations" and in "Religious Musings."

63. Herbert Piper, "The Pantheistic Sources of Coleridge's Early Poetry," p. 49; J. A. Appleyard, *Coleridge's Philosophy of Literature,* p. 51.

64. *Collected Letters,* I, 197.

65. See, for example, *Monthly Review,* xx (1796), 194–199, and *Annual Register,* xvii (1797), 265.

66. Geoffrey Yarlott, *Coleridge and the Abyssinian Maid,* p. 100.

67. "Coleridge, Hartley, and the Mystics."

68. *Collected Letters,* I, 126.

69. *Collected Letters,* I, 236.

70. *Collected Letters,* II, 686.

71. *Collected Letters,* II, 703.

72. *Collected Letters,* II, 768.

73. *Collected Letters,* II, 749.

74. *Inquiring Spirit,* p. 27.

75. *Biographia,* I, xxiv.

76. Since his object was a joke, too much weight should not be given to Coleridge's often quoted remark in a letter to Southey in December, 1794: "I am a compleat Necessitarian—and understand the subject as well almost as Hartley himself—but I go farther than Hartley and believe the corporeality of *thought*—namely, that it is motion—. Boyer thrashed Favell most cruelly the day before yesterday—I sent him the following Note of consolation. 'I condole with you on the unpleasant motions, to which a certain uncouth Automaton has been mechanized; and am anxious to know the motives, that impinged on it's optic or auditory nerves, so as to be communicated in such rude vibrations through the medullary substance of It's Brain, thence rolling their stormy Surges

into the capillaments of it's Tongue, and the muscles of it's arm. The diseased Violence of It's thinking corporealities will, depend upon it, cure itself by exhaustion—In the mean time, I trust that you have not been assimilated in degradation by losing the atarxy of your Temper, and that the Necessity which dignified you by a Sentience of the Pain, has not lowered you by the accession of Anger or Resentment'" (*Collected Letters*, I, 137–138).

77. David Hartley, *Observations on Man*, II, 280.

78. Hartley, I, 33.

79. Hartley, I, 110–112.

80. Hartley, I, 33–34.

81. In arguing for the materiality of mind, Priestley began by denying the conventional notion of matter as a solid inert substance. The only observed properties of 'matter,' he insisted, were the 'powers' of attraction and repulsion. (*Disquisitions Relating to Matter and Spirit*, 1777). In this, Priestley's views had something in common with those which Coleridge adopted in his later philosophy of nature. Coleridge complained of Priestley in March, 1796 in terms very like many of his later attacks on pantheism: "He asserts in three different Places, that God not only *does*, but *is*, everything . . . with no *unity of consciousness*" (*Collected Letters*, I, 192).

82. Hartley, I, 368.

83. Hartley, I, 74–75.

84. Hartley, I, 371.

85. Hartley, II, 19.

86. Hartley, II, 19.

87. Hartley, I, 114.

88. Hartley, II, 22.

89. Hartley, II, 280. Pistorius' comment to which Coleridge also refers for support is largely a repetition of Hartley's arguments, but he concludes: "Former defenders of the pure love of God, a Fenelon and a Madame Guyon, if they had not found fewer antagonists, would have been treated with more respect by them, had they known, like our author, how to give a clear explanation of it, deduce it from fundamental laws of the human mind, and illustrate it from analogy and experience" (*Notes and Additions to Dr. Hartley's Observations on Man* [London, 1801], p. 669). The comment well describes a major element in Hartley's attraction for Coleridge.

90. *Notebooks*, III, #3847.

91. *Notebooks*, III, #3935.

Chapter 4 (pages 112–153)

1. J. H. Muirhead, *Coleridge as Philosopher*, p. 44.
2. Herbert Read, *The True Voice of Feeling*, p. 164.
3. J. B. Beer, *Coleridge the Visionary*, p. 164.
4. *Collected Letters*, I, 209.
5. *Collected Letters*, I, 256.
6. *Collected Letters*, I, 320.
7. *Collected Letters*, I, 213.
8. See A. D. Snyder, "Books Borrowed by Coleridge from the Library of the University of Göttingen, 1799."
9. *Notebooks*, I, #389.
10. Clement Carlyon, *Early Years and Late Reflections*, I, 101.
11. See Carlyon I, 90: "[Hartley and Berkeley] were in fact the frequent subjects of his conversation, not only during our Alpine tour, but in our evening walks on the ramparts of Göttingen"; and I, 95: "*Jeremy Taylor* was an author from whose works Coleridge always professed to have derived the greatest possible delight; and he more particularly referred us to his 'Ductor Dubitantium,' and his 'Holy Living and Dying.' . . . Butler's Sermons were commended by him; and as not irrelevant to this discourse on divinity, he spoke with general approbation of *Burnet's* 'Theory of the Earth,' and *Browne's* 'Religio Medici.'"
12. Carlyon I, 140: "I must candidly confess, that in discussing the merits of the 'Rime of the Ancient Mariner' it did happen that 'there pass'd a weary time,' or something very like it, for I was unable to follow him to my certain satisfaction either in the verse or the accompanying colloquy, and yet 'Day after Day—Day after Day,' he was at one time fond of returning to it, but either my mind was not 'in the right temper,' or from some defect or other, I could not fully appreciate the mysteries of the Albatross . . . [I prefer reading it when] unattended by the author and his bewildering metaphysics."
13. Elisabeth Schneider has argued (in *Coleridge, Opium and Kubla Khan*) that "Kubla Khan" also belongs to this period. But see *Collected Letters*, I, 348 note, and *Notebooks*, III, 3997 for evidence supporting the date of 1797.
14. See *Collected Letters*, I, 531 and note.
15. *Collected Letters*, I, 535.
16. *Collected Letters*, I, 549.
17. See Griggs's concise summary of the situation in *Collected Letters*, I, 631 note.
18. *Collected Letters*, I, 631 note.

19. *Collected Letters*, I, 631 note.

20. *Collected Letters*, I, 656.

21. *Collected Letters*, I, 658.

22. *Collected Letters*, II, 714.

23. *Philosophical Lectures*, p. 179.

24. See above Chapter 1, note 25.

25. *Collected Letters*, I, 623.

26. *Collected Letters*, II, 668.

27. *Collected Letters*, II, 815.

28. *Collected Letters*, II, 831.

29. *Collected Letters*, I, 535.

30. *Collected Letters*, I, 632.

31. *Collected Letters*, II, 671.

32. *Collected Letters*, II, 707.

33. *Collected Letters*, II, 927.

34. *Collected Letters*, II, 947.

35. *Collected Letters*, II, 1113.

36. See p. 15.

37. *Notebooks*, III, #3744.

38. See *Monthly Repository*, XII (1817), 268–272 for a Unitarian criticism of Coleridge on this point.

39. *Notebooks*, I, #922. It is interesting to note also the increasing uneasiness in Coleridge's letters to his Unitarian friend Estlin, to whom he wrote in July, 1802: "In these [proposed letters] you will see my *Confessio Fidei*, which as far as regards the Doctrine of the Trinity is *negative* Unitarianism—a non liquet concerning the nature & being of Christ —but a condemnation of the Trinitarians as being wise beyond what is written. . . . believe no idle reports concerning me/ *if* I differ from you, & wherein I differ from you, it will be that I believe *on the whole more* than you, not less" (*Collected Letters*, II, 821–822).

40. *Notebooks*, I, #920.

41. See p. 70.

42. *Collected Letters*, I, 470–471.

43. *Collected Letters*, II, 916.

44. *Collected Letters*, II, 746.

45. See p. 14.

46. *Collected Letters*, II, 1195–1196.

47. Boehme, I, i, 38–39.

48. Boehme, I, i, 44–47.

49. Boehme, I, i, 22.

50. Boehme, I, ii, 16.

51. *Notebooks*, II, #2784.

52. Miss Coburn concludes: "The statement here, of the centrality of the self, in various degrees of consciousness, in any attempt to solve the

problem of the unity of thought and the diversity of things, ornamented though it is with etymological and pictorial play, is basic in Coleridge's philosophy to the end" (*Notebooks*, II, #2784 note).

53. See p. 13.

54. Boehme, I, ii, 211.

55. *Notebooks*, II, #3159.

56. *Notebooks*, II, #3159 note.

57. *Notebooks*, II, #2453.

58. *Notebooks*, II, #3159 note.

59. See p. 4.

60. *Collected Letters*, II, 1196.

61. Boehme, I, i, 42.

62. *Anima Poetae*, p. 184.

63. According to René Wellek in "Coleridge's Philosophy and Criticism," p. 114, H. Nidecker's 1927 dissertation for the University of Basel deals with the influence of Schelling and Steffens on *The Theory of Life*. This I have not read. But while the influence mentioned is important and undeniable, an adequate study of Coleridge's philosophy of nature would have to take into account a large number of often obscure scientific and philosophical writers who formed a background for *both* Coleridge and Schelling.

64. Boehme, I, i, 40.

65. Humphry Davy, "An Essay on Heat, Light, and the Combinations of Light" (1799), in *Collected Works*, II, 85.

66. *Notebooks*, III, #4225.

67. See p. 12.

68. *Notebooks*, III, #4352.

69. Coleridge's notes to Davy's 1802 lectures are in *Notebooks*, I, #1098, and see *Collected Letters*, III, 172 and *Fragmentary Remains . . . of Sir Humphry Davy, Bart.*, ed. John Davy, p. 110.

70. Humphry Davy, "An Essay on the Generation of Phosoxygen and on the Causes of the Colours of Organic Beings," *Collected Works*, II, 107.

71. Humphry Davy, "Outlines of a View of Galvanism," *Collected Works*, II, 195.

72. *Collected Letters*, III, 172.

73. *Journal of Natural Philosophy, Chemistry, and the Arts*, XXII (1809), 66.

74. Humphry Davy, "Electro-chemical Researches on the Decomposition of the Earths."

75. *Collected Letters*, III, 38.

76. Boehme, I, i, 42.

77. Davy, "Electro-chemical Researches," p. 362.

78. *Notebooks*, I, #1098f21.

79. Boehme, I, i, 41–42. Coleridge's memory has obviously slipped and he has forgotten that Ammonia and Volatile Alkali are the same thing and omitted "muriatic acid Gas" (hydrogen chloride).

80. For Coleridge's reasons for this and other chemical coinages, see *Notebooks*, II, #3192, which begins "I will suggest to Davy the propriety of confining archè, to that which causes a compound to *begin* to be . . . ."

81. Boehme, I, i, 42.

82. See especially Schelling's *Darstellung meines Systems der Philosophie* (1805). See also Steffens' *Beyträge zur innern Naturgeschichte der Erde* (1801).

83. *Notebooks*, III, #3401.

84. *Notebooks*, III, #3605.

85. *Poetical Works*, II, 1112–1113.

86. *Notebooks*, I, #556.

87. *Notebooks*, I, #1561.

88. *Collected Letters*, II, 706.

89. *Collected Letters*, II, 709.

90. *Collected Letters*, II, 675 note.

91. *Collected Letters*, II, 675. For a further interesting comment on Wedgwood's work and Coleridge's relation to it, see *Collected Letters*, II, 787 and note.

92. Coleridge's refusal to be bound by Kant's limits has often been discussed, usually with the conclusion that he misunderstood what he borrowed. See Introduction, pp. 14–16, and note 35. There is also an interesting comment in Crabb Robinson's Diary for May 3, 1812: "To Kant his obligations are infinite, not so much from what Kant has taught him in the form of doctrine as from the discipline Kant has taught him to go through. Coleridge is indignant at the low estimation in which the Post-Kanteans affect to treat their master. At the same time Coleridge himself adds Kant's writings are not metaphysics, only a propaedeutic. Were Coleridge in Germany he would not be suffered to hold this language; he would be forced to make his election between the critical and the absolute philosophy, or he would be equally proscribed by both" (Morley, I, 70). Coleridge's refusal to "make his election" is a significant indication of his philosophical (or possibly *un*philosophical) attitude, and has led to his proscription by a number of critics.

93. See p. 15.

94. *Collected Letters*, I, 557.

95. *Collected Letters*, I, 590.

96. *Collected Letters*, I, 625.

97. *Collected Letters*, II, 678. It is possible that one reason Coleridge never wrote the later letters was that Wedgwood never replied to the earlier ones.

98. *Collected Letters*, II, 671.
99. *Collected Letters*, I, 625–626.
100. *Notebooks*, I, #383.
101. *Notebooks*, I, #1016.
102. *Notebooks*, I, #921.
103. *Collected Letters*, II, 961.
104. See p. 12.
105. *Collected Letters*, II, 706.
106. *Inquiring Spirit*, pp. 126–127.

Chapter 5 (pages 154–181)

1. Boehme, I, i, 22.
2. *Notebooks*, III, #4351.
3. *Notebooks*, III, #3947.
4. *Notebooks*, III, #4225.
5. *Notebooks*, III, #3962.
6. *Unpublished Letters*, II, 128.
7. *Collected Letters*, II, 865–866.
8. *Biographia*, I, 60.
9. *Biographia*, I, 59.
10. See p. 142.
11. *Biographia*, II, 12.
12. *Notebooks*, II, #3158.
13. *Notebooks*, III, #4066.
14. See pp. 128–129.
15. *Notebooks*, II, #2370.
16. *Biographia*, I, 202.
17. *Biographia*, I, 202.
18. Ernst Cassirer, *Language and Myth*, trans. Suzanne K. Langer, pp. 9–10.
19. Cassirer, p. 13.
20. Cassirer, p. 32.
21. Cassirer, p. 33.
22. I have been speaking, of course, in terms of Western languages. A most valuable study could result from an examination of the effect of syntactic forms in 'imaginative' poems written in non-Western languages.
23. T. M. Raysor, ed., "Unpublished Fragments on Aesthetics by S. T. Coleridge," p. 530.
24. *Anima Poetae*, p. 60.
25. *Shakespearean Criticism*, I, 216.
26. *Shakespearean Criticism*, II, 260.

27. *Shakespearean Criticism*, I, 213.

28. *Notebooks*, I, #1610.

29. Shedd, *Literary Remains*, p. 529.

30. *Biographia*, II, 107.

31. See pp. 148–150.

32. See p. 142.

33. "On Poesy or Art," *Biographia*, II, 259.

34. *Statesman's Manual*, Shedd, I, 437.

35. *Statesman's Manual*, Shedd, I, 437.

36. *Miscellaneous Criticism*, p. 30.

37. See pp. 47–48.

38. *Poetical Works*, I, 172 note.

39. *Collected Letters*, II, 864.

40. "Unpublished Fragments," p. 531.

41. *Philosophical Lectures*, p. 168.

42. *Philosophical Lectures*, pp. 193–194.

43. See p. 30.

44. See p. 53.

45. Wordsworth, "Preface to *Lyrical Ballads:* Appendix," *Poetical Works*, p. 742.

46. *Biographia*, II, 5–6.

47. *Notebooks*, III, #4046.

48. See p. 160.

49. *Collected Letters*, II, 867.

Postscript (pages 182–187)

1. *Notebooks*, III, #3312.

2. Wordsworth, Preface to *The Excursion, Poetical Works*, p. 590.

3. *Biographia*, II, 59.

4. *Philosophical Lectures*, p. 168.

5. *Letters*, II, 742–743.

6. *Notebooks*, III, #4371. The notebook gives a rough draft including a number of cancellations which I have omitted here.

Bibliography

The following list is limited to works actually cited in the Notes.

PRIMARY SOURCES

The following short titles are employed in the notes for primary sources.

Anima Poetae: Anima Poetae, from the unpublished notebooks of Samuel Taylor Coleridge, ed. E. H. Coleridge. Boston and New York, 1895.

Biographia: Biographia Literaria, ed. J. Shawcross. Oxford, 1907, 2 vols.

Boehme: Coleridge's unpublished marginalia in *The Works of Jacob Behmen*. London, 1764–1781, 4 vols., British Museum C 126 k 1. References are to volume, part number, and page. References to Boehme's own text are to title, chapter, and paragraph. The marginalia will be published in the forthcoming *Collected Coleridge*.

Brinkley: *Coleridge on the Seventeenth Century*, ed. Florence Brinkley. Durham, N. C., 1955.

Collected Letters: Collected Letters of Samuel Taylor Coleridge, ed. E. L. Griggs. Oxford, 1956–, four (of six) vols.

Inquiring Spirit: Inquiring Spirit; a new presentation of Coleridge from his published and unpublished prose writings, ed. Kathleen Coburn. London, 1951.

Letters: Letters of Samuel Taylor Coleridge, ed. E. H. Coleridge. Boston, 1895, 2 vols.

Literary Remains: The Literary Remains of Samuel Taylor Coleridge, ed. H. N. Coleridge. London, 1836–1839, 4 vols.

Miscellaneous Criticism: Coleridge's Miscellaneous Criticism, ed. T. M. Raysor. London, 1938.

Morley: *Henry Crabb Robinson on Books and their Writers*, ed. Edith J. Morley. London, 1938, 3 vols.

Notebooks: The Notebooks of Samuel Taylor Coleridge, ed. Kathleen Coburn. London and New York, 1957–, three (of six) vols.

Philosophical Lectures: Philosophical Lectures of Samuel Taylor Coleridge, ed. Kathleen Coburn. London, 1949.

Poetical Works: The Complete Poetical Works of Samuel Taylor Coleridge, ed. E. H. Coleridge. Oxford, 1912, 2 vols.

Shakespearean Criticism: Coleridge's Shakespearean Criticism, ed. T. M. Raysor. London, 1930, 2 vols.

Shedd: *The Complete Works of Samuel Taylor Coleridge*, ed. W. T. Shedd. New York, 1868, 7 vols.

"Unpublished Fragments": "Unpublished Fragments on Aesthetics by S. T. Coleridge," ed. T. M. Raysor. *Studies in Philology*, XXII (1925), 529–537.

Unpublished Letters: Unpublished Letters of Samuel Taylor Coleridge, ed. E. L. Griggs. London, 1932, 2 vols.

SECONDARY AND MISCELLANEOUS SOURCES

APPLEYARD, J. A. *Coleridge's Philosophy of Literature*. Cambridge, Massachusetts, 1951.

ABRAMS, MEYER. "The Greater Romantic Lyric." *From Sensibility to Romanticism*, ed. F. W. Hilles and H. Bloom. New York, 1965. pp. 527–560.

———. *The Mirror and the Lamp*. New York, 1953.

BEER, J. B. "Coleridge and Boehme's *Aurora*." *Notes and Queries*, X (1963), 182–187.

———. *Coleridge the Visionary*. London, 1959.

BLAKE, WILLIAM. *The Complete Writings of William Blake*. Oxford, 1966.

BLOOM, HAROLD. *The Visionary Company*. New York, 1961.

BODKIN, MAUDE. *Archetypal Patterns in English Poetry*. London, 1934.

BOULGER, JAMES D. *Coleridge as Religious Thinker*. New Haven, 1961.

BRETT, R. L. "Coleridge's Theory of the Imagination." *English Studies* N.S., II (1949), 74–90.

BURKE, KENNETH. *A Grammar of Motives*. New York, 1945.

———. *The Philosophy of Literary Form*. New York, 1957.

CARLYON, CLEMENT. *Early Years and Late Reflections*. London, 1836.

CASSIRER, ERNST. *Language and Myth*, trans. Suzanne Langer. New York, 1946.

———. *The Philosophy of Symbolic Forms*, trans. Ralph Manheim. New Haven, 1953.

CHAMBERS, E. K. *Samuel Taylor Coleridge*. Oxford, 1938.

CHAYES, IRENE. "A Coleridgean Reading of 'The Ancient Mariner'" *Studies in Romanticism*, IV (1965), 81–103.

CUSTANCE, JOHN. *Wisdom, Madness, and Folly*. London, 1951.

DAVY, HUMPHRY. *Collected Works*, ed. John Davy. London, 1839–1840.

———. "Electro-chemical Researches on the Decomposition of the Earths." *Philosophical Transactions of the Royal Society*. London, 1808. pp. 333–370.

————. *Fragmentary Remains . . . of Sir Humphry Davy, Bart.*, ed. John Davy. London, 1858.

DE QUINCEY, THOMAS. *Collected Writings of Thomas De Quincey*, ed. Masson. Edinburgh, 1890.

EMMET, DOROTHY M. "Coleridge on the Growth of the Mind." *Bulletin of the John Rylands Library*, XXXIV (1952).

FOGLE, R. H. *The Idea of Coleridge's Criticism.* Berkeley and Los Angeles, 1962.

FRYE, NORTHROP. *Fearful Symmetry.* Princeton, 1947.

GÉRARD, ALBERT. "Counterfeiting Infinity: The Eolian Harp and the Growth of Coleridge's Mind." *Journal of English and Germanic Philology*, LX (1961), 411–422.

———— "The Systolic Rhythm: The Structure of Coleridge's Conversation Poems." *Essays in Criticism*, X (1960), 307–319.

HARDING, D. W. "The Theme of 'The Ancient Mariner.'" *Scrutiny*, IX (1941), 334–342.

HARPER, G. M. "Coleridge's Conversation Poems." *Spirit of Delight.* New York, 1928. pp. 3–27.

HARTLEY, DAVID. *Observations on Man.* London, 1791, 2 vols.

HARTMAN, GEOFFREY. *Wordsworth's Poetry.* New Haven, 1964.

HAVEN, RICHARD. "Coleridge, Hartley, and the Mystics." *Journal of the History of Ideas*, XX (1959), 477–494.

————. "Coleridge and Jacob Boehme." *Notes and Queries*, XIII (1966), 176–178.

HORT, F. J. A. "Coleridge." *Cambridge Essays.* London, 1856. pp. 292–351.

HOUSE, HUMPHRY. *Coleridge.* London, 1953.

HOWARD, CLAUDE. *Coleridge's Idealism.* Boston, 1924.

HUXLEY, ALDOUS. *The Doors of Perception.* London, 1954.

————. *The Perennial Philosophy.* London, 1946.

INGE, W. R. *Studies of English Mystics.* London, 1905.

JAMES, WILLIAM. *The Varieties of Religious Experience.* New edition, London, 1952.

JUNG, C. G. *The Interpretation of Nature and the Psyche.* Bollingen Series LI. New York, 1955.

LAING, R. D. *The Politics of Experience.* New York, 1967.

LEUBA, J. H. *The Psychology of Religious Mysticism.* London, 1925.

LINDENBURGER, HERBERT. *On Wordsworth's Prelude.* Princeton, 1963.

LOWES, JOHN LIVINGSTON. *The Road to Xanadu.* London, 1930.

MARITAIN, JACQUES. *Creative Intuition in Art and Poetry.* New York, 1953.

————, and RAISSA MARITAIN. *The Situation of Poetry.* New York, 1955.

MERCER, DOROTHY. "The Symbolism of *Kubla Khan.*" *Journal of Aesthetics and Art Criticism*, XII (1953), 214–266.

MUIRHEAD, J. H. *Coleridge as Philosopher*. London, 1930.

NEUMANN, ERICH. *The Origins and History of Consciousness*, trans. R. F. C. Hull. 2 vols. New York, 1962.

NICOLSON, MARJORIE. *Mountain Gloom and Mountain Glory*. Ithaca, New York, 1959.

OTTO, RUDOLF. *Mysticism East and West*. New York, 1962.

PIPER, HERBERT. "The Pantheistic Sources of Coleridge's Early Poetry." *Journal of the History of Ideas*, xx (1959).

POWELL, A. E. *The Romantic Theory of Poetry*. London, 1926.

READ, HERBERT. *The True Voice of Feeling*. London, 1953.

————. *The Forms of Things Unknown*. Cleveland and New York, 1963.

RICHARDS, I. A. *Coleridge on Imagination*. New York, 1950.

ROBBERDS, JOHN W. *Memoir of the Life and Writings of the late William Taylor of Norwich*. 2 vols. London, 1843.

SAYERS, DOROTHY. "The Beatrician Vision in Dante and other Poets." *Nottingham Medieval Studies*, ii (1958), 3–23.

SCHELLING, F. W. J. VON. *Darstellung meines Systems der Philosophie*. Sammtliche Werke, i. Stuttgart, 1860.

SCHNEIDER, ELISABETH. *Coleridge, Opium, and Kubla Khan*. Chicago, 1953.

SCHORER, MARK. *The Politics of Vision*. New York, 1959.

SCHULZ, MAX. *The Poetic Voices of Coleridge*. Detroit, 1963.

SMITH, JOHN. *Select Discourses*. London, 1660.

SNYDER, A. D. "Books Borrowed by Coleridge from the Library of the University of Göttingen, 1799." *Modern Philology*, xxv (1928), 377–380.

SOLOMON, DAVID, ed. *LSD: The Consciousness Expanding Drug*. New York, 1964.

STACE, WALTER T. *Mysticism and Philosophy*. New York, 1960.

STALLKNECHT, NEWTON P. *Strange Seas of Thought*. Durham, North Carolina, 1945.

STEFFENS, HENRIK. *Beyträge zur innern Naturgeschichte der Erde*. Freyberg, 1801.

STEPHEN, LESLIE. "Coleridge." *Hours in a Library*. London, 1892. iii, 339–368.

STOLL, E. E. "Symbolism in Coleridge." *PMLA*, LXIII (1948), 214–233.

SUTHER, MARSHALL. *Visions of Xanadu*. New York, 1965.

UNDERHILL, EVELYN. *Mysticism*. London, 1948.

WARREN, ROBERT PENN. "A Poem of Pure Imagination." *The Rime of the Ancient Mariner*. New York, 1946.

WELLEK, RENÉ. *Immanuel Kant in England*. Princeton, 1931.

————. "Coleridge's Philosophy and Criticism." *The English Romantic Poets*, ed. T. M. Raysor. New York, 1956. pp. 110–137.

WHALLEY, GEORGE. "The Bristol Library Borrowings of Southey and Coleridge, 1793–1798." *Library*, IV (1949), 114–132.

———. "Late Autumn's Amaranth." *Transactions of the Royal Society of Canada*, II (1964).

———. "The Mariner and the Albatross." *University of Toronto Quarterly*, XVI (1947), 381–398.

WILLEY, BASIL. *The Seventeenth Century Background*. London, 1940.

WIMSATT, W. K. *The Verbal Icon*. Lexington, Kentucky, 1954.

YARLOTT, GEOFFREY. *Coleridge and the Abyssinian Maid*. London, 1967.

ZAEHNER, R. C. *Mysticism Sacred and Profane*. Oxford, 1961.

Index